STALINGRAD

Anatomy of an Agony

by
V. E. Tarrant

LEO COOPER
LONDON

Dedicated to My Mother
Whom I Cherish

First published in Great Britain in 1992 by
LEO COOPER
190 Shaftesbury Avenue, London WC2H 8JL
an imprint of
Pen & Sword Books, Ltd,
47 Church Street, Barnsley, South Yorkshire S70 2AS

ISBN: 0 85052 307 9

CONTENTS

MAPS

ACKNOWLEDGEMENTS

During 1960, when I was fourteen years old, I read Heinz Schröter's emotive account of Stalingrad. The momentous events which resulted in the encirclement of the 267,000 men of the German 6th Army in the Stalingrad *Kessel* (cauldron), and the subsequent horrors suffered by these men, captured my imagination and has haunted me ever since. I was, therefore, highly delighted when Bob Tanner, my literary agent at International Scripts, negotiated a contract with Leo Cooper on my behalf to write a reappraisal of Stalingrad to commemorate the 50th Anniversary of the battle.

Having drawn on a wealth of both German and Russian sources, I am indebted to Mr. Kenneth Marsh for assistance in translating German source material and to my brother, Lieutenant David Parry RN, whose mastery of the Russian language has proved invaluable in the preparation of this book. I also owe a debt of gratitude to Annette Lewis, BSc (Hons), for proof-reading the first draft of my manuscript, and to my Pastor, the Rev. Stuart Ryce-Davies BD, for his encouragement and support through difficult times and for much good talk. Last but not least, and with much love, I have to thank my wife Val, who has patiently borne the all-consuming effort which engulfed the bigger part of eight months which the writing of this book required.

When drawing from published sources, even when English translations are available, I have as far as possible referred to the original German and Russian editions, and grateful acknowledgement is made for permission to quote from the copyright material indicated:

Michael Joseph Ltd., from Heinz Schröter's *Stalingrad* and General Kurt Zeitzler's account of Stalingrad in Richardson and Freidin's *The Fatal Decisions*; Macdonald & Co., from *Marshal Zhukov's Greatest Battles*, and Cajus Bekker's *The Luftwaffe War Diaries*, and Walter Kerr's *The Secret of Stalingrad*; Oxford University Press, from Barry Leach's *German Strategy Against Russia, 1939-41*; Routledge, Chapman & Hall Ltd., from Walter Görlitz's *Paulus and Stalingrad*; Cassell, from Liddell Hart's *The Other Side of the Hill*, and General von Mellenthin's *Panzer Battles*; Harrap Ltd., from Paul Carell's *Hitler's War on Russia*; Penguin Books Ltd., from Joachim Fest's *Hitler*; Nizhnye-Volzhskoye Knizhnoye Izdatelstvo, from Marshal Vasili Chuikov's *Nachalo puti*; Brassey's Defence Publishers Ltd., from

Louis Rotundo's *Battle for Stalingrad*; Sigbert Mohn Verlag, from *Letzte Briefe aus Stalingrad*; Macmillan Ltd., from Alan Clark's *Barbarossa; The Russian-German Conflict*; Hamish Hamilton Ltd., from Alexander Werth's *The Year of Stalingrad*; Greenhill Books, from Field-Marshal von Manstein's *Lost Victories*. In a few instances I have been unable to trace the copyright holder of works where the publisher has ceased trading. In these cases I apologize for any unintentional breach of copyright.

All the photographs come from private collections either in Germany or the Soviet Union.

V.E.Tarrant
1992

INTRODUCTION

Here is wisdom. Let him who has understanding calculate the
number of the beast, for it is the number of a man: His number
is 666.

(Revelation 13:18)

THE VISION

In Biblical times numerical values were assigned to the letters of the Greek
and Hebrew alphabets, and by the time the Apostle John wrote the Book
of Revelation 777 had come to symbolize absolute perfection in the form of
the Holy Trinity. The antithesis of perfection in the gematrical scheme was
expressed as 666 — the mark of the beast, the Antichrist who would appear
in various human personifications throughout history. Applied to Adolf
Hitler, the very incarnation of the beast, the triune of the gematrical
expression took the form of a trilogy of obsessive delusions — anti-Semitism,
anti-Bolshevism and the geopolitical concept of Germanic colonization of the
east *(Lebensraum)*.

None of these concepts originated in Hitler's twisted mind: anti-Semitism
and Lebensraum had run pandemically through German history, and
anti-Bolshevism was common coinage in Weimar Germany. What was
unique to Hitler was the transformation of these three politically
commonplace notions into inordinately radical ones. The religious bias of
political anti-Semitism he perverted into a racial doctrine with extermination
as its goal. Then, by re-defining Bolshevism as a Jewish conspiracy for world
domination, he was able to radicalize anti-Bolshevism and the German
imperialist drive for autarky in the form of Lebensraum, into a crusade to
liberate Russia from its allegedly Jewish rulers. In effect a fusion of all three
of Hitler's radical obsessions into one concept, which became the cornerstone
of his grand strategy and foreign policy.

Literally translated Lebensraum means 'living space', but for Hitler it had
a far more complex significance. The obvert appeal of Lebensraum in the
east was a cure for the German economic ills of the day, and 'to create a
rational relation between the number of (German) people and the space for
them to live in.'[1] In a speech delivered at a Nuremberg Rally in 1936, Hitler

spelled out the economic gains of Lebensraum: 'If we had at our disposal the incalculable wealth and stores of raw material of the Ural Mountains and the unending fertile plains of the Ukraine to be exploited under National Socialist leadership... our German people would swim in plenty'.[2] But to Hitler *Lebensraumpolitik* offered much more. It not only satisfied the Germanic militaristic aspirations, in that it offered such gains as autarky and the re-establishment of the buffer states Ludendorff had fleetingly established in the Treaty of Brest Litovsk in 1918, it also satisfied Hitler's lust for struggle and power, to seize and defend a great Germanic Empire. Hitler spelled out this aspect of Lebensraum to a small circle of the Party faithful in 1932: 'I am not thinking in the first instance of economical matters. Certainly we need the wheat, oil and the ores... But our true object is to set up our rule for all time, and to anchor it so firmly that it will stand for a thousand years.'[3] Moreover, the conquest of Russia was associated in Hitler's mind with an apocalyptic final struggle between Aryans and Jews. In his lunatic phantasmagoric vision, Jews and Bolsheviks were not only identical, but he seriously believed that all Russia had somehow become captive of the Jews. In *Mein Kampf* he wrote: 'In Russian Bolshevism we must see the attempt undertaken by the Jews in the twentieth century to achieve world domination.'

Although the economic goals, geographic limits and military objectives were only expressed in vague terms, there can be no doubt that the conquest of Soviet Russia was Hitler's *ideé fixe*; a great preconceived plan from which he did not waver after committing his vision to paper in *Mein Kampf* during 1924. As Barry Leach concludes: 'Hitler did indeed follow a preconceived plan. Throughout his career, though he used the flexible methods of an opportunist, he adhered rigidly to the aim of winning a great eastern empire.'[4]

The road to Midsummer's Day, 1941, when Hitler finally unleashed his legions against the Soviet Union, was as long, twisted and contingent as the road to the extermination camps. Hitler's foreign policy, from 1933 to the outbreak of war, is what General Halder described as 'a chaos of improvisation'.[5] During those six turbulent years Hitler, with the consummate skill of the supreme opportunist in judging the mood of the democracies and exploiting their weaknesses, consolidated his power base by rearming Germany, snatching back most of the territories lost in the Treaty of Versailles, and assimilating Austria and the larger part of a dismembered Czechoslovakia into the Reich. The complexity of the creation of *Grossdeutschland* partly veiled his consistency of purpose, but Hitler never lost sight of his grand strategic plan of winning a great eastern empire: an unwavering pursuit of a vision to which he adhered with limpet-like fixity for nearly twenty years, that would eventually be torn asunder at Stalingrad.

THE ILLUSION

What Hitler regarded as the penultimate machination in his Lebensraum strategy — the attempt to convert Poland into a German satellite — proved to be the first of his fatal miscalculations. Throughout the winter and summer of 1939, Poland, emboldened by British and French guarantees of her national integrity, resisted Hitler's diplomatic pressures to make territorial concessions (Danzig and the Polish Corridor), or to accede to the Anti-Comintern Pact, which would, in effect, make her an accomplice in Hitler's grand strategy. Wedged between Germany and Russia, Poland's geographical position blocked Hitler's means of launching his military crusade, which required, as a pre-requisite, a common boundary with the Soviet Union, causing him to gamble recklessly to remove this last encumbrance.

Deluding himself that Britain and France would not honour their guarantees to the Poles unless they could obtain Russia's support, Hitler employed his recurrent principle whereby 'circumstances must be adapted to aims', by cynically effecting a *rapprochement* with Stalin in the form of a non-aggression pact laced with a secret protocol in which he agreed to partition Poland between Germany and Russia. In his own words it was 'a pact with Satan to drive out the devil'.

But his conviction that Britain would be prepared to abandon her traditional 'Balance of Power' policy and tolerate a German hegemony in Europe, was an error in which ideological dogma superseded rational calculation. At a military conference held at Obersalzberg, 18 days before he unleashed his legions across the Polish frontier, Hitler informed his select audience that while political and military successes could not be achieved without taking risks, he was certain that Great Britain and France would not fight. He became a victim of his own crude Machiavellianism, because his certainty that the Allies would not honour their guarantees proved to be an illusion.

Hitler's grand strategy was suddenly turned upside down. He now found himself fighting the wrong war, not against the East, but henceforth against the West. For nearly twenty years his thinking had been dominated by a diametrically opposite idea, and for the next twenty-two months his direction of the war was governed by the endeavour to turn this topsy-turvy situation back on its correct course again — the 300-year-old German dream of *Drang nach Osten* (the drive towards the East).

Ironically, the wrong war in which Hitler found himself embroiled led to his most spectacular military victories. There was nothing surprising in the outcome of the campaign against Poland, which was little more than a military formality. The 800,000 men, 225 small tanks and 313 obsolete aircraft of the notoriously ill-equipped Polish Army, which was wedded to hopelessly archaic strategic and tactical doctrines, stood little chance against the 1,512,000 troops, 2,977 tanks and 1,300 modern aircraft, employing far more sophisticated tactics, which was hurled against it. Moreover, Poland suffered from an acute geographical disadvantage in that her Western reaches formed a huge salient, outflanked by East Prussia in the north and German-occupied Czechoslovakia in the south. In great annihilating battles of encirclement, the Wehrmacht had already decisively beaten the Poles, when, on 17 September, the Soviet Army invaded from the east: a stab in the back which only served to hasten the Polish capitulation. Within 28 days it was all over, at a cost to the Germans of 10,572 servicemen killed, 30,322 wounded and 3,409 missing: 2.93 per cent of the total force employed.

Six months after the fall of Poland the Wehrmacht overran Norway and Denmark, the former in the space of a month, the latter in a day, at a cost of 1,317 killed, 1,604 wounded and 2,375 missing. Neither of these small neutral countries had any place in Hitler's grand strategy, but by the spring of 1940 the strategic situation had developed in such a way as to make the occupation of Norway imperative. In November, 1939, Russia attacked Finland and Hitler feared that, under the pretext of aiding the Finns, the Allies might violate Norwegian neutrality with the object of threatening Germany's northern flank, and interfering with the traffic in iron ore from Sweden which was vital to the Reich's war effort. The inclusion of Denmark was desirable to close the Skagerrak and dominate the Baltic, and to gain valuable fighter bases for an extension of the Luftwaffe's defence network covering Germany.

The rapid conquest of three poorly defended countries by a vastly superior power contained no imponderables. But both the speed and decisive manner in which the Wehrmacht defeated France and hurled the British Expeditionary Force off the Continent was as much a surprise to Hitler and his generals as the rest of the world. Indeed, before the attack in the West commenced, both Hitler and the General Staff expected to win only 'territory in Holland, Belgium and Northern France as a base favourable for waging extensive air and sea warfare against Britain and as a wide protective belt before the essential Ruhr area.'[6]

Numerically, the combined French, British, Dutch and Belgian Armies had a decided advantage over the German forces which invaded France and the Low Countries on 10 May, 1940. They had a 980,000 superiority in troops (3,740,000 to 2,760,000); a 1,026 superiority in tanks of at least equal calibre (3,600 to 2,574); and a 3,800 superiority in artillery pieces (11,500 to 7,700). Only in aircraft did the Germans have a distinct and decisive advantage (2,750 to 1,616); a German superiority of 1,134 machines. Yet, despite their numerical disadvantage the Germans decided the battle in their favour within ten days, the Allies having lost 50 per cent of their forces on the Continent, and some 74 per cent of their best equipment. Fighting ceased on the forty-sixth day of the campaign.

This astonishing triumph of German arms, which was achieved at the light cost of 27,074 dead, 111,034 wounded and 18,384 missing (5.67 per cent of the total force employed), had been bought by a highly innovative form of attack: fast, furious and decisive manoeuvre had shattered the outdated Allied linear defence strategy, which was little more than a hangover from the strategic and tactical doctrines of the First World War.

The revolutionary form of attack employed by the Germans became known retrospectively as *Blitzkrieg*. This term was a piece of pure journalese, first coined by the western press to explain the inexplicable. For although Blitzkrieg ('lightning war') is a German word it was not a German military expression, and was never used in their military manuals prior to or during the war. The term only gained universal currency after 1945. Blitzkrieg is essentially a doctrine of attack on a narrow front by a concentration of panzer (armoured) divisions supported by low-flying fighter and bomber aircraft, trained to drive forward through a gap punched in the enemy defences, followed by a deep thrust without concern for extended flanks, which was aimed at the paralysis rather than the physical destruction of the enemy forces.

Ironically, within the fruit of victory lay the seeds of the Third Reich's doom. Within nine months Hitler had conquered Poland, Norway, Denmark, Holland, Belgium, Luxembourg and France, at a total cost to the Wehrmacht of 38,963 killed, 142,960 wounded and 24,168 missing. The grand total of 206,091 is better understood in the meaningful context of comparison to the German casualties suffered in the single Battle of Verdun in the 1914-18 conflict, which amounted to 281,333. Apart from swelling still further Hitler's unbridled belief in his own infallibility, in that his grandiose contempt for facts became hysterical to the point that he was unable to reconcile large-scale plans conceived in a flash of inspiration with concrete situations and requirements, the intoxication of victory also unbalanced the judgement of the German generals, whose mood swung from one of the pessimistic truculence of being dragged into a general European war into one of excessive optimism, over-confident zeal and an inflated belief in the invincibility of what could be achieved with the forces at their disposal. All these factors were to have far-reaching effects on the subsequent planning and conduct of the operations against Russia.

The heady, intoxicating effect of victory on Hitler and his generals was only one aspect of the portents of doom. Surprisingly, despite the proven success of deep unsupported thrusts by the panzer divisions demonstrated during the campaign in the West, the German Army was never formally converted to the Blitzkrieg doctrine. On the contrary, the majority of the

General Staff and Officer Corps remained adherents of a more traditional strategic concept first expounded by General Graf von Schlieffen, the Chief of the German General Staff from 1891 to 1905.

In basic terms, Schlieffen established a doctrine of decisive manoeuvre which he called *Vernichtungsgedanke*, a strategic method designed to avoid costly frontal attacks whereby fast, far-reaching concentric encircling movements, launched from the enemy's flanks, sought to bring about annihilating *Kesselschlacten* (cauldron battles). The primary aim of Schlieffen's doctrine was the physical destruction of the enemy, as opposed to the paralysis of the enemy, by rendering inoperative his power of command, enshrined in the Blitzkrieg doctrine.

Although decisive manoeuvre was the common denominator of both strategies, this was their only affinity, and in all other respects there was a direct conflict between the two concepts. For ease of understanding, the fundamental differences can be tabulated as follows:

Vernichtungsgedanke	Blitzkrieg
Method.	
Well-coordinated flanking and encircling movements by the mass of the army, aimed at creating cauldron battles.	Deep penetration into the enemy's rear, through a narrow gap punched in the weakest point of the enemy's front.
Fundamental Rules of Operation.	
Guarded flanks and unbroken, if strained, lines of communication.	Surprise and high-velocity forward thrusts, leaving the far-extended flanks unguarded.
Primary Condition of Command.	
Centralized control.	Independent action.
Primary Instrument of Victory.	
Mass infantry armies with the panzers acting in concert, with the aim of causing the physical destruction of the enemy.	Panzers in the form of a relatively small attacking force, unhindered by the slower mass of the field army which had the subordinate task of mopping up the isolated pockets of resistance and capturing the large numbers of disorganized and demoralized enemy troops. The aim was to cause the paralysis of the enemy.

The division of opinion between the Generals on the relative merits of the traditional and the new revolutionary strategy remained unresolved during both the planning of the invasion of Russia and the subsequent operations on the Eastern Front. This conflict of convictions had no arbitrator in the victories so far achieved. Although Blitzkrieg had yielded spectacular results in the West, the advocates of the traditional strategy could point to its success in the conquest of Poland, which had been attained without the risks inherent in the long exposed flanks left by the panzers' deep unsupported thrusts during the campaign in France, which had caused great consternation, even to Hitler, necessitating a number of halt orders to allow the plodding infantry to catch up. For, contrary to popular belief, the Polish campaign had been planned, fought and won strictly in accord with the strictures of Vernichtungsgedanke, and was not the first demonstration of Blitzkrieg. The panzers had only been exploited in a very limited fashion, in secondary thrusts used to outflank the Poles in their eastern reaches in full accord with the plan to annihilate the Polish Army in great Kesselschlacten battles. This was pure Schlieffen.

The upshot of all this was that the basis of the detailed planning for the invasion of Russia was not founded wholly on either of the strategic alternatives — a lack of clear professional purpose, resolve and opinion, which gave rise to Hitler, the amateur military strategist, meddling in the complex planning process, and precipitating a situation whereby the Lebensraum crusade eventually degenerated into the static strategy of attrition fought at Stalingrad with bloody and fatal consequences.

During the tidal wave of victories, the obsessive intensity of the vision of Eastern Lebensraum never deserted Hitler. A week after the conquest of Poland he gave a clear indication of this when he ordered General Keitel (Chief of the *Oberkommando der Wehrmacht*) and the Quartermaster-General of the Army, General Eduard Wagner, to ensure that the roads, railways and lines of communication in Poland were to be preserved intact because: 'the territory is important to us from a military point of view as an advanced jumping-off point and can be used for the strategic concentration of troops.'[7] Further evidence is provided in a conversation Hitler held with General von Rundstedt and his Chief of Staff, von Sodenstern, at the time the British Expeditionary Force was surrounded at Dunkirk. He informed them that he expected Britain would come to a 'sensible peace arrangement' and that he would at last have his hands free 'for his real major task, the conflict with Bolshevism.'[8] Then, on 21 July, 1940, less than a month after the French Armistice, and despite the fact that Britain remained undefeated, Hitler called upon General Brauchitsch (Commander-in-Chief of the Wehrmacht) to make 'mental preparations' for a war against Russia. Ten days later, to justify the relentless pursuit of his aim to his generals, Hitler played the role of the master strategist by expounding a series of political exaggerations and inconsistent strategic rationalizations to Halder (Chief of the General Staff):

England's hope is Russia and America. If the hope of Russia is eliminated, America is eliminated also, because elimination of Russia will be followed by an enormous increase in the importance of Japan in the Far East.... Russia need tell England no more than that she does not want to have Germany great, and England will hope like a drowning man that in six or eight months the whole situation will be changed. But if Russia is smashed, England's last hope is wiped out. Then Germany is the master of Europe and of the Balkans. Decision: In the course of this war Russia must be finished off. Spring 1941.[9]

This was not the muddled rationalization of an opportunist recoiling from his inability to invade Britain and force a conclusive conclusion to the campaign in the West. The fact was that Hitler had not developed any ideas for the continuation of the war against Britain, simply because this war did not fit into his grand design for eastern Lebensraum. The seemingly incomprehensible and suicidal intention to leave an undefeated, albeit maimed and isolated, opponent in his rear while withdrawing the bulk of the Wehrmacht eastwards reveals Hitler's impatience to detach himself from the wrong war, in which he had enmeshed himself, as quickly as possible, and to twist, however tortuously, his grand design on to its correct course – the East.

While the planning involved in the invasion of Russia was being formulated, Hitler developed an ad-hoc strategy of attempting to force Britain to come to terms by attempting to defeat the RAF and win air superiority, cripple Britain's industrial potential and psychologically crush the populace by a bombing campaign and starve her into submission by a U-Boat blockade. All of these stratagems failed, with the result that the Germans eventually found themselves fighting a two-front war, a fear that Hitler had dismissed as hardly legitimate in the heady days of the summer of 1940, since Britain would be powerless to intervene in the campaign in Russia, which was to be concluded in the course of one season.

The limpet-like fixity of Hitler's obsession with his Lebensraumpolitik was responsible for yet another fatal flaw. In his reasoning, bringing Britain to terms was largely dependent on an indirect means – the defeat of Russia.

1

DELUSION AND REALITY.

... and behold a white horse. He who sat on it had a bow; and a
crown was given to him, and he went out conquering and to
conquer.

(Revelation 6:2)

THE PLAN

Two main plans had evolved, amongst a host of minor appreciations,
within seven weeks of Hitler's instruction to prepare preliminary studies for
the invasion of Russia. The first of these, dated 1 August, 1940, was drafted
by General Erich Marcks, Chief of Staff 18th Army. The Marcks plan had
a two-fold aim. The first was physically to destroy the bulk of the Russian
Army, which he assumed would be forced to stand and fight west of the
Pruth, Dniester, Dnieper and Dvina rivers, in order to defend the main
centres of the Russian war economy which lay in the food and
raw-material-producing areas of the Ukraine and Donets Basin and the
armament industries of Moscow and Leningrad. The second aim was to
paralyse the enemy by the capture of Moscow which constituted 'the
economic, political and spiritual centre of the USSR'.[1] It's capture, Marcks
believed, would 'destroy the co-ordination of the Russian State'.[2] To achieve
these aims Marcks proposed that the bulk of the army be concentrated in two
main offensive thrusts spearheaded by the panzer divisions. The forces
assigned to each thrust were to be divided north and south of the Pripet
Marshes, a vast swampland 150 miles in width and over 300 miles in depth,
which lay directly in the centre of the proposed front. The northerly thrust
was to advance directly on Moscow, with a portion of the forces wheeling
left to capture Leningrad and envelop the Russian troops in the Baltic States.
The southerly thrust was to capture Kiev, and then wheel north to link up
with the right flank of the northern thrust to create an enormous cauldron
battle with the bulk of the Soviet forces in Western Russia trapped inside,
who, 'fighting isolated battles' would 'soon succumb to the superiority of
German troops and leadership'.[3] In contrast, a plan drafted by
Lieutenant-Colonel Bernhard von Lossberg, dated 15 September, 1940,
envisaged a single main offensive thrust spearheaded by the bulk of the

panzer divisions to the north of the Pripet Marshes. The objective of the thrust was Moscow, but only after cauldron battles had been created by inward-wheeling pincer movements in the areas of Minsk and Smolensk. Like Marcks, Lossberg also envisaged a portion of the main thrust forces wheeling north after crossing the Dvina with an identical object.

After considering the relative merits of both plans, Halder commissioned General Friederich Paulus, the *Oberquartiermeister 1* (Deputy Chief of the General Staff), to draft a third solution, expanding on Marcks' proposal by including a subsidiary third thrust with an axis of advance on Leningrad through the Baltic states, employing forces independent from the northernmost of Marcks' two main drives. In its final form the solution proposed by Paulus, which was far more detailed in specifics, enlarged the subsidiary thrust on Leningrad proposed by Halder into a third major prong of the attack to be launched from East Prussia. To provide the necessary forces for this additional thrust, Paulus employed the simple expedient of drawing on the large number of reserve divisions (40, including 4 panzer) envisaged in the Marcks plan.

The Paulus solution envisaged the paralysis of the Soviet high command structure by the capture of Leningrad, Kiev and, most important of all, Moscow as the ultimate objectives, but only after the mass of the Russian Army had been physically destroyed in cauldron battles during the first stage of the invasion.

To achieve, in the first instance, localized paralysis of the enemy command and to effect the outer, far-reaching concentric encircling movements on the enemy flanks, each of the three main thrusts was to be spearheaded by Panzer Groups. Army Group 'North' was to be spearheaded by Panzer Group 4 driving hard for Leningrad via Dvinsk, while the infantry of the 16th and 18th Armies would destroy the enemy forces enveloped between the panzer drive and the Baltic Coast. Panzer Groups 2 and 3, spearheading Army Group 'Centre' was to lunge for Moscow after enveloping Soviet forces in the area of Minsk, an envelopment to be completed by the infantry of the 4th and 9th Armies. Army Group 'South', attacking from south of the Pripet Marshes, was to achieve a double envelopment of the Soviet forces in the Ukraine with Panzer Group 1, followed by 6th Army, pushing hard for Kiev and then south east − along the western bank of the Dnieper River to meet the advance of 12th Army from Rumania, while 17th Army completed the encirclement by pinning down the enemy between the two enveloping arms.

In the Paulus solution the central of the three thrusts was to be by far the most powerful to effect 'the decisive advance on Moscow',[4] the centre of Stalin's power, to ensure the general paralysis of the enemy high command structure. Indeed Paulus proposed that Army Groups 'North' and 'South' were to concentrate their weight on the flanks of Army Group 'Centre' to

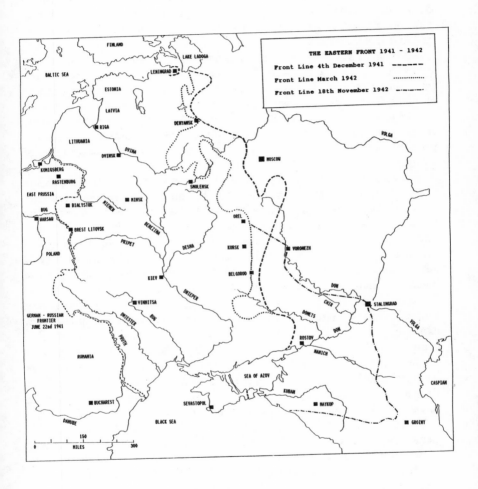

THE EASTERN FRONT 1941 - 1942

Front Line 4th December 1941 -------

Front Line March 1942 ....

Front Line 18th November 1942 -----

FINLAND

LAKE LADOGA

BALTIC SEA

LENINGRAD

ESTONIA

LATVIA

RIGA

DEMYANSK

VOLGA

LITHUANIA

DVINA

DVINSK

MOSCOW

KONIGSBERG

RASTENBURG

SMOLENSK

EAST PRUSSIA

MINSK

BUG

NIEMEN

BIALYSTOK

WARSAW

BREST LITOVSK

BEREZINA

OREL

VORONEZH

PRIPET

DESNA

KURSK

POLAND

BELGOROD

DON

KIEV

DNIEPER

CHIR

VINNITSA

DONETS

STALINGRAD

GERMAN - RUSSIAN
FRONTIER
JUNE 22nd 1941

DNIESTER

BUG

PRUTH

DON

VOLGA

ROSTOV

MANICH

RUMANIA

SEA OF AZOV

CASPIAN

KUBAN

BUCHAREST

SEVASTOPOL

MAYKOP

DANUBE

BLACK SEA

GROZNY

150

0   MILES   300

ensure that the 'ultimate and decisive advance on Moscow' was achieved 'at the latest by the fortieth day of the campaign'.[5]

In both the Paulus and Marcks solutions, and to a lesser extent in the Lossberg plan, the paralysis of the enemy command capabilities, inherent in the capture of Moscow, was the ultimate operational objective, but the physical destruction of the enemy in huge cauldron battles to the west of the Dvina and Dnieper rivers, designed to prevent the mass of the Soviet Army withdrawing largely intact into the vast interior of the country, was in the first instance imperative.

Both objectives were entirely dependent on decisive manoeuvre, and although this was the common denominator of both the Blitzkrieg and the traditional Vernichtungsgedanke strategic concepts, the conflicting primary methods of obtaining a decisive result enshrined in both was not relied on in a pure form. Rather, a division of the essential elements of both strategic creeds were thrown together in that the planners sought to achieve the primary motive of each: both the paralysis and the physical destruction of the enemy.

The traditional ingredient predominated to the extent that the panzers were to be subject to centralized control. The panzer commanders, especially General Heinz Guderian, the principal architect of armoured warfare and the Blitzkrieg doctrine, protested vehemently. Citing the experience gained during the campaign in France, they stressed the necessity of accepting the principle that the panzers should be employed as an independent entity in autonomous long-range operations, and they firmly rejected the idea that the panzer formations should be placed under centralized army command. However, and to the detriment of the campaign in Russia, the conservatively minded General Staff regarded this as an extreme solution which risked exposing the flanks of the central thrust on Moscow to massive counter-attacks by over-extending the depth of the Panzer Groups' attacks in the vast expanse of Western Russia. To put it succinctly, the panzers were to be kept on a leash and restrained from making an all-out dash for the ultimate geographical objectives, by being tied to a policy of operating in close co-operation with the mass of the infantry.

When the Paulus plan was submitted to the Führer the blunted Blitzkrieg element was emasculated still further by Hitler's insistence that the capture of 'Moscow was of no great importance'[6], and his assertion that the primary aim had to be the envelopment of the Soviet forces in cauldron battles. For these reasons Hitler decided to weaken the forces allocated to Army Group 'Centre' by diverting a part of them to the north to assist in the drive on Leningrad (which Hitler rated a higher priority than the Soviet capital), and a part of them to Army Group 'South' to ensure a decisive envelopment in the Ukraine. The motivations behind this tampering were ideological and economic. Hitler was drawn away from the military strategic realities by the emotive title deeds of Leningrad — the cradle of Bolshevism. His emphasis on the northern drive also allayed his psychological aversion to treading the same road as Napoleon in 1812, who captured Moscow but allowed the Russian Army to withdraw intact into the interior with nightmare consequences. The attraction in the South was motivated quite simply by greed, the rich economic and material gains in the Ukraine and the Don Basin proving an irresistible magnet.

The interference of the fanatical amateur in the Paulus solution not only involved a dispersion of the main effort, contrary to sound military strategy, which was to have been concentrated in the centre but was now to be diverted towards the Baltic and Black Sea, but also radically altered the method in that practically all vestiges of the Blitzkrieg concept were to be totally subordinated to the traditional modus operandi. The inveterate political gambler was hedging his bets on military orthodoxy. 'So with a stroke of the pen,' wrote General Walter Warlimont (Deputy Chief of the Wehrmacht Operations Staff), 'a new concept of the main lines of the campaign against Russia was substituted for that which the OKW had worked out as a result of months of painstaking examination and cross-checking from all angles by the best military brains available.'[7]

Despite the fact that the generals continued to regard the capture of Moscow as the main and most vital objective, Hitler's priorities were, without remonstration, duly incorporated into the final directive of Operation Barbarossa, as Hitler code-named the campaign (a name laced with overtones of medieval barbarity). Hitler's nefarious influence was encapsulated in a single paragraph of the Army High Command (Oberkommando des Heeres) final deployment directive of 31 January, 1941:

> The first intention... is, by means of swift and deep thrusts by strong mobile formations north and south of the Pripet Marsh, to tear open the front of the mass of the Russian Army... The enemy groups separated by these penetrations will then be destroyed.... *The conduct of operations will be based on the principles proved in the Polish Campaign.'*
> (author's italics)[8]

The principles were those of Vernichtungsgedanke: the concept of decisive manoeuvre around the enemy's flanks to achieve a double envelopment, ending with the annihilation of the enemy in *Kesselschlacten* (cauldron battles). The import was that instead of the panzers playing first fiddle in a Blitzkrieg, driving as deep as they could into the enemy rear as fast as they could, which had paid such rich dividends in France, they were reduced, in the main, to playing second fiddle to the mass of the infantry. Victory now rested firmly on a strategic concept formulated at the turn of the century by Schlieffen, long before tanks were even dreamt of. The result was that

Barbarossa, after spectacular initial success, deteriorated into a broad frontal advance which only served to push the Russians deep into the interior, the very contingency that Hitler feared most and was desperate to avoid at all costs. His meddling in the planning made Stalingrad inevitable.

THE MEANS

Writing after the war, General Gunther von Blumentritt (Chief of Staff, 4th Army) expressed the opinion that Germany's best hope of defeating Russia lay in the pure Blitzkrieg strategy expounded by Guderian:

Guderian had a different idea — to drive deep, as fast as possible, and leave the encircling of the enemy to be completed by the infantry forces that were following up. Guderian urged the importance of keeping the Russians on the run, and allowing them no time to rally. He wanted to drive straight on to Moscow, and was convinced that he could get there if no time was wasted. Russia's resistance might be paralysed by the thrust at the centre of Stalin's power. Guderian's plan was a very bold one — and meant big risks in maintaining reinforcements and supplies. But it might have been the lesser of two risks. By making the armoured forces turn in each time, and forge a ring around the enemy forces they had by-passed, a lot of time was lost.[9]

However, it is doubtful if this application would have proved any more successful than the strategy actually employed. The bottom line was that the Third Reich simply did not possess the military or economic means necessary to defeat the Soviet Union.

On the eve of Barbarossa the German forces committed to the invasion numbered 3,050,000 men, 3,350 tanks, 7,184 artillery pieces, 600,000 motor vehicles and 625,000 horses, disposed in 148 divisions (114 infantry, 19 panzer and 15 motorized). This amounted to 75 per cent of the existing German Field Army. In addition, 2,770 aircraft were committed to the campaign, representing 65 per cent of the Luftwaffe's first-line strength of 4,300 machines.[10]

Impressive as this force might seem at first glance, it was only 290,000 men, 776 tanks and 20 aircraft stronger than the forces committed to the campaign in the West in May, 1940, and deficient by 516 artillery pieces. When this force is equated to the relative geographical factors of space, the small increase in strength is completely negated. The decision in the West was achieved in an area of 50,000 square miles, while the area in which it was hoped to force a decision in the Western reaches of Russia amounted to some 1,000,000 square miles. Reduced to representational mathematical terms the relation of density in men and tanks to the square mile in the West amounted to 55.2 and 3.05 respectively: in Russia the density diminished to an infinitesimal 0.05 in men and 0.003 in tanks. Moreover, the relation of the number of tanks to the vast space involved was only one aspect which militated against a successful Blitzkrieg campaign in Barbarossa.

Conscious of the relative paucity of the forces available in relation to the enormity of his great undertaking, Hitler resorted to the naive contrivance of doubling the number of panzer divisions that had been employed in May, 1940. When it was made clear to him that German industrial capacity was not sufficient to produce the large number of tanks necessary for this level of expansion, he fulfilled his aim by the artificial means of mutilating the composition of the panzer formations. By removing one tank regiment from each of the ten existing divisions, ten new ones were formed on these 'ribs'. This self-deceiving dilution resulted in the normal divisional organization of two panzer regiments with a total establishment of about 280 tanks being reduced to a single tank regiment of about 140 tanks. To complete the illusion of a more imposing panzer divisional order of battle, the numerical strength of the divisions was topped up to the normal ration strength by increasing the lorry-borne infantry from one to two regiments. The reality was that 'the punch' that each division could deliver was substantially reduced, for of its 17,000 men only some 2,600 remained tank crews.

Hitler's fraudulent attempt to increase his apparent strength fundamentally flawed the effectiveness of the panzer divisions, because the bulk of their regimental elements, being trackless, lacked cross-country mobility and were thus devoid of the tanks' ability to move over open terrain without dependence on hard-surfaced roads. The full extent of this disability was soon to become apparent due to the primitive state of the roads in the Soviet Union. Of the 850,000 miles of Russian roads, 700,000 were hardly more than cart tracks which turned to quagmires of mud in heavy rain; and of the 150,000 miles of allegedly all-weather roads, only 40,000 miles had a hard surface.

The appalling road conditions, which were to act as a brake on the speed of the advance, was only one of the many unpleasant surprises to greet the Germans; the size and quality of the Soviet tank park was another. *Fremde Heere Ost* (Foreign Armies East), the General Staff intelligence-gathering section for the Eastern Front, estimated that the Soviets possessed some 10,000 tanks. However, all of these were considered to be qualitatively inferior to the German panzers. In fact the true figure was nearer 24,000, and although the vast majority were indeed obsolete, the first of two new series of main battle tanks — the 25-ton T-34 medium and the 43-ton KV heavy — were to make their appearance, albeit in small numbers, within a month of the German attack. These super, armoured monsters completely outclassed the Reich's main battle tanks (PzKw IIIs & PzKwIVs) in both firepower, armour protection and speed, rudely shattering the German illusions of technical superiority. This undreamt-of qualitative superiority was matched by the Russian production capabilities. During 1941 Soviet industry churned out a total of 6,590 tanks, nearly double Germany's total of 3,790 tanks and self-propelled guns. During the following year the Russian total of 24,446 dwarfed the Reich's 6,180 by sixty-six per cent. A similar situation existed with regard to aircraft. The Soviet air park on the eve of the invasion numbered 17,745, and although some 80 per cent of the first-line strength was obsolete and of crude design by German standards, new aircraft which proved a match for the German machines were shortly to enter service in meaningful numbers, being produced in quantities nearly double that of the Reich. Through 1941/1942 the Soviets manufactured 33,857 combat aircraft, compared to Germany's 18,890. This kind of ratio existed in all other aspects of military hardware. For instance Russia produced 75 per cent more artillery pieces through 1941/42 (169,300 to 33,857).

Apart from Russia's greater industrial base, this great disparity in the relative production figures was to a large extent attributable to the Reich's economy being geared to the principle of 'armament in width' rather than to 'armament in depth,' a principle explained by Alan Milward:

> [Germany]... had organized her economy to maintain a relatively high level of ready armaments [armament in width], but had not undertaken the basic investment and redevelopment necessary to produce the level of armaments sufficient to bring success in a war against the greater mass-productive powers [armament in depth]. She had a high degree of armament readiness, but a low degree of armaments-producing potential. Her interest was in the production of ready armaments but not in increasing her armaments-producing machinery. 'Guns and butter' was Hitler's aim.[11]

With only a superficial grasp of economics, Hitler had a blind disregard for the difficulties involved in demanding the simultaneous production of a relatively high level of ready-to-use armaments and the maximum production of consumer goods designed to ensure the maintenance of high morale amongst the German populace.

From the outbreak of war through the defeat of France this policy had worked perfectly, due simply to the rapid nature of the individual campaigns. 'Business as usual' was the motto, and the Nazi propaganda machine was loud in proclaiming that the intense economic pressures of war on the nation's economy had been avoided. Indeed, for the first two years of the war the output of consumer goods from German industry actually rose above their pre-war levels.

To 'crush Soviet Russia in a quick campaign' was the first imperative in Führer Directive 21, for the author was acutely aware that his 'armaments in width' policy could only sustain a lightning campaign, and was in no way geared to a long war of attrition with a power whose economic strength was as great as that of the USSR.

A rapid and decisive conclusion to Barbarossa was also essential to deny the Russians the time and opportunity to mobilize their vast reserves of manpower. The Greater German population of 1941 was 78 million, and Hitler could not afford to get bogged down in a war of attrition with a country which possessed a population sixty per cent larger (194 million). Moreover, although the Germans were fully aware of the Soviet *Osoaviakhim*, a nationwide paramilitary organization numbering some 36 million members (equivalent to nearly half the population of the Reich), who were trained to defend local areas and would provide a ready reservoir of militarily competent reserves, Hitler dismissed the possibility that this great latent strength could be brought to bear in time. His gaze was riveted on the immediate strength of the Red Army gathered in the frontier districts, which he was convinced the Wehrmacht could defeat in a summer campaign. It was a myopic view that did not penetrate into the vast space of the Russian hinterland, which was pregnant with harsh and terrifying realities.

Red Army strength in the border districts facing the German front, running for 930 miles from the Baltic to the Black Sea, was, according to the latest appreciation prepared by Fremde Heere Ost (dated 13 June) about 3,000,000 men. This was a realistic estimate, as Soviet accounts give the strength as 2.9 million men, almost equal to that fielded by the *Ostheer*, as the German field army on the Eastern front was named. But, still basking in the illusion of invincibility fostered by the spectacular victory over superior numerical armies in France, the German generals had few doubts that the Ostheer could destroy the Red Army in the Western districts within the first few weeks of the campaign and achieve a decisive victory in little more than two months. Although their view was not as myopic as Hitler's, they nonetheless deluded themselves in the absurd conviction that the seemingly inexhaustible reserves of Russian manpower were valueless because they lacked effective leadership.

Up to a point this belief had some substance. Between 1937 and 1939 the paranoid Stalin, with no other motive than ensuring his grip on absolute power, carried out a purge of the military. Altogether some 35,000 officers were either dismissed, imprisoned or shot during this fearful reign of terror. The Red Army lost all of its military district commanders, all its corps commanders, nearly all of its divisional and brigade commanders and nearly half of its regimental commanders. The best of the military brains along with the most experienced officers were simply swept away, and their places were filled by largely inexperienced men who had no understanding of the fundamental principles of decisive manoeuvre employed by the Germans. However, Halder's contention that *'Die Rote Armee ist führerlos'* (the Red

Army is leaderless) was stretching the point too far and soon proved to be as irrational as Hitler's belief that Russia was a 'clay colossus without a head'.

Most of the military leaders were inclined blithely to accept Hitler's underestimation of Soviet Power, which was summed up in a typical remark he made to von Rundstedt: 'You have only to kick in the door [of Russia], and the whole rotten structure will come crashing down.' Like Hitler, they too were lured by the vision of a great autarkic German state and the total mastery of Europe. Those who harboured doubts suppressed them because they could offer no alternative to the problem of an undefeated Britain, and because they too suffered from the infectious delusion that the victory in Russia would be so swiftly won that the risks of a two-front war would be short-lived.

The illusion was total, for no studies had been made to provide alternative plans should the campaign, as it was conceived, fail in any of its main essentials. The consensus of opinion prevailing on the eve of Barbarossa was encapsulated in the braggadocio of General Alfred Jodl (Chief of Operations OKW): 'The Russian colossus will be proved to be a pig's bladder; prick it, and it will burst.'

Strangely and uncharacteristically, the only glimmer of reality to break through the soaring clouds of fantasy was the signs of depression and nervous agitation that suddenly gripped Hitler on the day before the invasion. Amidst the bustle of last minute preparations in the Wolfsschanze, the Führer's command post situated deep in a mosquito-infested forest ten miles outside the East Prussian town of Rastenburg, Hitler gloomily remarked: 'I feel as if I am pushing open the door to a dark room never seen before, without knowing what lies behind the door.'[12] But he was not the kind of man to be deterred from realizing his life's dream on account of an intrusive stab of reason. Consequently at 0315 the following morning (Sunday, 22 June, 1941) a gigantic flash of lightning, followed a split second later by a deep thunderous roar, rippled along the 930 miles of the German front as guns of all calibres simultaneously belched fire and the Ostheer lurched forward into the unknown of the Russian enigma. Following in the wake of the troops came the *Einsatzgruppen*, four special squads each 3,000 men strong, whose sole object was the murder of the Jews, the Communist Commissars and the intelligentsia in the territory wrested from the Red Army. These Einsatzgruppen fulfilled the racial element of Hitler's lunatic phantasmagoric vision of the apocalyptic final struggle between the Aryans and the Jewish-Bolshevik hordes. The Devil was loose and riding high.

THE REALITY

The success of Barbarossa depended entirely on the destruction of the Red Army in huge cauldron battles west of the Dvina and Dnieper Rivers, the nearest reaches of their courses lying just over 200 miles to the east of the Germans' jumping-off positions.

By 10 July, *Heeresgruppe Nord* (Army Group North) was well beyond the Dvina, its spearhead (4th Panzer Army) having advanced 300 miles in nineteen days of slashing its way through the Baltic States towards Leningrad. The mailed fist of *Heeresgruppe Mitte* (Centre), in the form of 2nd and 3rd Panzer Armies, had reached the upper stretches of both the Dvina and Dnieper, while the lead units of 1st Panzer Army of *Heeresgruppe Süd* (South) were within 50 miles of Kiev (situated on the middle reaches of the Dnieper).

The distances covered were indeed impressive, but the conquest of territory was not the yardstick of success. Although huge chunks had been torn out of both the Red Army's front and order of battle, the hard fact was that the mass of the Russian forces had not been destroyed west of the Dvina and Dnieper. This crucial factor in the German plan had not been achieved because neither Heeresgruppe North or South had been able to bring about a single, all important, cauldron battle, while the inner armoured pincers thrown out by Heeresgruppe Centre in two attempted Kesselschlacten, in the Bialystok salient (3/5 July) and in the area of Minsk (9 July), were too slow in closing, with the result that over half the encircled forces in both were able to slip out before the net was drawn tight. Some 300,000 prisoners were taken, but with roughly the same number being able to withdraw to form new defensive blocks further east, neither envelopment could be rated as decisive.

The vast distances involved and the primitive state of the roads had acted as a decided check on the speed of the panzers' attempts to close the ring around the partially enveloped forces, aspects which were magnified in the Minsk cauldron by the onset of heavy rain which turned the sandy soil into mud. This proved a great handicap, since it not only cramped tactical manoeuvring across country, but held up strategic road movements. The 'only one good tarred road in the whole area was the new highway that ran past Minsk direct to Moscow, and that was only of partial service to Hitler's plan – which contemplated, not a race for Moscow, but a wide-cast encircling manoeuvre that had to use the soft-surfaced roads on either flank. Following the rain storms of early July, these quicksands sucked down the invader's mobility and multiplied the effect of the stubborn resistance offered by many isolated pockets of Russian troops within the area that the Germans had overrun.'[13]

With the failure to prevent the withdrawal of the mass of the Red Army over the Dvina and Dnieper, Hitler's dream of obtaining a quick decisive victory faded. But the reality of the situation did not impress itself on the Führer, who, blinded by the great depth and speed of the advance, boasted to Oshima, the Japanese Ambassador, that he 'did not think he would have to be fighting after the middle of September; in six weeks or so it would be pretty much all over.'[14]

The delusion continued to be fostered by the speed of the subsequent advance ever deeper into the endless spaces in the attempt to fulfil the will-o'-the-wisp vision of rounding up the Red Army in gigantic rings.

Between the beginning of August and the end of October five major Kesselschlacten were actually brought about, but although Russian army after Russian army was surrounded and technically destroyed, again and again the steel cord formed by the panzers was too thin to stop tens of thousands of enemy soldiers from breaking through and filtering east. By any conventional military standard, the Soviet forces were out-fought, out-manoeuvred and beaten. But the Russian soldiers fought on with a bitter tenacity, sucking the panzers ever deeper into the hinterland and into endless whirlpools of bloody battles.

The limitless reserves of Russian manpower, which the German generals had dismissed as valueless, were already beginning to make themselves felt. The Ostheer was learning to its cost that the Russian colossus was like a many-headed hydra: for every dozen divisions they destroyed, the Russians simply threw in another dozen ad infinitum.

By the second week of November the war of decisive manoeuvre, on which Hitler had banked all, had degenerated into the nightmare of a broad, almost continuous front which had expanded by a third from the original 930 miles to 1,490 miles. Not only was the Ostheer stretched perilously thin over this vast line, they had also been drawn 600 miles into the interior.

The achievements had been great, but not great enough, and had been bought at a terrible price. Since the invasion began the Ostheer had suffered 743,112 casualties (not counting the sick), which represented 24.36 per cent of the original force, and was equivalent to one regiment in every division. To put the losses in context, they were 72.27 per cent in excess of the casualties incurred in all the campaigns from the conquest of Poland through the fall of France. The seriousness of this scale of attrition was calculated by Field-Marshal Keitel: 'The monthly losses of the [Ostheer]... averaged 150,000 to 160,000 men. Of these only 90,000 to 100,000 could be replaced. Thus the army in the field was reduced in numbers by 60,000 to 70,000 men each month. It was a piece of simple arithmetic to work out when the German front would be exhausted.'[15]

As far as obtaining a quick and decisive victory was concerned, the Ostheer had shot its bolt. It no longer possessed the strength, in men or armoured vehicles, to concentrate the necessary forces on any one section of the extended front to create major cauldron battles. Not only had mobility been compromised by the loss of 50 per cent of the load-carrying vehicles, but the losses in tanks had been particularly severe. Combat was only partially responsible, and no greater, comparatively, than in the French campaign. Wear and tear, caused by the huge distances that had to be traversed in conjunction with the shocking state of the roads and the terrain, was the main culprit. By early November, despite replacements, the panzer formations as a whole had only 35 per cent of their normal establishment of armoured vehicles fit for action. Such was the state of affairs that OKH rated the 136 divisions on the Eastern Front as equivalent in real terms to no more than 83 full-strength divisions.

The severity of the German casualties were, nonetheless, a drop in the ocean compared to the horrendous mutilation suffered by the Red Army. By the beginning of November the number of killed, wounded and missing amounted to a staggering 5 million, while a further 3 million had been taken prisoner and 21,000 tanks, 32,000 artillery pieces and some 5,000 aircraft had been destroyed.

Russia had suffered the greatest catastrophe in her history, for the military casualties were only one aspect of the tragedy. The advancing German tide had engulfed 900,000 square miles of Western Russia, along with 45 per cent of the total population, some 88 million souls, one-third of the factories, 47 per cent of the land under grain crops and almost half of the railway network. Yet, incredibly, considering the speed of the German onslaught, the Soviets had not only evacuated over 136,000 items of heavy plant for the aviation, tank, weapons and ammunition industries from the threatened areas to new hastily erected factories to the east of the Ural Mountains, but they had also managed to mobilize huge numbers of reserves (5 million between 22 June and 1 July alone).

The result was that, by mid-November, the Red Army was still able to field 4.2 million men in the front line, along with 1,984 tanks (a 531 superiority over the Germans' 1,453 runners at that stage). And that was not all, for behind the front stood an immediate reserve of 123 divisions, 31 brigades and 16 independent regiments, with a further nine reserve armies in the process of being formed and trained. In addition 18 divisions of crack Siberian troops and 9 tank brigades (1,700 tanks) were being withdrawn from the Soviet Far East and would soon be thrown into the affray. But the application of brute force in the form of sheer numbers was only one aspect of the nightmare for the Ostheer. During early November Russia's great and perennial ally, 'General Winter', began to curl its cruel and merciless fingers around the throat of the invader.

The climatic ally of the Russians descended on the battle front with more than average severity, the temperatures falling far below the seasonal norm. Throughout November and December daytime temperatures rarely rose much above -25°C, falling to as low as -40°C at night. At the start of the campaign Hitler declared that the issue of winter clothing was totally unnecessary as Russia would be finished long before the winter set in. This arrogant boast condemned the Ostheer to shiver and freeze in the murderous cold, clad in nothing more than their thin denim summer uniforms. The existing but totally inadequate stocks of warm clothing was immediately dispatched from the Reich. But it took an inordinate length of time to reach the front because the congested, over-extended supply lines could not cope with the extra burden. For example, Heeresgruppe Centre required a minimum of 31 trains a day carrying rations, ammunition and other essentials, but on average only 16 a day managed to reach the forward supply bases. Simple everyday items such as razor blades, soap and shoe-repairing materials had all but disappeared in the Ostheer, with the result that all ranks were filthy and bearded, and had no way of changing their dirty, rotting and verminous underclothes, or their regulation boots which in most cases were falling to pieces. It was not until January that winter clothing began to reach the frozen troops in meaningful quantities, and for thousands it proved too late.

Exhausted by the hundreds of miles of marching and bitter fighting, weakened by dysentery which was rampant throughout the Ostheer, and surviving on an inadequate scale of rations, 'General Winter' was able to reap a rich harvest of misery and death amongst the insufficiently clad, half-starved troops who had plumbed the depths of wretchedness.

Forced to squat in the open in the sub-zero temperatures to relieve the compelling effects of dysentery, thousands died as a result of a congelation of the anus. Frostbite accounted for thousands more. Of the 100,000 frostbite cases which had to be withdrawn from the front, 14,357 required amputation of one or more limbs. The cold was particularly merciless on the wounded who died where they fell, not from their wounds but from the rapid onset of frostbite occasioned by loss of blood.

To add to the miseries, the oil in the recoil systems of the artillery became solidified and machine-guns and automatic rifles failed for the same reason. So severe was the unimaginable cold that, unless muffled, tank and lorry engines iced up while they were running and fires had to be kept burning under them while stationary.

In comparison, the hardy Red Army troops, who were fully acclimatized to the rigours of the extreme conditions, had the advantage of being well fed and suitably attired in felt boots, fur caps and thickly quilted garments. They were also abundantly provided with materials and munitions from supply bases only 20 miles to their rear.

Hitler's dream of Lebensraum was slowly freezing and bleeding to death. Knee-deep in the ruins of the Barbarossa plan, he nonetheless clung to an irrational conviction that the Red Army was at the end of its tether, and that a final lunge by Heeresgruppe Centre to capture Moscow – the objective he had dismissed in the planning stage as 'of no great importance' – would salvage the situation.

On 15 November, began what became known as the *flucht nach vorn* (the flight forward). Moscow lay only 50 miles from the German front, but to the frozen, exhausted, wretched German troops it was too far. Clawing their way forward into the face of fanatical Soviet resistance, through blinding snow blizzards and temperatures that dropped as low as -56°C, the advance ground to a halt 20 miles short of Moscow 17 days later.

The extremes of cold, the infinite horizons of the hostile terrain, and the toughness and indomitable tenacity of the Russian soldiers had ground Hitler's war machine to a standstill. But the Ostheer was not to stand still for long.

At 0300 on the morning of Friday 5 December, in temperatures of minus 25° – 30°C and with snow lying three feet deep, Stalin unleashed a massive counter-offensive on the Moscow front. In five weeks Heeresgruppe Centre was hurled back for distances of between 100 and 200 miles.

Rejecting all appeals by his generals to carry out a controlled tactical withdrawal from untenable positions, Hitler, suffering his first severe set-back since the war began, demanded that every soldier stand fast and fight with dogged resistance 'without regard for enemy breakthroughs on the flanks and rear'. When Guderian remonstrated against the senseless sacrifices this order entailed, Hitler retorted: 'You stand too close to the events. You have too much pity for the soldiers. You ought to disengage yourself more.'

This cynical disregard for the lives of the troops was motivated quite simply by the 'dread of the enormous psychological effects that would necessarily follow the shattering of his image of personal invincibility'.[16] Whole divisions were overrun or surrounded and cut to pieces when a timely withdrawal would have saved them. Yet, as some of the German generals reluctantly admitted, Hitler's brutal insistence that the armies stand and fight probably did avert a rout developing in which Heeresgruppe Centre would have disintegrated and been buried in the snow.

The success of the Moscow counter-offensive goaded Stalin, against the advice of his General Staff, to order a general offensive along practically the whole length of the 1,500 mile front. The result of attempting the impossible was a predictable failure. Two 100-mile-deep salients were punched into the front (in the north near Demyansk, and in the south near Izyum), but the effort involved in achieving these limited gains exhausted the Soviet resources and sucked in the bulk of the precious reserves.

By the middle of March, 1942, the offensive had spent itself and the Soviets found themselves back on the defensive. If, instead of a general offensive, Stalin had concentrated the entire effort against Heeresgruppe

Centre a huge 600-mile chunk would have been ripped out of the German front, effectively wrecking Hitler's dream of Lebensraum. The dispersion of effort left the Ostheer mauled but basically intact, and after licking its frozen wounds, fit enough to launch another offensive — on Stalingrad.

2

THE MAGNET

And they had as king over them the angel of the bottomless pit,
whose name in Hebrew is Abaddon (destruction), but in Greek
he has the name Apollyon (destroyer).

(Revelation 9:11)

CASE BLUE

The Soviet winter offensive of 1941/42 had been halted, primarily, by the
very factors that had proved so baneful to the Germans: exhaustion, lack of
transport, harsh climatic conditions, mud and snow, and difficulties caused
by the rapidly lengthening and uncertain lines of communication. The
stubborn, rigid defence by the Ostheer was the secondary factor, but the
Nazi propaganda machine was quick to proclaim to the German people that
the Führer, in ordering the troops to stand fast, was solely responsible for
halting the Soviet counter-offensive and bringing the Army safely through
the winter. It was hailed in the Nazi press as 'a success of unequalled
magnitude'.

The fostering of yet another illusion only served to convince Hitler that
he was a military genius and that any crisis could be weathered by sheer
will-power in conjunction with strategic and tactical rigidity. The apparent
success of this policy before Moscow became a justification for an obdurate
and often senseless attitude towards German withdrawals, which was to find
its full, disastrous expression at Stalingrad.

Hitler's conceited belief in his own genius had a more serious deleterious
effect. When Field-Marshal von Brauchitsch requested to be relieved from
his post as Commander-in-Chief of the Army, Hitler seized the opportunity
to elevate himself into the position of *Feldherr* (Warlord) by donning the
mantle vacated by Brauchitsch. From this moment on the Führer's control
of operations became paramount and his generals, as Halder complained in
his diary, were henceforth reduced to little more than postmen purveying
Hitler's orders based on his singular and inept conception of strategy.

It was from this Olympian position that Hitler began planning ways and
means of getting his derailed drive for Lebensraum back on the tracks again.
The means at his disposal were slender. Between June, 1941, and the middle

of March, 1942, Hitler's vision of a great Germanic Empire in the East had cost the Ostheer 1,005,636 casualties (killed, wounded, missing and sick – of which 228,000 were frostbite cases). A full 33 per cent of the original number which invaded Russia had been wiped from the German order of battle. During the same period some 800,000 replacements had been fed into the Ostheer, bringing the total number of German troops on the Eastern front in March, 1942, to 2.8 million. But of these 150,000 were in Finland, and a further 200,000 were policing the occupied areas of Soviet territory. The net result was that Hitler had only 2.4 million troops at his disposal on the Eastern front proper. True, Germany's allies were fielding an additional 510,000 troops (330,000 Rumanians; 70,000 Hungarians; 68,000 Italians; 28,000 Slovakians and 14,000 Spanish 'volunteers'), but these were proving to be more of a liability than an asset. They were a constant drain on German resources, especially weaponry, and they were mainly employed in the rear areas or in defensive positions on relatively 'quiet' sectors of the front. A further 300,000 Finnish troops were strung out across their own border.

To give the illusion of greater strength than he actually possessed, Hitler, who was inclined to think in terms of numbers of divisions rather than in the real terms of the actual number of troops, once again resorted to the contrivance of dilution to conjure up an increase of 20 infantry and 3 panzer divisions greater than the Ostheer possessed in June, 1941. This illusion was created by reorganizing the infantry divisions on the basis of 7 battalions instead of 9, and reducing company strength from 180 to 80 soldiers; while the 3,300 tanks in the existing panzer formations (360 less than in June 1941) were thinned out to invent the three new divisions. In comparison to the enemy's ever-increasing strength, Hitler's balance-sheet of a basically fictitious divisional strength represented a precarious foundation for a new offensive.

Despite the previously wildly inaccurate estimations of Soviet strength provided by Fremde Heere Ost, Hitler took blind comfort in the latest estimate provided by the incompetent intelligence gathering section. It not only once again hopelessly underestimated current Red Army strength, but came up with the completely erroneous statement that the Soviets had mobilized all their available manpower resources and were unable to raise any additional tank forces.

Nothing could have been further from the truth. Despite heavy losses sustained during the winter offensive, Red Army strength had actually increased from the 4.2 million men fielded in November, 1941, to 4.9 million by the spring of 1942. But that was not all. By the end of June this prodigious number would climb to 5.5 million troops, supported by 55,600 artillery pieces and mortars, with a mailed fist of 6,000 tanks. This amounted to the equivalent of 410 divisions (239 in excess of Hitler's contrived 171 divisions).

In addition a reserve of 152 divisions, 107 brigades and 225 independent regiments were in the process of being formed. Only in combat aircraft did the Germans have a marginal superiority – 2,750 to 2,600. In all other respects they were hopelessly outnumbered.

Hitler, thanks to the bungling of Fremde Heere Ost, was blithely unaware of the true situation. But with his contempt for reality there is a certainty in reasoning that he would have rejected such unpalatable facts even if they had been presented to him. Von Blumentritt gives graphic evidence of this: 'Intelligence had information that 600 to 700 tanks a month were coming out of the Russian factories in the Ural mountains and elsewhere. When Halder told him of this, Hitler slammed the table and said it was impossible. *He would not believe what he did not want to believe.*' (author's italics)[1] Even in this respect Fremde Heere Ost got it wrong. Far from being impossible, the number of tanks suggested was only a third of the actual number. Throughout 1942 the Soviets churned out an average of 2,037 tanks a month – 75 per cent more than the Reich (515 a month). Russian artillery production was even more impressive in the comparative sense: an average of 10,583 pieces a month – 82 per cent more than the Reich (1,933 a month). This does not take into account the war materials Russia received from the Western Allies. By the end of the war they supplied the Soviets with 427,000 motor vehicles, 10,000 tanks and nearly 19,000 combat aircraft, amongst a host of other materials totalling 17,499,861 tons.

The savage, bloody realities of 1941 had pricked the bubble of the generals' excessive zeal and confidence. Jolted into a more rational and realistic frame of mind, they began to exhibit marked misgivings about the resumption of a full-scale offensive. They even mooted the idea that the Ostheer should withdraw all the way back to the original jumping-off positions in Poland. General Adolf Heusinger describes the generals' dilemma: 'For a long time Halder examined the idea of whether we should not definitely go over to the defensive in the East, since further offensive operations seemed to be beyond our strength. But it is impossible even to mention this to Hitler. What then? If we let the Russians get their second wind...then we have surrendered the initiative to the enemy and we shall never get it back again. We can therefore do only one thing – try once more in spite of all drawbacks.'[2]

They had no choice but to try again. Hitler would have it no other way. His abiding obsession with Lebensraum, the fundamental rationale of the war, made the slightest suggestion of withdrawal from the one-million square miles of Russia already conquered not only repugnant but totally inconceivable. Alternatively, to anchor the Ostheer in its present position was inviting a war of attrition which even Hitler had enough sense to realize he could not win. Unable to step back or remain inert, he could only push forward, deeper and deeper into the Russian interior, with the aim of wiping out 'the entire defence potential remaining to the Soviets, and to cut them off, as far as possible, from their most important centres of war industry'.[3]

The form the new offensive was to take was dictated by the Reich's need for sources of crude oil. The campaign in Russia had so far swallowed up 176 million gallons of motor fuel and had cut so deep into the stockpiles that it would compel a sharp cutback in the amount that could be issued to the Ostheer in 1942. As this would adversely affect the mobility of the Army, the successful prosecution of the war was dependent on Germany securing and utilizing the huge supply of crude oil flowing from the Caucasian oilfields.

On 18 March Halder and his staff in OKH began work on a draft plan for the new offensive, based firmly on objectives and methods of accomplishment dictated by Hitler. The results were refined into Führer Directive 41 by Hitler's personal operations staff in OKW, which he signed on 5 April, 1942, but only after he had made substantial revisions and amendments. In its final form Directive 41 had the nature of an untidy disarray of disconnected thoughts containing many asides and irrelevancies. Entangled in this confused hotch-potch of strategy and tactics, the acquisition of the Caucasus emerged as the ultimate objective but not the first objective.

Just over 300 miles to the east of the German front line lay the city of Stalingrad, and the ideological title deeds inherent in the name – 'the City of Stalin' – exerted a magnetic effect on Hitler's banal, obsessive mode of thought.

During the civil war which resulted from the Russian revolution, the city, which was then called Tsaritsyn, had been held by Red forces during part of 1918 by Voroshilov, Budenny and Stalin. All three claimed the victory when the White forces were repulsed, but when Stalin came to power and history was rewritten, the defence of Tsaritsyn was elevated to legendary proportions with the entire credit being imputed to Stalin, who vaingloriously renamed the city Stalingrad in 1925.

The provocative symbolism of the name perverted the nature of Hitler's planning to the degree that the capture of the city became the first objective in the offensive, while the ultimate objective – the securing of the Caucasian oilfields – was deemed to depend firstly on dominating Stalingrad, ostensibly to protect the north-east flank of the drive into the Caucasus from Soviet counter-attack.

Although Stalingrad was an important industrial and communications centre, Hitler's insistence on its seizure had little basis in reason, since its capture would not assist in the destruction of the Red Army west of the River Don or further the occupation of the Caucasus. His argument that the holding of Stalingrad would offer the advantages of providing security to the north-east flank, and cut the important Volga River traffic to interdict the supply of oil from the Caucasus to the north of the country, had the nature of excuses. Both these aims could be achieved by dominating an area to the south of Stalingrad. In any case cutting the Volga traffic further downstream would have the additional advantage of cutting the Soviets' only remaining rail artery with Astrakhan (north-east Caucasus), while the cutting of the rail communications at Stalingrad had no decisive importance as Stalingrad could be by-passed by the rail link to Saratov (200 miles north-east of Stalingrad).

That Hitler was once again subordinating strategic realities to ideological dogma is evinced by his continuing obsession with Leningrad. Rather than concentrate all the main weight of his available forces on the offensive in the south, he dispersed his strength by adding the capture of Leningrad to his immediate aims. In his directive he insisted that: 'In pursuit of the original plan for the eastern campaign, the armies of the central sector will stand fast, while those in the north will capture Leningrad and link up with the Finns.'[4] Typically, he was once again overestimating the capabilities of his own forces and underestimating the strength of the enemy forces, but this time the end result would be far more calamitous than the reverses suffered in the winter. In blind arrogance he was hurling a mauled and weakened Ostheer into a venture that would break its back and from which it would never recover.

In its final form *Fall Blau* (Case Blue), as the offensive in the south was code-named, called for three consecutively launched parallel thrusts. The first and most northerly thrust was to capture Voronezh (some 300 miles north-west of Stalingrad), and while the infantry consolidated the north-eastern flank the panzers were to wheel south-eastwards to move rapidly down the west bank of the Don, rolling up the enemy from north to south, to link up with the spearhead of the second (central) parallel thrust in the area of Millerovo (200 miles west of Stalingrad). The two united thrusts were then to strike out eastwards along the banks of the upper Don to approach Stalingrad from the north-west, to link up with the panzer spearhead of the third and southernmost parallel thrust approaching Stalingrad from the south-west. The infantry of the latter thrust was to protect the southern flank by confining the enemy to the area of the Sea of Azov. Only after Stalingrad had been captured was the advance into the Caucasus, the ultimate objective, to be carried out.

During the advance of the three thrusts the bulk of the Soviet forces were to be destroyed in cauldron battles. However, the huge Kesselschlachten envisaged in the Barbarossa plan had no place in Fall Blau. In Hitler's reasoning: 'Experience has sufficiently shown that the Russians are not very vulnerable to large operational encircling movements. It is therefore of decisive importance that...individual breaches of the front should take the form of close pincer movements. We must avoid closing the pincers too late, thus giving the enemy the possibility of avoiding destruction.'[5]

The strategic concepts of the eternal corporal in his self-appointed role as *Feldherr* now predominated. What he intended was to destroy the Red Army in a large number of small tactical encirclements. He simply did not appreciate that he did not have enough forces available to create enough of these small cauldrons to achieve a decisive result. Halder was appalled at the prospect: 'The situation is getting more and more intolerable. There is no room for any serious work. This "leadership", so called, is characterized by a pathological reacting to the impressions of the moment and a total lack of any understanding of the command machinery and its possibilities.'[6]

With his Caesaristic tendencies of thinking in absolutes and maniacally subordinating military principles to his grandiose goals, Hitler was completely oblivious to the limitations of pursuing an offensive strategy with limited strength in unlimited space. The original length of the front from which the three thrusts were to be made stretched for some 500 miles from Orel in the north to Taganrog in the south. But what he was attempting would rapidly expand the front into a massive 1,500-mile salient stretching from Orel through Stalingrad, south through the area of the Grozny oilfields, and then back again along the foothills of the Caucasus Mountains to the Sea of Azov. The forces available were simply not adequate to stretch along this enormous frontage.

For the execution of Fall Blau Hitler amassed 38 infantry, 9 panzer, 5 motorized and 2 Waffen SS motorized divisions. These 54 divisions were disposed in 5 armies:

	Panzer	Motorized	Infantry
6th Army	2	1	15
2nd Army	–	1	4
17th Army	1	1	6
1st Panzer	3	2	7
4th Panzer	3	2	6

On account of the vast distances involved (the salient would be almost as long as the entire existing front in Russia), the five armies were divided into two new army groups: Heeresgruppe 'B' under the command of Field-Marshal Fedor von Bock (4th Pz, 2nd and 6th Armies), and Heeresgruppe 'A' under the command of Field-Marshal Wilhelm List (1st Pz and 17th Army).

All of the 54 divisions were brought up to full strength, but this was achieved at the expense of the remaining 117 divisions along the rest of the Eastern Front. Of the 2.4 million men in the Ostheer strung out along the 1,500 miles of the main front just over a million (42 per cent) were assigned to the 54 divisions earmarked for Fall Blau. This brought the average divisional establishment to some 18,500 men. In comparison the remaining divisions in the Ostheer averaged 11,900 men (64 per cent of full establishment).

The situation regarding the panzers was comparable. Each of the 9 panzer divisions had about 140 tanks each; the remainder (some 230) of the 1,495 tanks assigned to Blau (45 per cent of the total in the Ostheer) were disposed among the 7 motorized divisions.

That all vestiges of Blitzkrieg had disappeared from German operational planning is illustrated by the fact that, instead of being concentrated within the two panzer armies, three of the nine panzer divisions were dispersed among two of the infantry armies, while three of the seven motorized divisions were distributed among three infantry armies. In other words one-third of the mechanized units were scattered instead of being concentrated as they should have been.

Moreover, the panzer armies included large numbers of infantry divisions in their order of battle. Six of 4th Panzer Army's eleven divisions were mainly reliant on horses, and seven of 1st Panzer Army's twelve were similarly handicapped.

In line with Hitler's intoxication with the number of divisions marked on his situation maps, he included a number of allied divisions in the general framework of the forthcoming operations to give the illusion of greater strength than he actually possessed. But the 20 allied divisions included (6 Hungarian, 8 Rumanian and 6 Italian infantry divisions) had an establishment only half that of the German divisions and were deficient in arms, equipment, training, leadership and organization. In the opinion of General Paulus: 'The allied troops were not fit to take part in a major, modern war, and particularly in one fought in the severe climatic conditions of a Russian winter. Furthermore, opinion in allied countries was opposed to the sending of their troops to the Volga and the Don. Nor could it have been easy to explain to, say, an Italian soldier why he should be called upon to fight in the depths of the Russian steppes – and under climatic conditions which were all but intolerable to him. The same applied, generally speaking, to all the other allies. The 2nd Hungarian Army was composed of units plucked haphazardly from the whole of the Hungarian Army and of men recruited for the most part from the territories which Hungary had but recently acquired. The weakness inevitable in a force of this composition will be immediately apparent.'[7]

This obvious weakness Hitler was able to brush over by relegating them, in the main, to the role of occupying and safeguarding the new territories to be conquered, and by propping up the flanks of the German armies. Only the Rumanians, who supplied the major contingent, were to participate in any considerable numbers in the actual offensive operations. That at least was the theory, but when it was found necessary to include all of these allied divisions in vital areas of the front line the whole security of the vast salient was undermined with disastrous repercussions.

Another cause of the forthcoming tragedy was Hitler's failure to appreciate the inadequate nature of the supply lines replenishing the 74 German and allied divisions. There were not enough railheads in the areas over which the offensive was to unfold, a problem compounded by lack of locomotives and rolling stock to run the available railways at anything near full capacity. Nor could much reliance be placed on motor transport, for the availability of trucks and fuel was limited. The panzer and motorized divisions had only 85 per cent of their organic transport vehicles, and the infantry divisions had an even lower percentage available.

Neither did Hitler have much of an inkling of actual Soviet strength deployed to oppose his designs. On the eve of Fall Blau, German intelligence calculated that the Soviets were fielding 91 rifle divisions, 32 rifle brigades, 20 cavalry divisions and 44 tank brigades along the fronts of Heeresgruppe A and B. This was fairly realistic as far as unit numbers went. Actual Red Army order of battle was 81 rifle divisions, 38 rifle brigades, 12 cavalry divisions and 62 tank brigades which were dispersed among 16 armies in 4 'Fronts' (the Soviet equivalent of a German army group).[8]

However, Fremde Heere Ost believed all of these formations to be far below normal strength, and simply did not appreciate that the total strength of these forces amounted to 1.7 million men: almost half a million more than the combined German and allied troops. With regard to tanks the Soviet superiority was even more pronounced: 3,472 were concentrated on the axis of the German offensive (1,977 more than the Germans) of which 2,300 were KVs and T-34s.

In addition a further 17 rifle divisions, 3 rifle brigades, 3 cavalry divisions and 3 tank brigades were in the Caucasus, while 9 reserve armies were situated behind the front, and beyond these new armies were forming. While, lurking in the shadows behind all this, was the sinister form of Stalin who, with a kind of primitive Oriental shrewdness, was gambling on Hitler's arrogance to stretch the already overstretched Ostheer to breaking point.

DRAMATIS PERSONAE

Of the five German armies in Fall Blau, two, 4th Panzer and 2nd Army (supported by 4 Rumanian divisions and the 2nd Hungarian Army) were assigned to the northern thrust, and two, 1st Panzer and 17th Army (supported by 4 Rumanian divisions and the 8th Italian Army) to the southern thrust. This left only the German 6th Army to carry out the central thrust. During operations in Poland, France and on the southern wing of

Barbarossa 6th Army had earned the reputation of being a corps d'elite. To achieve the objectives outlined in Fall Blau it was reinforced with new divisions which had been raised in the Reich, and a few veteran divisions brought up to full establishment and transferred from France. With a final holding of 18 divisions (all German), which represented 33.33 per cent of the German divisions in Heeresgruppe A and B, it was the largest in the whole German Army.

The man chosen to command this huge army of 330,000 men, 500 tanks and some 7,000 guns and mortars, was fatefully ill-suited to the position. Fifty-two-year-old Friedrich Wilhelm Ernst Paulus had been chosen purely and simply on account of favouritism rather than ability.

During his tenure as Chief-of-Staff of 6th Army (1939 – 1940) Paulus had become a firm favourite of Field-Marshal Walther von Reichenau, and when the latter was promoted from the command of 6th Army to the command of Heeresgruppe South, he used his influence to persuade Hitler to give Paulus, who had served as Quartiermeister I from the summer of 1940, the command of 6th Army. As Hitler had long regarded Reichenau as absolutely loyal to his cause, including its more brutal excesses, he accepted the recommendation and Paulus duly assumed command of the 'crack' army on 5 January, 1942. No doubt Hitler's decision was influenced in large measure by the fact that Paulus was essentially a man who obeyed orders without question, and he had made it known that he was convinced of Hitler's infallible military genius.

Although a gifted staff officer, Paulus had never commanded a regiment, let alone a division or corps. Indeed his last appointment in direct command of troops had been in peacetime when he was OC of a rifle company for two years in the early 1920s, and the brief command of a motor transport section in 1934. With the Führer in command of the army, seniority and experience obviously counted for nothing, for an officer who had never commanded a unit in active wartime operations suddenly found himself tribune over corps commanders in 6th Army who were not only senior to him on the army list, but were far more competent by virtue of their combat-experience.

Six-foot four tall, slim, painstakingly well groomed, habitually wearing gloves because he hated dirt, and in the habit of taking a bath and changing his uniform twice a day, Paulus was sarcastically nicknamed 'The Noble Lord' and 'Our Most Elegant Gentleman' by his peers in 6th Army. But despite his aristocratic bearing he was never the 'von' frequently but mistakenly attributed to him by numerous historians. In fact he was of middle-class yeoman stock hailing from the province of Hesse-Nassau, his father being nothing more than a minor civil servant.

A gifted staff officer, with a flair for the intellectual aspects of the profession of war, Paulus undoubtedly was, but a ponderous mastery of detail and a fascination with figures and grand strategy are not the virtues of a field commander. Intuition, inspiration and incisive reactions and decisions in the whirling confusion and smoke of battle are the necessary attributes of a master of fluid situations. In comparison Paulus proved to be uninspired and incapable of making balanced judgements independent of and contrary to Hitler's inept strategic concepts. As Quartiermeister I he had observed at first hand the 'insanity' of Hitler's leadership, but incredibly his belief in Hitler's 'genius' remained unshaken. Colonel Heim, who served as Chief of Staff 6th Army under Reichenau and for five months under Paulus until he was relieved by Colonel Arthur Schmidt in May, 1942, has provided a graphic vignette of Paulus:

> Within a few days the new C-in-C 6th Army had firmly grasped the reins that had slipped from his deceased predecessor's grasp (Reichenau died of a heart-attack on 17 January). He sat in the same chair as the late Field-Marshal and he used the same pens and pencils; and he was every inch a soldier, with a superb mastery of his profession. And yet, in appearance, how utterly different he was from Reichenau. Well groomed and with slender hands, always beautifully turned-out with gleaming white collar and immaculately polished field-boots, he presented such a contrast to his rugged and always deliberately battle-stained predecessor. Before me there now stood not a massive body on sturdy legs but a slender, rather over-tall figure, whose slight stoop seemed somehow to be a gesture of goodwill towards those of smaller stature. Instead of the fresh face of the Field-Marshal, with his small yet sparkling light blue eyes, were the slender head and features. Was it the face of an ascetic? For that it was hardly severe enough. Rather, I would say, it was the face of a martyr. And the characters of Reichenau and Paulus were as different as were their physical attributes. Where before a broad and worldly wisdom had been in command, taking seemingly snap decision, but decisions which so often turned out to be unerringly correct, there now ruled a trained mind, sober, cool and calculating. In the place of an agile intellect, quick to grasp the essentials of any problem, there was now a brain which examined every aspect from every possible angle, which painstakingly separated the wheat from the chaff, which advanced slowly, logically, step by step, until absolute clarity led it, almost laboriously, to the correct decision. And instead of categorical orders, we now had irrefutable, convincing argument and proof.[9]

The final negative in this catalogue of negatives is that when this extremely methodical and overly-meticulous man reached a decision which he believed to be right, he adhered to it unswervingly, exhibiting obstinacy and rigidity of Hitlerian proportions which was to seal the doom of 6th Army.

TOO MUCH, WITH TOO LITTLE, ALL AT ONCE.

At 0215 on 28 June, 1942, one year and six days since Hitler invaded Russia, the northern thrust of Fall Blau smashed through the Russian front lines. Nine days later the tanks of General Hoth's 4th Panzer Army had reached their first objective — Voronezh — more than 100 miles from the jumping-off position.

Two days after the northern thrust lurched forward, 6th Army struck out from the area around Kharkov and two days later (2 July) achieved the first of the planned small tactical encirclements to the east of Stary Oskol, some 50 miles from the original front line. Despite this favourable start Fall Blau began to misfire. The northern thrust encountered stiff Soviet resistance at Voronezh and von Bock was reluctant to let 4th Panzer Army wheel south-east as planned until the large enemy forces on his north-east flank had been subdued. Consequently he only released one corps of 4th Panzer to drive down the west bank of the Don, and this did not prove powerful enough to form an inner pincer to envelop the great flood of Russian troops falling back in front of 6th Army, which was advancing across the open, sun-baked steppe beyond the Donets River into the great bend of the Don.

Hitler was furious when he discovered that the whole of 4th Panzer had not wheeled south-east, and he ordered von Bock to hold Voronezh with the 2nd Army and to set all the panzers rolling south in a desperate attempt to prevent the mass of the Soviet forces escaping east across the Don. But already the effects of the inadequate supply lines began to be felt. Lack of fuel forced the panzers to a halt on a number of occasions, and it was not until 13 July that 4th Panzer reached Boguchar, 150 miles south of Voronezh and 200 miles north-east of Stalingrad. They were too late, because the bulk of the Red Army, retiring in front of the relentless pressure of 6th Army, had already escaped across the Don and only 80,000 were cut off. On account of this failure Hitler relieved von Bock of his command of Heeresgruppe B and appointed General Maximilian von Weichs in his place.

In an attempt to save the situation Hitler ordered a radical departure from the original plan. Convinced that the Red Army must have withdrawn to the lower Don to a position north of Rostov, where 17th Army of the southern thrust was meeting stiff resistance, he ordered 4th Panzer to drive south across the rear of 6th Army to cross the lower Don in conjunction with 1st Panzer Army to form an inner pincer on the Soviet forces facing 17th Army. This proved to be a fatal mistake, as General von Kleist, commanding 1st Panzer Army, complained: 'The 4th Panzer was advancing on my left. It could have taken Stalingrad without a fight in mid-July, but was diverted south to help me in crossing the lower Don. I

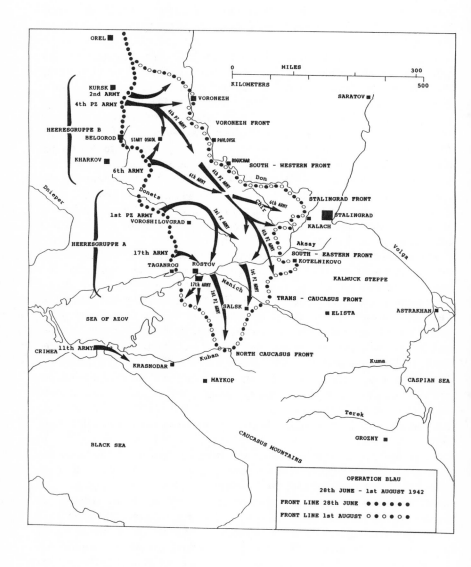

OPERATION BLAU
28th JUNE – 1st AUGUST 1942
FRONT LINE 28th JUNE ● ● ● ● ● ●
FRONT LINE 1st AUGUST ○ ● ○ ● ○ ●

did not need it's aid, and it merely congested the roads I was using. When it turned north again, a fortnight later, the Russians had gathered sufficient forces at Stalingrad to check it.'[10]

The diversion of 4th Panzer Army away from Stalingrad, which it could have taken off the march, was a fatal mistake, for it achieved nothing south of the lower Don, the Russian forces rapidly withdrawing eastwards before the armoured pincer could close on them, while the armies of Heeresgruppe B could not reach Stalingrad in the absence of 4th Panzer. The 2nd Army was tied down by a Soviet counter-offensive around Voronezh; 2nd Hungarian Army was defending 100 miles of front along the Don from Voronezh to Pavlovsk, while 6th Army was trying to cover and defend its 100-mile left flank running south-east from Pavlovsk, and at the same time advance 250 miles through the Don Bend on Stalingrad. It was a task beyond its means because 6th Army's only panzer corps (40th) had been transferred to 1st Panzer Army. In return Paulus received 8th Italian Army from Heeresgruppe A, which took over the defence of 6th Army's northern flank on the sector of the front south-east of Pavlovsk. By the time this was effected and 6th Army was able to resume its advance the Soviets had thrown in substantial forces from their reserves to defend the approaches to Stalingrad. The capture of the city, which could have been achieved with hardly a fight, was shortly, on account of Hitler's 'genius', to turn into one of the bloodiest battles in history.

It had by now become apparent that the three thrusts of Fall Blau had largely punched into thin air. Hardly any of the small, tight envelopments designed to destroy the mass of the Red Army had been realized. Halder believed that the Russians were systematically avoiding contact and had adopted an elastic, mobile defence, avoiding encirclements by surrendering territory in timely and planned withdrawals. Hitler dismissed this inference as nonsense. He was convinced that the Russians were in full flight, reeling from the blows dealt by the three thrusts, and that the mass retreat was akin to a rout symptomatic of organizational and moral collapse. Confident that victory was in sight and completely obsessed by the belief that the Red Army had already been decisively defeated, Hitler now committed the cardinal tactical sin of splitting his forces and sending them off in two directions at right angles to each other. Henceforth Heeresgruppe A and B would be conducting separate campaigns, each having to be sustained independently without either being fully independent of the success or failure of the other.

The extent of Hitler's departure from reality is illustrated in the opening paragraph of Führer Directive 45, which was issued on 23 July, 1942: 'In a campaign which has lasted little more than three weeks, the deep objectives outlined by me for the south flank of the Eastern Front have been largely achieved. Only weak enemy forces have succeeded in escaping encirclement and reaching the further bank of the Don.'[11] On the basis of this masterly piece of self-deception, Hitler launched into the soaring heights of wishful thinking which completely ignored the limits of the possible by ordering Heeresgruppe A (1st Panzer and 17th Army) to advance southward into the Caucasus to take possession of the oil resources in the Grozny and Baku areas. At the same time Heeresgruppe B was 'to develop the Don defences and, by a thrust forward to Stalingrad, to smash the enemy forces concentrated there, to occupy the city, and to block the land communications between the Don and the Volga as well as the Don itself.'[12]

In the original plan the drive into the Caucasus was not to be attempted until Stalingrad and the north-east flank had been secured. Now both the first and the ultimate objectives were to be attained simultaneously. It was a classical case of attempting too much with too little all at once. General Kurt Zeitzler sums up the situation:

> Military objectives must always correspond to the forces and other means available for the attainment. From a purely tactical point of view it is not enough simply to reach an objective: consolidation upon the objective is also essential. If this is not achieved, the forces involved will have over-reached themselves, and the offensive operation, no matter how attractive the target, will contain within itself and from the beginning the germ of failure if not of actual defeat....The question now arose whether there were sufficient forces at present available to capture two such remote and distant objectives (being some three hundred and fifty miles apart, the two operations must diverge). The answer was plainly in the negative.[13]

In his diary Halder confided that: 'His [Hitler's] persistent underestimation of the enemy's potential is gradually taking on grotesque forms and is beginning to be dangerous.' When a report was read to Hitler showing that Stalin could still muster from one to one-and-a-quarter million fresh troops in the region north of Stalingrad and west of the Volga, and a further half-a-million men in the Caucasus, and which provided proof that Russian output of front-line tanks amounted to at least 1,200 a month, Hitler flew at the man who was reading the report with clenched fists and foam in the corners of his mouth and forbade him to read any more such idiotic twaddle. When Halder pointed out to Hitler that it did not require the gift of a prophet to foresee what would happen when Stalin unleashed those million-and-a-half troops against Stalingrad and the Don flank, Hitler dismissed him from his post as Chief of the Army General Staff. Such was the nature of Hitler's military genius.

HIGH SUMMER ON THE STEPPES.

The 'thrust forward to Stalingrad' was to be made by 6th Army in a frontal advance supported by 4th Panzer Army which was to approach Stalingrad from the south-east flank after a 175-mile drive from its present position in the north Caucasus.

As 6th Army was devoid of panzer and motorized divisions Hitler ordered General Hoth to transfer the 14th and 24th Panzer Corps and the 51st Infantry Corps from 4th Panzer Army to Paulus. Both armies were supported by the Fliegerkorps VIII (8th Air Corps) of nine fighter, nine bomber and three Stuka dive-bomber groups.

The axis of 6th Army's advance would carry it over wild, sun-baked, grassy steppes, scorched into a light-brown hue by the unremitting sun and stifling heat of high summer. This flat, barren desolation, broken only by a few rectangular patches of cultivated farmland, was dissected by the great bend of the River Don. This huge loop was formed by the river turning sharply eastwards from its southerly flow and continuing eastwards for 150 miles before dropping southwards for some 50 miles and then swinging south-east to wind its way to Rostov where it flowed out into the Sea of Azov. The easternmost reach of the great bend occurred opposite Stalingrad, forming a forty-mile-wide isthmus between the Don and the Volga.

By 28 July 6th Army was deep into the Don bend, but was immobilized by lack of fuel, an acute shortage of ammunition and stiff enemy resistance. Half of the army's daily supply tonnage had been diverted to Heeresgruppe A by General Wagner, the Quartermaster-General, who had not taken into account the transfer of the two panzer and one infantry corps to Paulus. Hitler had to rectify the situation by ordering 1st Panzer Army to relinquish 750 tons of its transport capacity to get 6th Army moving again. Even then it was ten days before the spearhead of 6th Army could start rolling again.

By this stage the majority of the Soviet forces had fallen back over the Don, but the Russian First Tank and Sixty-second Armies had formed a large bridgehead on the west bank in front of Kalach. These two armies were blocking 6th Army's direct route towards Stalingrad. To smash this barrier Paulus mounted a classical battle of encirclement. The left or northerly pincer was mounted by 14th Panzer Corps (16th panzer and two motorized divisions), while the right or southerly pincer was formed by the 24th Panzer Corps (24th panzer and one motorized divisions). To complete the envelopment a frontal attack was made by 11th and 51st Infantry Corps.

While the rival armoured forces manoeuvred and blazed away at each other over the sandy, grassy desolation of the steppe, the cloudless sky above the Don became the scene of fierce fighting between the opposing air forces. But the Red Air Force was unable to prevent the Luftwaffe from mercilessly hammering the Russian forces on the ground and blowing up their ammunition columns and fuel dumps. On 11 August the spearheads of the panzer pincers linked up to complete what proved to be the very last cauldron battle that the Germans would achieve on the Eastern Front. Although

Russian losses — 35,000 killed and taken prisoner — were substantial, and the divisional constitution of both armies was destroyed, enough troops managed to evade or fight their way out of the cauldron in small groups to reform the Sixty-second army on the east bank of the Don. It incorporated whatever units remained of First Tank Army and was reinforced by a rifle division from Sixty-fourth Army.

Hitler's ideological obsession with the capture of Stalingrad was now matched by Stalin's determination to deny the city which bore his name to the fascist hordes. On 28 July, Stalin issued his *"Ni shagu nazad!"* (not a step back) order. The terms of the order were draconian:

> In each Front [army group] area, from one to three punishment battalions of five hundred men each are to be created. Into them are to be placed all intermediate and senior commanders and political officers of comparable ranks who have shown themselves guilty of cowardice, of not preserving discipline, or of not maintaining resistance to the enemy. They will be committed in especially dangerous situations so that they may expiate their crimes against the homeland with their blood.
>
> Corps and division commanders who allow troops to retreat without an order from the army commander are to be unconditionally removed from their posts. They will be turned over to the military councils of the Fronts to be condemned by courts martial.
>
> In each army area, three to five well-armed blocking detachments of approximately two hundred men are to be created. They will be stationed directly behind unreliable divisions, and it will be their duty, in the event of panics or unauthorized retreats, to shoot spreaders of panic or cowards on the spot.
>
> In each army area three to five punishment companies of one hundred and fifty to two hundred men are to be created in which all enlisted men and junior officers are to be placed who are guilty of cowardice, not preserving discipline, or of failing to maintain resistance to the enemy. They will be committed in especially dangerous situations so that they may expiate their crimes against their homeland with their blood.[14]

The 'not a step back' order effectively ended the highly successful mobile defence tactics employed by the Soviets during Blau, in favour of the rigid, linear defence tactics which had proved so disastrous in 1941. But it was a temporary expedient, designed to wear down the over-stretched German forces in a huge battle of attrition at Stalingrad. With a shrewd appreciation of military reality, Stalin planned to fight the battle by deploying forces for the defence of the city on the principle of the minimum necessary instead of the maximum possible, thereby preserving the strength of the considerable reserves at his disposal for a massive counter-stroke against the exhausted, thinly spread German armies.

On the other side of the front Paulus was preparing for the final lunge on Stalingrad. The door to the most direct route to the city had been burst open at Kalach. But after the terrain of this axis of advance had been thoroughly reconnoitred by the Luftwaffe, Paulus decided not to exploit it. The steppe between Kalach and Stalingrad was better suited to defence than offensive action. It was criss-crossed by *balkas*, deep gullies that would force the panzers to make lengthy detours and which could be used as trenches by the enemy. Moreover, the Soviets were still in possession of a narrow bridgehead in the north-eastern loop of the Don bend on a line running between Kletskaya and Peskovatka. As these forces, from the Fourth Tank Army, would threaten 6th Army's left flank if it advanced via the Kalach route, Paulus decided to order 14th and 24th Panzer Corps to move north to eradicate the bridgehead, while 8th Infantry Corps would follow through to establish German bridgeheads on the east bank of the river, prerequisite for an advance on Stalingrad from the area north of Peskovatka.

In accord with this plan the panzers cleared the entire loop of the Don by 17 August, and the 76th and 295th Infantry Divisions established two small bridgeheads on the east bank at Luchinskoy and Vertyachiy, some 10 miles north of Peskovatka, where the Don was about 100 yards wide and flowed between steep banks. However, on 18 August the Russians counter-attacked with five divisions of First Guards Army and succeeded in establishing another bridgehead on the west bank which ran for twenty miles between Kremenskaya and Sirotinskaya, less than 10 miles from the newly won German bridgeheads.

This turn of events presented Paulus with the choice of either accepting a prolonged contest for the Don bend or making the drive on Stalingrad from the two bridgeheads leaving his deep left flank exposed. He chose the latter course, reasoning that an imminent threat to Stalingrad would force the Russians to withdraw the substantial forces from 6th Army's exposed northern flank to defend the approaches to the city.

On the evening of 19 August Paulus issued a lengthy order to his corps commanders, setting out his plan of attack on Stalingrad in detail:

The Russians will defend the Stalingrad area stubbornly. They hold the high ground on the east bank of the Don and west of Stalingrad and have built defensive positions in great depth there. It must be assumed that the enemy has assembled forces, including armoured brigades, ready to counter-attack, both in the Stalingrad area and in the area north of the isthmus between the Don and Volga. Therefore in the advance across the Don towards Stalingrad the Army must reckon not only with frontal enemy resistance but also heavy counter-attacks against the northern flank of our advance. It is possible that the annihilating blows struck during the past few weeks will have destroyed the enemy's means of fighting a determined defensive action.

6th Army will occupy the isthmus between the Don and Volga north of the railway line Kalach–Stalingrad and will protect its own northern and eastern fronts. With this intention the Army will cross the Don between Peskovatka and Ostrovsky. The point of main effort will be on either side of Vertyachiy. With standing protection being provided along the northern flank, armoured and motorized formations will advance over the high ground between Rossoshka and Samofalovka into the area immediately north of Stalingrad, and then to the bank of the Volga, while at the same time forces will be detached to fight their way into and occupy Stalingrad from the north-west. This advance will be accompanied by a subsidiary advance on the southern flank by a detached force advancing along the central reaches south of Rossoshka. This force will establish contact south-west of Stalingrad with the mobile troops of the 4th Panzer Army advancing on the city from the south-west. Initially a weak covering force will hold a line facing south-west towards the area between Rossoshka and the Karpovka River. This area will be mopped up by an advance from the north-east as soon as the forces of 4th Panzer Army advancing towards the Karpovka have reached the river.

With the progress of the advance on the east side of the Don, the forces stationed along the west bank of that river below Malye will be steadily reduced in strength, since their task will then be that of a security force. This force will later cross the Don on both sides of Kalach and participate in the destruction of the enemy forces in that area.

Objectives:

24th Panzer Corps will hold the west bank of the Don from the Army's right-hand boundary to Luchinskoy and, with the 71st Infantry Division, will prepare to leave a minimum security force to hold the Don while establishing a bridgehead on either side of Kalach from which 71st Infantry Division will advance eastwards. 51st Infantry Corps will seize a further bridgehead across the Don on either side of Vertyachiy. For this purpose the following units at present under 24th Panzer Corps will be temporarily placed under command of 51st Corps, viz: artillery, engineer, traffic control, anti-tank and the necessary signals units.

As soon as the 14th Panzer Corps has advanced eastwards from the bridgehead, 51st Corps will become responsible for covering the right flank of the advance. With this intention the 51st Corps will attack towards Rossoshka to occupy the high ground west of Stalingrad, and will temporarily establish south-westerly contact with the advancing mobile forces of 4th Panzer Army on our right flank. The 51st Corps will then capture and occupy the central and southern parts of Stalingrad. Meanwhile weak forces will form a covering line between Peskovatka and Nijni-Alexeievski (some 10 miles south-east of Peskovatka). A special Army Order will decide when the time has come to annihilate the Russian forces located south of this line and north of the Karpovka River.

14th Panzer Corps, after the capture of the bridgehead by 51st Corps, will push forward through the bridgehead, advancing eastwards over the high ground north of Malrossoshka to the Volga north of Stalingrad. It will prevent all river traffic and cut all rail communications immediately to the north of the city. Elements of the Corps will attack Stalingrad from the north-west and occupy the northern parts of the city. Tanks will not be used for this purpose. In the north a covering line will be established running along the high ground south-west of Yersovka and south of the Gratshevaia stream. While so doing closest contact will be maintained with the 8th Infantry Corps advancing from the west.

8th Infantry Corps will cover the northern flank of the 14th Panzer Corps. It will launch a sharp attack in a south-easterly direction from the bridgehead captured between Nijni-Gerassimov and Ostrovsky, and then, swinging steadily north, will form a line, which must so far as possible be proof against attack by armoured forces, between Kuzmichi and Kachalinskaya. Close contact will be maintained with 14th Panzer Corps.

11th Infantry Corps will cover the northern flank of the Army. 11th Corps will hold the line of the Don from Melov-Kletskaya to left Army boundary. 11th Corps will release 22nd Panzer Division, as soon as possible, to Army reserve. This division will be assembled ready for action in the area Perelazovky-Orekhovsky-Selivanov.

Fliegerkorps VIII will give air support to the Army's attack with the point of the main effort initially in 51st Infantry Corps' sector, later switching to the line of advance of 14th Panzer Corps.[15]

The success of Paulus' plan of attack depended in large degree on the forces of 6th Army's right flank linking up with the advanced panzer formations of General Hermann Hoth's 4th Panzer Army, which should approach Stalingrad from the south-west. It was intended that this link-up would envelop the Russian forces defending the east bank of the Don.

However, by the time Paulus' plan was being formulated, Hoth's army was a panzer army in name only. Two of Hoth's panzer corps (14th and

24th) had been transferred to Paulus, and the 40th Panzer Corps, which Hoth had obtained from 6th Army earlier in the campaign, had in turn been transferred to Heeresgruppe A to reinforce the drive into the Caucasus. In consequence Hoth's effective armoured strength had been reduced to General Werner Kempf's 48th Panzer Corps, consisting of one panzer and one motorized division. The remainder of the army was made up of 4th Infantry Corps (General von Schwedler) with three infantry divisions, and the Rumanian 6th Infantry Corps (General Dragalina) of four under-strength infantry divisions. An army with only one of its nine divisions being armoured clearly did not rate as a panzer army.

On 31 July, during its 175-mile north-easterly advance across the sun-scorched Kalmuck Steppe, conforming roughly to the direction of the single railway track in the area which ran from Krasnodar in the north-west Caucasus to Stalingrad, 4th Panzer Army crashed into the flimsy Russian Fifty-first Army. As this army was composed of nothing more than five under-strength rifle divisions, Hoth was able to push it aside without much difficulty. But five days later Hoth ran into the eastern flank of the Sixty-fourth and the western flank of Fifty-seventh Armies to the north of Abganerovo railway station, some 50 miles south-east of Stalingrad. Not only was 4th Panzer Army's advance ground to a halt, but a violent counter-attack forced Hoth to give ground. It was the first retreat by German forces since the opening of Operation Blau.

Enemy action was only a part of Hoth's problems. Shortages of fuel and ammunition continually plagued 4th Panzer Army, and the troops were exhausted. In a letter to Colonel Heusinger, Chief of Operations OKH, dated 19 August, Hoth explained the predicament:

Here on the border between steppe and desert the troops live and fight under unspeakably difficult conditions. In spite of shimmering heat that does not let up at night, in spite of indescribable dust and lack of rest at night owing to vermin and air raids, in spite of the absence of any kind of shade or ground cover, in spite of scarcity of water and poor health, they are doing their best to carry out their assigned missions.[16]

When Hitler learned that Hoth's drive on Stalingrad had stalled, he juggled his forces around by ordering Paulus to relinquish 24th Panzer division, which then had to burn up precious fuel on a sixty-mile journey over the lower Don to reinforce Hoth's ailing army. Until this division could form up, and fuel, ammunition and supplies could be flown in by the Luftwaffe to supplement the inadequate tonnage arriving on the single rail track, 4th Panzer Army would have to remain on the defensive.

THE SOVIET RESPONSE

To counter the double threat to Stalingrad which had developed to the west of the city (6th Army) and from the south-west (4th Panzer), Stalin stiffened the front with 26 divisions from the reserve armies. It has been argued that this response was motivated less by military considerations and more by an emotive reaction on Stalin's part to prevent the capture of the city bearing his name. Doubtless there is some substance in this claim, but the emotive element in Stalin's calculations did not predominate to the extent that it clouded the strategic realities. In comparison to Hitler, the hot, emotionally unstable, intuitive and reckless gambler, Stalin was a cold, ruthless, political professional with a firm grasp of the military realities. The reserves he committed were carefully measured within the bounds of the principle of the minimum necessary to mount a stubborn and effective defence, while the maximum possible were being preserved for 'the opportune moment of greatest potential, a potential rapidly developing by the ever-increasing concentration of German forces on the Stalingrad axis. For Stalingrad, being the hub of a communications network, afforded an easy supply and rapid reinforcement potential, and was consequently advantageous to both effective defence and the mounting of a counter-attack.

The Russian direction of the battle was firmly in Stalin's hands. He was as much the de facto supreme commander of the Soviet armed forces as Hitler was the Feldherr of the Wehrmacht. Stalin ruled the Stavka (*Stavka Glavnovo Komandovaniya* — High Command Headquarters), in the same manner as Hitler dominated the Oberkommando der Wehrmacht. Stalin was the centre of all activity and decision-making in the Stavka's command and signals centre in the Kremlin buildings, and as he was in constant touch with his field commanders via the telephone and high frequency radio, he made Stavka as much an instrument of extreme centralization as the German OKW.

Because both dictators employed the same methods of absolute command, the battle for Stalingrad would be fought in the manner of a titanic struggle of will between the two most evil men in history. They were to play a gruesome game of chess in which the lives of countless thousands of German and Russian troops counted for nothing, as they were manoeuvred and sacrificed on the vast chess board of the steppes.

In mid-July Stalingrad could have been taken off the march by 4th Panzer Army if Hitler had not made the fatal mistake of sending it off on a wild goose chase over the lower Don. At that time only negligible Soviet forces were defending the city. But now, on the eve of the offensive, a total of 8 Russian armies were deployed against Paulus and Hoth.

These eight armies were deployed in two Fronts. The Stalingrad Front, under the command of General Gordov, was comprised of four armies: Sixty-third, Twenty-first, First Guards and Fourth Tank. This Front ran from Malye on the northern flow of the Don Bend (on the left flank of 6th

Army) and followed the line of the river round to the Don—Volga isthmus, with its southern flank anchored on a line drawn on the map running from Kalach to the Tsaritsa River which flowed east through the centre of Stalingrad and out into the Volga.

This line formed the boundary between the Stalingrad Front and the South-east Front. The latter, under the command of General Fillip Golikov, was comprised of four armies: Sixty-second, Sixty-fourth, Fifty-seventh and Fifty-first. This Front covered a line running due south from the Don—Volga isthmus across the Kalmuck Steppe and came to an end on the right flank of 4th Panzer Army.

Both Fronts were under the overall, co-ordinating command of General Andrei Ivanovich Yeremenko. This resulted in a cumbersome local command structure. Yeremenko, with his own staff and command centre, exercised unified command over his two deputies, Gordov and Golikov, who with two Fronts and two staffs were defending the same objective. To add to the confusion, the initiative of all three local commanders was restricted and stultified by Stalin, who, through the agency of Stavka far from the theatre of operations, directed the day-by-day struggle in the smallest detail.

By 22 August Yeremenko had a total of 42 divisions manning the 400 miles of front on the Stalingrad axis. With a total of 577,970 troops in the two Fronts the average divisional establishment numbered 13,761.

The comparative strength of the opposing forces on the eve of the German attack was as follows:-
On the Stalingrad Front

	Soviet	German
Divisions	26	28
Manpower	414,700	427,735
Tanks	200	440
Guns & mortars	1,969	5,270

The marginal German superiority in manpower facing the Stalingrad Front (13,035) became a crushing advantage when the comparative strengths are narrowed down to the 31-mile axis of the main German blow against Stalingrad:-

	Soviet	German
Divisions	5	10
Manpower	39,132	129,635
Tanks	113	275
Guns & mortars	556	2,105

However, this 70 per cent German advantage was reversed on the Southeast Front.
On the Southeast Front.

	Soviet	German

Divisions	16	12
Manpower	163,270	158,200
Tanks	70	595
Guns & mortars	1,390	2,110

The Soviet marginal superiority of 5,070 troops on this front became a clear 32.52 per cent advantage on the 21-mile axis of the main German blow:-

	Soviet	German
Divisions	4	7
Manpower	134,490	90,760
Tanks	70	440
Guns & mortars	990	1,210

But this still left the Germans with an overall advantage of 37.48 per cent on the combined axis of the advance against the flanks of the two Soviet Fronts which added up to 52 miles. Moreover, the Germans possessed a 74.41 per cent superiority in tanks and a 56.08 per cent superiority in guns and mortars on the 52-mile main axis.

The considerable advantages of concentration of forces is always bestowed on the attacker, simply because he alone knows where the blow will fall. Conversely, the disadvantages of the Soviet dispersion were a result of having to cover all the areas of the front with roughly equal density, because the direct and most obvious line of advance on an objective is not necessarily the enemy's chosen point of main effort. It behoved Stalin to wait for Paulus and Hoth to show their hands.

3

THE GATES OF HELL

'... and behold, a pale horse. And the name of him who sat on it
was Death, and Hell followed with him. And power was given to
them over a fourth of the earth to kill with the sword, with hunger,
with death, and by the beasts of the earth.'

(Revelation 6:8)

THE CITY OF STALIN

In August, 1942, Stalingrad was sweltering in temperatures that soared to
70°C (above 100° Fahrenheit). Although no rain had fallen on the city for
two months, its position on the banks of the River Volga produced high
humidity which was not only sticky and uncomfortable but totally
enervating. Sprawling for some 25 miles along the high cliffs of the western
bank of the river, some a thousand feet high, the city was no more than 2½
miles wide anywhere along its great north-south length. This huge, dusty
metropolis, possessing 120 schools and 17 hospitals, was normally the home
of half-a-million souls, but the population had been swelled to 600,000 by
the influx of refugees driven east by the advancing German tide of conquest.

Slightly to the south of the city centre was the Mamaev Hill, an ancient
Tartar *Kurgan* (burial mound). This grassy, rock-studded hill, shown on
military maps as 'Height 102' (it was 102 metres (331 feet) high), was the
dominant topographical feature and it afforded a view of almost the entire
lay of the city. To the west was a twenty-nine mile arc of woodland, a mile
wide at its thickest point, which had been planted decades before to protect
Stalingrad from the dust clouds and snowstorms blown in on howling winds
from the desolate steppes beyond. To the east was the mighty Volga, a mile
wide in places, crowded with hundreds of tugs, barges and steamers
navigating this great artery which linked Moscow and the north with the
Caucasus in the south, and beyond the table-flat sandy steppes of Kasakstan
stretching into infinity.

To the far south of Mamaev Kurgan was the residential suburb of Dar
Gova, a jumble of wooden houses, overshadowed by grain silos, a massive
concrete grain elevator, a sugar refinery, lumber mills and rotund oil storage
tanks crowded together in an industrial complex to the north of the suburb.

These southern districts were divided from the centre of Stalingrad by the Tsaritsa River running through a two-hundred-feet-deep gorge from the west out into the Volga.

The heart of the city encompassed some hundred or so large office and apartment blocks and department stores, along with Red Square around which were clustered unprepossessing stone and concrete government buildings, the main railway station, a waterworks and a power plant.

The northern boundary of the city centre was provided by the deep ravine of the Krutoy Gully. Beyond this was the awesome, eleven-mile-long heavy-industrial complex, which contained, among a myriad host of smaller plants, the Lazur chemical plant; the huge maze of foundries and calibration shops of the Krasny Oktyaber (Red October) small arms plant; the Barrikady Gun Factory producing artillery pieces of all calibres; and the Dzerhezinsky Tractor Works, which had switched from the manufacture of farm machinery to being the principal producer of T-34 tanks (this factory alone was more than a mile in length).

Bordering this eleven-mile industrial complex, with its railway yards and innumerable tall chimneys belching out constant clouds of filthy smoke and showers of soot, lay the settlements housing the thousands of workers and their families. The dwellings ranged from small wooden hovels to six-storey tenement blocks, amongst which nestled clusters of small, carefully manicured communal parks.

Such was Stalingrad, founded as the fortress of Tsaritsyn in 1589, which had grown into the third largest industrial city in the Soviet Union, and was destined to become the blood-soaked tomb of Hitler's dream of Lebensraum.

THE NORTHERN THRUST

The night of 22/23 August was clear and starry, and a light mist lay over the Don. Darkness brought no relief from the torrid heat of the day to the long columns of tanks, armoured vehicles and sweating, dust-caked troops as they moved up to their jumping-off positions for the assault on Stalingrad. Throughout the night 400 tanks, armoured troop-carriers, scout cars and vehicle and horse-drawn artillery of the 16th Panzer Division (under the command of the one-armed General Hube), and the 3rd and 60th Motorized Divisions, which together made up the 14th Panzer Corps, crossed the Don over a 20-ton pontoon bridge into the 3-mile-long, 1½-mile-deep bridgehead around Vertyachiy, the perimeter of which was being defended by the infantry of the 295th Division. The crossing was illuminated by numerous burning vehicles, smashed by Russian bombers which made a total of 76 attacks on the bridge that night but failed to destroy it.

While the armour trundled over the pontoon, the infantry of the three divisions were ferried across the river in 112 assault boats and 108 rubber

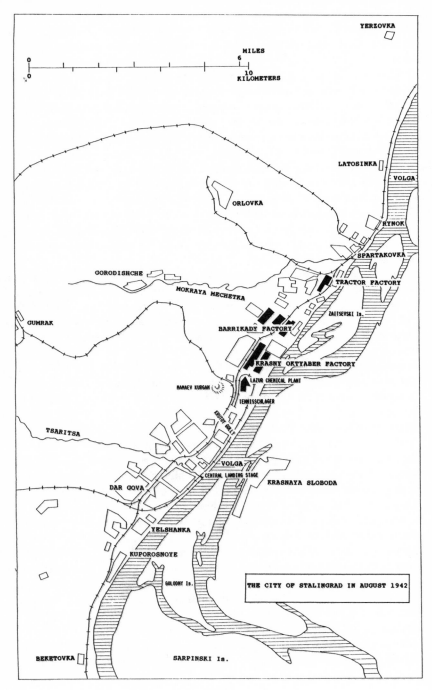

Kapok rafts of the 912th Assault Boat Commando. During the crossing 76 troops were killed and 351 wounded by Soviet artillery and Katyusha rocket mortar fire, which pounded the crossing points and the bridgehead on the east bank.

Dawn on Sunday, 23 August, was announced by a brilliant red and violet hue rising above the eastern steppes of Asia. At 0430 the tanks of 16th Panzer lurched forward in a broad wedge, striking out due east across the scorched grass of the dusty steppe for the northern suburbs of Stalingrad some 36 miles distant. Opposing them was a single Russian rifle division of the Sixty-second Army. By 0800 all effective, organized resistance by this division, the 98th, had collapsed under the onslaught of the panzers and a rain of bombs from Stukas diving out of the sky with their sirens screaming.

With the dazed and demoralized troops of the Russian 98th surrendering or scattering in all directions, the tanks of Hube's 16th Panzer sped forward across the steppe, hindered only by isolated nests of resolute resistance. These were dealt with by German reconnaissance aircraft which pinpointed their positions by radio or smoke markers, and drew upon the Russians dive-bomber attacks and combat groups hived off from the main wedge of the attack.

By midday the skyline of Stalingrad was visible on the right-hand side of the lead panzers. Above the tall factory chimneys, the high office blocks and the onion-topped spires of the churches billowed huge clouds of thick, black smoke from fires started by a massive bombing attack on the city.

During the course of that fateful Sunday Luftwaffe bombers with strong fighter support flew 1,600 sorties and dropped 1,000 tons of bombs on Stalingrad, with the loss of three aircraft and a claim of 91 Russian aircraft shot down. The main point of the bombing effort was directed against the residential districts and the administrative centre, in what was a pure terror raid, designed to kill as many civilians as possible, overload all the essential services, create panic and demoralization and disrupt the supplies and reinforcements passing through the city to the front-line troops.

When the bombs rained down on the southern suburb of Dar Gova, the resulting flames spread like wildfire through the narrow jumbled streets of tinder-dry wooden houses, so that the whole area was quickly engulfed. When the flaming holocaust eventually burnt itself out all that was left was a grotesque forest of smoke-blackened brick chimneys standing as stark monuments to mark the spots where homes once stood.

In the city centre the explosions caused the high office blocks and government buildings to collapse into piles of rubble. The waterworks, the telephone exchange and the main hospital were among the buildings destroyed. By the evening fires were raging along the entire 25-mile length of Stalingrad. The industrial complex in the north was hit, and the squat oil storage tanks spewed out rivers of liquid fire which spread across the great width of the Volga to the eastern bank. Thousands died in this inferno of destruction.

While Stalingrad burned Hube's panzers approached the northern suburb. The three regiments of 16th Panzer Division advanced on a broad front. On the northern flank was the 79th Panzer Grenadier Regiment (lorry-borne infantry), attacking in the direction of Rynok; the southern flank was occupied by the 64th Panzer Grenadier Regiment, which was attacking in the direction of Spartakovka, while the single tank formation of the division, the 2nd Panzer Regiment, advanced in the centre to a position on the Volga between Rynok and Spartakovka.

In the last few miles separating the 2nd Panzer Regiment from the river, the lead tanks ran into a group of anti-aircraft batteries which depressed their guns to engage the sudden appearance of the enemy. All 37 emplacements were manned by female workers from the Barrikady Gun Factory, who, being members of the para-military *Osoaviakhim*, had received rudimentary training in AA defence but had no idea of how to use their guns against ground targets. Despite an heroic stand by the Russian women para-militaries, their positions were quickly overrun and they were wiped out. The route to the 300-feet-high western bank of the Volga was wide open and at 2310 that night Paulus, ensconced in 6th Army H.Q. at Ossinovskoy, received the following signal from Hube:

> Battle Group 79th Panzer Grenadier Regiment first German troops to reach Volga 1835 hours. One company 2nd Panzer Regiment occupied Spartakovka. Enemy resistance initially weak, but strengthening. Strong attacks from the north expected. Outstanding support was given by Fliegerkorps VIII.[1]

Within an hour of the dispatch of this signal, Hube received a personal order from Hitler, who was keeping a close eye on events from the *Wehrwolf* command post situated at Vinnitsa in the Ukraine some 600 miles to the west of Stalingrad: '16th Panzer Division will hold its positions in all circumstances.' This was easier said than done, for Hube's panzers had perched themselves precariously on the end of a very long limb and were under attack by the Soviet 87th Rifle Division from the north.

The advance of 3rd Motorized Division, which had been following in the wake of the speeding panzers, was blocked by the 35th Guards Division and the 169th Tank Brigade which poured into the 12-mile gap between 3rd Motorized and the rear of 16th Panzer. 60th Motorized was 10 miles further back barely half way across the isthmus, bogged down in fierce fighting with the Soviet 214th Rifle Division, which had held the northerly flanking position of the smashed 98th Division. By nightfall all three divisions were forced to leaguer in hedgehog (circular) defence positions, to replenish with

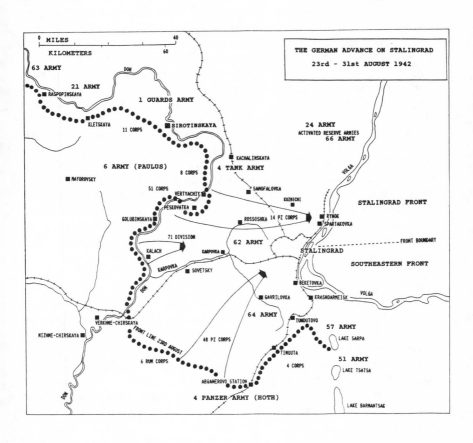

fuel and ammunition, in three separate islands completely isolated from each other. Strung out along a 36-mile-wide corridor between the Don and the Volga, the three divisions were hard pressed by the Soviet counter-attacks, which were gathering in strength and intensity.

All through the night of 23/24 August, the exhausted troops of the three divisions, which were under constant attack and Soviet artillery fire, dug in, laid mines and serviced and refuelled their vehicles and tanks. They worked under the illumination of a hellish red glow from the sea of flames sweeping across the entire length of Stalingrad.

That night the Luftwaffe delivered its heaviest single blow on the Eastern Front, in numbers of aircraft employed and the weight of bombs dropped, since 22 June, 1941. Every available aircraft capable of delivering a bomb load in General Wolfram Freiherr von Richthofen's Luftflotte IV (of which Fliegerkorps VIII was a part), which was covering both Heeresgruppe A and B, was unleashed against the city in another terror raid. With many of the aircraft making up to three sorties, the attack was equivalent to a 1,000 bomber raid. Half the bomb load was made up of incendiaries and the effect was terrifyingly spectacular. Nearly every wooden building not destroyed in the daylight raid was set alight, including the acres of workers' settlements running parallel to the eleven-mile-long northern industrial complex. So great was the conflagration that some German troops on the banks of the Don, forty miles distant were able to read newspapers by the light of the fiery red glow. Thousands more civilians, men, women and children, died in this fearsome raid.

THE CENTRAL AND SOUTHERN THRUST

Simultaneous with 14th Panzer Corps' crossing of the Don at Vertyachiy during the night of 22nd/23rd, the 71st Infantry Division forced a crossing of the river in assault boats and Kapok rafts 25 miles to the south, and obtained a bridgehead at Kalach at a cost of 56 dead and 100 wounded.

Soviet resistance was stiff and the 71st was unable to begin an advance on Karpovka, situated midway between the Don and central Stalingrad, until the morning of 25 August. Progress was slow and costly and it took the 71st seven days to push back the Russians 20 miles to a position just east of Karpovka.

The advance from the south-west by Hoth's 4th Panzer Army, designed to link up with 6th Army's right flank and envelop the Russian Sixty-Second and Sixty-fourth Armies and destroy them in a cauldron battle between the Don and Stalingrad got off to a bad start. On 20 August General Kempf's 48th Panzer Corps (24th and 14th Panzer and 29th Motorized Divisions) spearheaded an attack striking north-east from the area of Abganerovo. The advance quickly ground to a halt when Kempf's panzers ran into Russian defence positions established in deep echelon along a line of hills around Tundutovo. It was manned by divisions of the Sixty-fourth Army reinforced by armoured units of First Tank Army and workers' para-military formations. Despite repeated costly attacks Kempf's three divisions failed to breach the strong Russian defensive positions.

The three infantry divisions of von Schwedler's 4th Infantry Corps (94th, 371st and 297th Divisions), which were strung out in a long flanking line running from Tinguta railway station, on 48th Panzer Corps' left, southward along the single railway track to Abganerovo, were also experiencing resolute Soviet resistance and counter-attacks.

The stubborn Russian defence around Tundutovo prevented Hoth from seizing the Volga heights between Beketovka (3 miles south of Stalingrad) and Krasnoarmeisk (2½ miles south of Beketovka). These heights were one of the most important − perhaps the most decisive − areas in the whole operational area of Stalingrad, and from these hills the Germans could have dominated the whole knee of the Volga. Krasnoarmeisk was also the southern cornerstone of the Soviet Stalingrad defences. At no other point would the appearance of German troops on the Volga have been more disadvantageous to the Russians.

From the German point of view their operations in and around Stalingrad, whether offensive or defensive, were made considerably more difficult with Krasnoarmeisk and Beketovka in Russian hands. These heights so dominated the Volga that they offered excellent observation positions towards the Kalmuck Steppes, and the concentration areas for Russian counter-attack on the southern flank of the forces fighting for Stalingrad.

It was therefore a difficult decision for Hoth to abandon the attack around Tundutovo, but with losses mounting alarmingly in repeated unsuccessful frontal assaults on the fortified Russian positions, he was left with no other choice but to break off the attack on 25 August, with the intention of launching a surprise attack from behind the left hanging wing of 4th Corps.

To achieve this, Kempf's three divisions were withdrawn from the front, unit by unit, at night and unseen by the enemy, between the 26th and 28th. Their positions were filled by the infantry of the 94th Division. It was not until 29 August that Kempf's Corps, having regrouped west of Abganerovo, was ready to launch the surprise attack, by which time the precarious corridor across the Don − Volga isthmus, formed by von Wietersheim's 14th Panzer Corps, was being subjected to a massive Soviet counter-attack which threatened to destroy it.

BOLTING THE GATES

When Stalin received the news of the German breakthrough to the Volga, he immediately radioed Yeremenko in his underground command bunker in the centre of Stalingrad:

> The enemy has broken our front with insignificant force. You have quite enough men at your disposal to destroy enemy units which have broken through... Jab into the breakthrough units by day and also by night use all your artillery and katyusha resources. The most important thing is not to let panic take hold, do not be afraid of the enemy thrusts and keep your faith in our ultimate success.[2]

In fact Yeremenko was already doing this and more. Apart from the Russian regular forces from Sixty-second Army 'jabbing' into the German corridor along the isthmus from the north, Yeremenko caused the City Defence Committee to call the populace to arms. Grey-haired veterans from the civil war of the 1920s, foundrymen, Volga boatmen and stevedores, railway men and shipbuilders, school teachers and office workers, even housewives, reported in their thousands to designated assembly points in the ruined, burning city, to collect weapons and to erect barricades and strong points in the factories and any other buildings that could be turned into miniature fortresses. A total of 50,000 civilian volunteers were incorporated into the 'People's Guard'; 75,000 inhabitants were assigned to Sixty-second Army; 3,000 young women were mobilized for service as nurses and as radio operators; while 7,000 boys aged between 13 and 16 were armed and fed into the Red Army fighting formations.

To reinforce the three infantry brigades, defending the northern suburb against Hube's 16th Panzer Division, 2,000 workers from the Dzerhezinsky Tractor Works, formed into rifle companies and armed with rifles, machine guns, anti-tank rifles and grenades and entrenching tools, marched out of the factory to take up positions on the north bank of the Mokraya Mechetka River which separated the Tractor Factory from Spartakovka. With the workmen marching to the front line rumbled brand new T-34 tanks, most of them still without a coat of paint or even gun-sights, which were driven straight off the assembly line into action, a lot of them crewed by the workmen who had built them.

Yeremenko was bolting the gates to the city, and to conquer Stalingrad the Germans would have to defeat not only the Red Army but the resolute resistance of a large part of the population, which were being spurred on by the revolutionary rhetoric of thousands of hastily printed posters which were hurriedly pasted up throughout the city:

> Dear Comrades!
>
> Native Stalingraders!
>
> Frenzied bands of enemy have reached walls of our native city.
>
> Once again, as 24 years ago, our city is living through difficult days.

Bloody Hitlerites are striving to reach sunny Stalingrad and great Russian river — Volga.

Troops of Red Army are selflessly defending Stalingrad.

All approaches to city are strewn with corpses of German-fascist occupiers.

Super-bandit Hitler is rushing more and more of his cutthroats into battle and trying to take Stalingrad at any cost.

Comrade Stalingraders!

We will not give up our native city, our native home, our native land.

We will turn every street in city into impenetrable barricades. We will make impregnable fortress of every home, every building, every street. Everybody, come out and build barricades. Organize brigades. Barricade every street. To build barricades, use whatever is at hand — stones, logs, iron, streetcars.

We will build barricades quickly so soldiers can annihilate enemy from barricades built by us.

Soldiers of the Red Army! Defenders of Stalingrad!

We will do everything so you can hold Stalingrad. Not a step back. Fight enemy without mercy. Take vengeance on Germans for every hearth destroyed, for every brutality committed, for bloodshed and tears of our children, our mothers, and our wives.

Defenders of Stalingrad!

In terrible year 1918 our fathers held Red Tsaritsyn from band of German mercenaries. In year 1942 we will hold Red Banner Stalingrad. We will hold it so you can throw back and then destroy bloody band of German occupiers.

Everyone to build barricades!

Everyone who can carry gun — to barricades — to defence of native city, our native home.[3]

And build barricades they did. They ran from the walls of office blocks or houses to walls on the other side of the street with a gap in the centre barely wide enough for the military traffic distributing reserves, supplies and ammunition to pass. Every street was barricaded, the piles of rubble from the bombed buildings providing ready material.

At midnight on the 23rd Yeremenko telephoned Stalin on the *Vysokochastotnyi* line, the direct high frequency link from the command bunker in the city with the Stavka operations room in the Kremlin (the Vysokochastotnyi line was commonly abbreviated to V Ch). Yeremenko raised the question of evacuating the industrial plant and the demolition of the industrial installations to prevent their capture. This Stalin expressly forbade on the grounds that it would imply to the population that a decision had been taken to surrender Stalingrad and weaken their will to resist. With this decision 'Stalin committed himself, the Red Army and the Russians at large to one of the most terrible battles in the whole history of warfare.'[4]

However, Yeremenko did make one decision without seeking Stavka consent. He ordered the evacuation of non-essential civilians – those too old or too young to work or fight – and between 24 August and 14 September some 200,000 people were ferried across the Volga to the safety of the east bank.

ENEMY AT THE GATES

At dawn on 24 August, squadrons of Stukas screamed out of the sky to divebomb the Russian positions on the north bank of the Mokraya Mechetka River. At 0440 the artillery and mortars of 16th Panzer Division also began to pound the Soviet front line. Then behind the curtain of exploding bombs and shells and the din of the screeching Stuka sirens, the tanks and grenadiers of a combat group of Hube's division hurled themselves forward with the intention of breaking into Stalingrad from the north and capturing the city.

The attack was met by a hurricane of artillery, Katyusha rocket, anti-tank gun, machine-gun and rifle fire, and the fanatical resistance of Red Army rifle brigades and workers' militia from the factories who were rooted to their positions by Stalin's 'Not a step back!' order.

Taf18positions proved impregnable. Every street and building was barricaded, and the north bank of the river was studded with pillboxes, machine-gun nests and mortar emplacements. Half of 16th Panzer was pinned down on the northern and western flanks of the 'hedgehog' resisting heavy attacks mounted by the 87th Rifle Division. These attacks were designed to relieve the pressure on the forces defending Stalingrad, with the result that the forces committed did not possess enough strength to break through into the city.

Not only did Hube's repeated attacks against the Mokraya Mechetka line fail to win an inch of territory, but late on that boiling hot afternoon a Russian counter-attack, spearheaded by T-34 tanks, actually threw the Germans back for 1½ miles, pushing them out of Spartakovka and Rynok. A small group of T-34s actually penetrated as far as the battle headquarters of 64th Panzer Grenadier Regiment, within the 'hedgehog', before they were knocked out.

By nightfall the fighting died down and Hube's tanks retired within the defence perimeter to refuel, repair and take on ammunition. The only success of the day, achieved by 16th Panzer, was on the north-eastern flank of the 'hedgehog', where a combat group captured the landing stage of the large Volga railway-ferry, thereby cutting the rail connection from Kasakstan on the east bank via the Volga to Stalingrad and Moscow. Digging in amongst large walnut and chestnut trees, the combat group's artillery took the river traffic under fire, and was well positioned to interdict the crossing of Russian reserves to the northern suburbs from the far bank.

Losses in tanks and men had been heavy during the day's fighting, making 16th Panzer's isolated position even more precarious. For Hube to comply with Hitler's order to hold his position in all circumstances, everything now depended on the 3rd and 60th Motorized Divisions fighting their way through to link up with 16th Panzer, and the six infantry divisions of 51st and 8th Corps following up in the rear to secure the corridor across the Don − Volga isthmus.

While the battle raged in the northern suburbs, the city was subjected to its third heavy air-raid. In accord with Yeremenko's decision to evacuate non-essential civilians, thousands had gathered on and around the central landing stage waiting to be ferried over to the east bank of the river by an armada of steamers, ferries, tugs and any small craft that could be pressed into service.

This congestion of terrified humanity was reported by German reconnaissance aircraft, and in an act of sheer murder squadrons of Stukas dive-bombed and machine-gunned this hapless mass of women, children, sick and aged. The landing stage and shore line were soon slippery with blood and became heaped with dead and mutilated bodies. The armada of crowded boats was also attacked. A lot were sunk or badly damaged and the Volga became strewn with floating bodies which were carried downstream on the current.

For the next four days 16th Panzer fought off Russian attacks on the northern and western flanks of its defence perimeter, while combat groups hammered away at the Russian positions in the northern suburbs of the city without success: the northerly gate to Stalingrad remained firmly locked.

By 28 August the effort had not only cost Hube's division a high price in men and tanks, it had also practically exhausted the supplies of fuel, ammunition and food. The situation of the isolated panzer division, precarious to begin with, had become critical and its toe-hold on the Volga untenable despite supply drops by the Luftwaffe. Summoning a meeting of his commanding officers, Hube spelled out the predicament:

The shortage of ammunition and fuel is such that our only chance is to break through to the west. I absolutely refuse to fight a pointless battle that must end in the annihilation of my troops and I therefore order a break-out to the west [to fall back on 6th Army lines on the Don]. I shall personally take responsibility for this order, and will know how to justify it in the proper quarters. I absolve you, gentlemen, from your oath of loyalty [to the Führer], and I leave you the choice of either leading your men in this action or of handing over your commands to other officers who are prepared to do so. It is impossible to hold our positions without ammunition. I am acting contrary to the Führer's orders.[5]

Hube was spared the unenviable consequence of incurring Hitler's wrath by making an unauthorized withdrawal, which would undoubtedly have cost him his command, by the arrival of a supply column of 250 lorries containing ammunition, fuel and food, following in the wake of the tanks and grenadiers of the 103rd Panzer Battalion of 3rd Motorized Division, which had succeeded in breaking through the Russian blockade.

During the break-through the panzer battalion overran a freight train which was in the process of being unloaded to the west of Kuzmichi. The train was loaded with brand new Ford lorries, jeeps, mines and other British and American war materials that had been shipped to Russia via the Arctic convoys. All of this was pressed into the service of 3rd Motorized Division.

However, the link-up with 16th Panzer only eased the situation, for the enlarged 'hedgehog' formed by the two divisions was still separated by an 18-mile gap from the rest of 6th Army. Furthermore, that very afternoon a fierce Russian attack widened the gap by tearing away three miles of the western flank held by 3rd Motorized. This caused von Wietersheim, commander of 14th Panzer Corps, to radio Paulus at his new HQ at Golubinskaya on the Don. 'It is not possible with present forces to stay on the Volga, and hold open communications to the rear... will have to pull back tonight. Request decision.'

Paulus's reply was uncompromising and laconic: 'Do not retreat.' But it was made in the knowledge that Russian resistance opposing 60th Motorized Division and the six infantry divisions of 51st and 8th Corps was crumbling.

Two days later 60th Motorized linked up with the isolated 'hedgehog' and the six infantry divisions bringing up the rear fanned out and completely sealed off the corridor across the isthmus between the two rivers. The sealing of the 40-mile-long, 5-mile-wide corridor, and the securing of the supply lines, was made in the nick of time, for the forces of a massive Soviet counter-attack on the northern flank were gathering.

On 27 August Stalin appointed General Georgi Konstantinovich Zhukov as Deputy Supreme Commander of the Red Army (making him second in rank only to Stalin), and ordered him to hand over his command of the Western Front to his chief of staff and to fly to Moscow. Zhukov recalls that:

I arrived at the Kremlin late that evening. Stalin was at work in his office. Several members of the State Defence Committee were with him. Posekrebyshev [chief of Stalin's secretariat] announced my arrival, and I was admitted at once.

Stalin said that the situation in the south was very bad and that the Germans might seize Stalingrad. It was no better in the Northern

Caucasus. The State Defence Committee had decided to appoint me Deputy Supreme Commander and to send me to Stalingrad. Vasilevsky [Chief of the General Staff], Malenkov [Politburo member] and Malyshev [arms commissar] were there already. Malenkov was supposed to remain there with me and Vasilevsky was to return to Moscow.

'How soon can you take off?' Stalin asked me.

I said I needed a day to study the situation and would fly to Stalingrad on the 29th.

'Well, that's fine,' Stalin said, adding, 'Aren't you hungry? It wouldn't hurt to have a little refreshment.'

Over tea Stalin briefed me on the situation as of 8pm on August 27th. Having told me quickly about developments at Stalingrad, where German troops had crossed the Don in force, Stalin said he had decided to transfer the Twenty-fourth Army, the First Guards Army and the Sixty-sixth Army to the Stalingrad Front (24th and 66th were activated from the reserve armies, while 1st Guards would have to disengage from its present position on the northern loop of the Don). The Twenty-fourth Army was commanded by General Kozlov, the First Guards Army by General Moskalenko, and the Sixty-sixth by General Malinovsky.

The First Guards Army was to be shifted to Loznoye, north of Stalingrad, and open an attack on September 2nd against the Germans' Volga River wedge in an effort to link up with the Sixty-second Army.

Stalin then said, 'Under the cover of Moskalenko's army you must then promptly move the Twenty-fourth and Sixty-sixth armies into battle. Otherwise we may lose Stalingrad.'

It was clear to me that the Battle for Stalingrad was of the utmost military and political importance. The fall of the city would enable the German command to cut off the south of the Soviet Union from the rest of the country. We might lose the great waterway of the Volga River, on which a heavy flow of goods was moving from the Caucasus.

The Supreme Command had moved everything it had, except for the newly formed strategic reserves intended for subsequent operations, into the Stalingrad area. Urgent measures were being taken to speed the production of planes, tanks, guns, munitions and other supplies in order to have them ready in time for the defeat of the enemy forces that had broken through to Stalingrad.[6]

By the time Zhukov arrived at the Stalingrad Front HQ at Malaya Ivanovka, at midday on the 29th, the situation had taken a serious turn for the worse.

At dawn on the 29th the two panzer and one motorized divisions of Kempf's 48th Panzer Corps, having regrouped to the west of Abganerovo, struck northward across the Kalmuck steppe, outflanking the rear of the Russian forces engaging the three infantry divisions of the 4th Corps and by-passing the heavily fortified hills of Beketovka and Krasnoarmeisk. Smashing through the Russian 126th Rifle Division, which was taken completely by surprise, Kempf's panzers advanced 20 miles on the first day.

By the next morning they had crossed the Karpovka River at Gavrilovka, only 30 miles south-west of Stalingrad and some 25 miles from the southern flank of 6th Army's corridor. When von Weichs, commanding Heeresgruppe B, learned of the development he immediately appreciated the opportunity that had presented itself to trap the entire northern wing of the Sixty-fourth and all of Sixty-second Army between two pincers and the Don.

At noon on the 30th he transmitted an urgent signal to Paulus:

> In view of the fact that 4th Panzer Army gained a bridgehead at Gavrilovka at 1000 hours today, everything now depends on 6th Army's concentrating the strongest possible forces in spite of its exceedingly tense defensive situation... on its launching an attack in a general southerly direction... in order to destroy the enemy's forces west of Stalingrad in cooperation with 4th Panzer Army. This decision requires the ruthless denuding of secondary fronts.[7]

Everything depended on Paulus sending his fast formations on a southerly drive to link up with Kempf's panzers and close the pincers on the two Russian armies. But this Paulus could not do. The hiving off of a strong armoured group formed from the five panzer battalions in 14th Panzer Corps would so weaken the corridor against the constant, suicidal Soviet counter-attacks that Paulus feared his northern front would collapse if he attempted an armoured thrust to the south.

By the evening of 31 August 24th Panzer Division of Kempf's corps had driven even deeper into the Soviet rear, cutting the railway line south of Pitomnik at a point less than 20 miles west of Stalingrad. On the following day von Weichs shot off another signal to Paulus, fearing the opportunity in the offing would be lost:

> The decisive success scored by 4th Panzer Army on 31.8 offers an opportunity for inflicting a decisive defeat on the enemy south and west of the Stalingrad—Voroponovo—Gumrak line. It is important that a link-up should be established quickly between the two Armies, to be followed by a penetration into the city centre.[8]

But still Paulus felt unable to take the gamble. On 1 September General Kempf's 14th Panzer and 29th Motorized Division struck out for Pitomnik, less than 10 miles from the southern flank of the corridor, but it was too late. On the following morning reconnaissance units of the two divisions discovered that the bulk of the enemy forces had melted away from the steppes west of Stalingrad, and all that remained were a few rearguards.

This was confirmed by the infantry divisions of Seydlitz-Kurzbach's 51st Corps on the southern flank of the corridor some 10 miles to the north-west of Pitomnik, and the 71st Division which was advancing from the Kalach bridgehead towards Karpovka 10 miles west of Kempf's spearhead. On the same day Soviet pressure on the northern flank of the corridor died down appreciably, finally allowing Paulus to dispatch an armoured formation from 14th Panzer Corps to drive south. On the following day (3 September) all the German formations to the west of Stalingrad linked up on a broad front less than five miles from the outskirts of the city. The manoeuvre envisaged in the plan formulated by Paulus on 19 August had been realized — forty-eight hours too late.

Yeremenko had been alerted to the danger posed by 4th Panzer Army's northward strike on 29 August by General Vasili Chuikov, deputy commander of 64th Army. To avoid the threatened envelopment of most of Sixty-fourth Army and all of Sixty-second Army, Yeremenko ordered both armies to abandon their heavily fortified defence positions, studded with strong points, wire obstacles, and the anti-tank ditches formed out of the balkas (deep gullies of dried-up river beds), and withdraw to a hastily improvised defence line on the outskirts of Stalingrad.

The northern wing of Sixty-fourth Army began to pull back on the night of 29/30 August, two of its rifle divisions (29th and 204th) being withdrawn into Army reserve, while Sixty-second Army began to disengage on the following night. Under the cover of darkness and rearguards formed out of punishment battalions, both armies escaped the German pincers and survived to form a *cordon sanitaire* around the city. Having weathered this crisis the Russians now pinned their hopes on prising the Germans away from the Volga with Zhukov's counter-offensive from the north.

ZHUKOV'S COUNTER-OFFENSIVE

Stalin had scheduled the counter-offensive to start on the morning of 2 September, but the difficulties of disengaging from the positions on the northern loop of the Don and regrouping in the new position around Loznoye, delayed the units of First Guards Army from reaching their jumping-off positions in time. Zhukov reported the fact to Stalin over the V Ch line:

The First Guards Army could not launch its offensive (today) because its units had been unable to reach their jumping-off points, to bring up munitions and fuel, and to organize for battle. Rather than send unorganized troops into battle and risk unwarranted losses, and after having inspected the situation on the spot, I have postponed the attack to 0500 (tomorrow) September 3rd. The attack by the Twenty-fourth and Sixty-sixth armies has been set for September 5th/6th. The operational plan is now being worked out in detail by commanders, and steps are being taken to insure a steady flow of supplies.[9]

Stalin raised no objections to the twenty-four hour delay, but it was still not long enough for First Guards to regroup properly. When the attack began on the morning of Thursday the 3rd, First Guards went into action in piecemeal fashion. Of its three Guards Divisions, the 39th was still on the march, while the 38th and 41st were in the vicinity but were still regrouping and were not fully concentrated. All five rifle divisions were in position but two of them, 84th and 315th, were in a disorganized state, and two of the three Tank Corps (4th and 16th) had only some 70 tanks each, far short of their full establishment of 200.

After a weak artillery bombardment of the German positions which began at 0700, General Moskalenko attacked with only two of his eight divisions (24th and 116th Rifle) and two of his three Tank Corps (the full-strength 7th and the weak 16th). The attack was launched at the right of centre of 6th Army's northern flank against positions defended by 14th Panzer Corps. The hurriedly committed forces were too weak to make any real impression and they ground to a halt after merely denting the German positions to a depth of a few thousand yards. When Stalin learned what had happened, he sent an urgent signal to Zhukov:

The situation in Stalingrad is getting worse. The enemy is three versts [a verst = 3,500 feet] from Stalingrad. They can take Stalingrad today or tomorrow, unless the northern group of troops gives help urgently. Get the commanders of the troops to the north and north-west of Stalingrad to attack the enemy without delay and get to the relief of the Stalingraders. No delay can be tolerated. Delay at this moment is equivalent to a crime. Throw in all aircraft to help Stalingrad. In Stalingrad itself there is very little aviation left. Report at once on receipt and on measures taken.[10]

This signal was sent after Stalin had been informed by Yeremenko of the link of the 6th Army and 4th Panzer Army to the west of the city, and it accounts for the tone of desperation. Zhukov immediately contacted Stalin on the V Ch line and informed him that the earliest possible moment he could commit all three armies to the offensive would be the following morning (4 September), because the two activated reserve armies were still in the process of taking up position on either flank of First Guards. Even then the troops would have to attack without adequate artillery support because sufficient ammunition stocks would not reach the front until the evening of the 4th. Zhukov also pointed out that more time was needed to coordinate the infantry operations with artillery, tank and air support, and unless this could be properly formulated it would result in the units being fed piecemeal and haphazardly into action with predictably negative results.

This sound reasoning was lost on Stalin: 'And you think the enemy is going to wait while you're getting organized? Yeremenko insists the enemy is going to take Stalingrad on his first try unless you strike from the north.' Zhukov retorted that he did not share this view, and was emphatic that the earliest possible moment that he could launch a successful offensive was on the morning of the 5th. Reluctantly Stalin agreed but with the proviso that:

> If the enemy begins a general offensive against the city, you are to attack him at once and not to wait until all your troops are ready. This is your main task: to draw the Germans away from Stalingrad, and, if you succeed, to eliminate the German corridor splitting the Stalingrad and South-eastern Fronts.[11]

Even the postponement to the morning of the 5th proved too ambitious. It did not allow sufficient time to reconnoitre the enemy's artillery positions necessary to aim the preparatory fire effectively. Neither did it allow enough time for an adequate quantity of shells to reach the Russian guns so that when the pre-attack barrage was laid on the northern flank of 14th Panzer Corps at 0600 on the morning of Saturday, 5 September, Zhukov, observing events from a forward observation post, could tell immediately that its density was too light, even in the sectors of the principal thrusts, to expect any deep penetration by the assault units.

Zhukov's fears were confirmed by the violence of the German counter-fire when First Guards attacked at 0630. The same withering artillery fire met the assault launched by Malinovsky's Sixty-sixth Army, on the right of First Guards, at 0900; while Kozlov's Twenty-fourth Army, on the left of the Guards, did not begin its assault until 1500, but once again it was met with a hail of shells from the German batteries which scythed down the advancing Russian infantry.

By nightfall, when the fighting died down, the deepest penetration of a mere 4,000 yards had been made by units of First Guards, while fierce German counter-attacks supported by heavy bombing had thrown back Twenty-fourth and Sixty-sixth armies, both of which were made up of elderly reserves, to their original start lines.

Despite the inability to achieve a breakthrough, Stalin was satisfied with the results because aerial reconnaissance had reported large groups of German motorized infantry, tanks and artillery moving northward from Gumrak, Orlovka and Bolshaya Rossoshka on the western outskirts of Stalingrad to reinforce 14th Panzer Corps. As this relieved the pressure on the city, allowing Yeremenko more time to strengthen his improvised defence line, Stalin ordered Zhukov to continue the attacks and keep up an unrelenting pressure in order to draw off as many German troops as possible from the vital sector.

Zhukov complied by hammering away in the north, but despite

horrendous losses his three armies were unable to achieve a breakthrough. Part of this failure was due to German air superiority over the battlefield which relentlessly bombed and strafed the Russian positions. In an attempt to rectify the situation four additional Russian fighter groups were thrown in to assist the hard-pressed ground troops, but despite countless dog-fights the Russian fighters were unable to stop the frightful slaughter being wreaked by the Luftwaffe. Zhukov also called on the services of a long-range bomber group to attack the German lines of communications at night.

The German reinforcements which had been drawn north quickly made their presence felt. Infantry, tanks and self-propelled guns dug in on dominant elevations along 14th Panzer Corps's threatened sectors, and these strong-points proved impregnable as Zhukov did not have enough heavy artillery pieces at his disposal to subdue them.

After touring the front lines on 10 September, Zhukov sent a despondent but realistic appreciation of the situation to Stalin:

> With the forces which are available to the Stalingrad Front we are not able to break through the corridor and link up with the troops of the South-eastern Front in the city. The German defensive front has been appreciably strengthened owing to the renewed movement of forces from the environs of Stalingrad itself. Further attacks with these forces and with this deployment would be pointless, and the troops would inevitably suffer heavy losses. We need reinforcements and time to regroup for a more concentrated frontal assault. Thrusts by individual armies are not sufficient to dislodge the enemy.[12]

On receipt of what was clearly an appeal to end the bloody assaults Stalin severely rebuked Zhukov for failing to press the attacks energetically enough and ordered him to fly to Moscow to report in person. Zhukov delayed his departure from the front for two days, giving him enough time to defuse Stalin's fury by composing, with Malenkov's assistance, a more detailed appreciation which was defensive if not obsequious in nature. It was teletyped to reach Stalin before Zhukov arrived in the Kremlin:

> We have not broken off the offensive operations begun by First Guards, Twenty-fourth and Sixty-sixth Armies and will persist with them. In these operations, as we duly reported to you, all available units and materials are participating in the continuing offensive.
>
> We have not succeeded in linking up with the defenders of Stalingrad, since we are weaker than the enemy in artillery and air strength. Our First Guards Army, which initiated the offensive, did not have a single artillery regiment as reinforcement, nor a single anti-tank regiment nor an anti-aircraft regiment.
>
> The situation at Stalingrad compelled us to commit Twenty-fourth and Sixty-sixth Armies on the 5th September, without waiting for them

1. Stalingrad exerted a magnetic effect on Hitler's obsessive mode of thought. *Left to right:* Generals Heusinger and Paulus, Hitler, and General von Weichs during the final planning of Operation Blau, May, 1942.

2. To smash the last Soviet barrier blocking 6th Army's direct route towards Stalingrad, Paulus mounted a classical battle of encirclement in the Don bend with two Panzer Corps.

3. Huge clouds of thick, black smoke from fires started by a massive bombing attack billow above Stalingrad. Panzer Grenadiers follow in the wake of the tanks during the advance into the northern suburbs of the city.

4. When German bombs rained down on the southern suburb of Dar
Gova on 23 August, huge fires quickly engulfed the jumbled streets
of wooden houses. All that remained was a grotesque forest of
smoke-blackened brick chimneys .

5. Russian civilians fleeing from Stalingrad. Between 24 August and
14 September all civilians who were too old or too young to work or
fight were evacuated from the city .

6. For a full twenty-four hours preceding the attack on Stalingrad, the Soviet defences were subjected to a pulverizing bombardment by 3,000 guns and mortars. This German mortar squad are firing from a bomb crater alongside a wrecked Russian T-34 tank.

7. One hundred thousand civilians reinforced the 54,000 regular Red Army troops defending Stalingrad. These Russian women are carrying supplies to the troops in the front line.

to concentrate properly and for their artillery to move up. The rifle divisions went into the attack straight from a 50-kilometre [31-mile] march.

Committing these armies to action in pieces and without support meant that we could not break the enemy defences and link up with the defenders of Stalingrad, though nevertheless our speedy blow compelled the enemy to turn his main force away from Stalingrad against our concentrations, thus relieving the situation of the defenders of the city which would have been taken by the enemy without our attacks. We had no other aim unknown to Stavka in mind.

We propose to mount a new operation on the 17th September, and about this Comrade Vasilevsky will report to you. The form of that operation and its timing will depend on the arrival of fresh divisions, bringing tank units up to strength, strengthening the artillery and moving up ammunition.

Today, as on other days, our units mounting the attacks have made little progress and have suffered heavy losses from enemy artillery fire and aircraft, but we do not think it possible to bring our offensive to a halt, since this would free the enemy's hands and leave him free for operations against Stalingrad.

We consider it obligatory for us even in these difficult circumstances to continue our offensive operations, to grind down the enemy, who no less than us, is suffering losses, and simultaneously we will prepare a more organized and more powerful blow.

In the course of our operations we have established that six German divisions are operating the first line against the northern group: three infantry, two motorized divisions and one tank division.

In the second echelon for operations against the northern group no less than two infantry divisions and from 150 to 200 tanks have been concentrated in reserve.[13]

Zhukov arrived at the Kremlin on the evening of 12 September, to find Stalin in a more reasonable frame of mind. In his personal report Zhukov repeated the gist of his teletyped message but added further weight to his argument by pointing out that although the three armies committed to the offensive were basically good fighting units, they were handicapped by the absence of reinforcements and shortages of heavy artillery and tanks. He also made reference to the extremely unfavourable terrain over which the armies were attacking. The open steppe dissected by balkas, which provided excellent cover for the enemy, was dominated by a number of commanding heights from which the German artillery observers could pin-point all the attacking units. In addition the commanding heights allowed the Germans to direct the fire of long-range artillery at the Russian positions from as far back as Kuzmichi and Akatovka. For these reasons and German air superiority, Zhukov concluded, the forces available were simply incapable of breaking through the enemy defences. To achieve a break-through, he contended, the three armies would have to be reinforced by at least one full-strength field army, a tank corps, three tank brigades, 400 heavy artillery pieces and at least one full air army.

The Chief of the General Staff, Vasilevsky, agreed with this assessment, in response to which Stalin began studying a map on which the dispositions of all the Stavka reserves were displayed to ascertain what forces he could release to comply with Zhukov's requirements.

At that point, Zhukov recalls, 'Vasilevsky and I stepped away from the table and, in a low voice, talked about the need for finding another way out. "What other way out?" Stalin suddenly interjected, looking up from the map. I had never realized he had such good hearing. We stepped back to the map table. "Look," he continued, "You had better get back to the General Staff and give some thought to what can be done in the Stalingrad area. Think about which troops and which areas they can be drawn from to reinforce the Stalingrad group... We will meet again tomorrow evening at nine." '[14]

Zhukov and Vasilevsky spent the whole of the following day (13 Sept.) with the General Staff, exploring the possibilities of the situation unfolding on the flanks of the German 6th and 4th Panzer Armies which had been sucked on to a very narrow front in the attempt to capture Stalingrad.

On the basis of front-line reports it had become apparent that both the northern and southern flanks of the two German armies were manned by weak satellite divisions which, through experience, the Soviets knew were less well armed, less experienced and had poor fighting qualities, even in defence, in comparison to the German units. It did not require a military genius to appreciate what heavy blows aimed at these vulnerable flanks could achieve, and this provided the basis of Zhukov's and Vasilevsky's solution.

A single day of deliberations did not provide enough time to formulate a detailed operational plan, but when the two men reported back to Stalin that evening they were able to present a clear objective. Their plan envisaged breaking through the weak enemy flanks and encircling the two German armies on the narrow front at Stalingrad, and establishing a solid outer Russian front to completely isolate the enveloped German divisions. When this had been achieved, the encircled enemy forces were to be annihilated while the outer front would beat off enemy attempts to break through the Soviet 'ring'. It was to be a classic cauldron battle brought about by decisive manoeuvre on the flanks. All that was required was for the necessary forces to deliver the two massive concentric blows into the operational rear of the two German armies. At that time the large forces envisaged were not available, but preliminary calculations showed that sufficient forces and equipment, including mechanized and tank formations from the strategic reserve equipped with newly produced KV and T-34 tanks, could be made ready and moved into position by mid-November.

Grasping the tremendous possibilities inherent in the plan, Stalin ordered Zhukov to return to the Stalingrad Front with instructions to keep up the pressure on 6th Army's northern flank with a new offensive by First Guards, Twenty-fourth and Sixty-sixth Armies, and to study the situation on the northern flank between the loop of the Don and Voronezh, to give detail to the proposed big solution. Meanwhile the situation on the southern flank of the German armies, opposite the South-eastern Front, would be studied by Vasilevsky.

Thus was borne the embryo of the 'Stalingrad counter-offensive' which was destined to deal the death blow to Hitler's dream of eastern Lebensraum. But its success depended entirely on holding Stalingrad and keeping the German forces locked in the contest for the city until the appointed hour.

THE ZENITH OF POWER AND DELUSION

On the very day Zhukov arrived in the Kremlin to report to Stalin, Paulus, in the company of von Weichs (commanding Heeresgruppe B) arrived in the Wehrwolf HQ at Vinnitsa. They had been summoned by Hitler to discuss the details of the final assault on Stalingrad.

By this time Paulus was already a very tired man and was visibly showing signs of the stress and strain of his command. An uncontrollable nervous tic was affecting his cheek, and he was plagued by 'Russian sickness' as dysentery had become euphemistically known on the Eastern Front.

Hitler opened the conference by stating that he believed victory was near and ordering the seizure of Stalingrad in an assault that was to begin on the following day. Neither von Weichs nor Paulus shared the Führer's confidence and expressed their anxieties regarding the inadequately protected northern flank of 6th Army, running for 350 miles along the line of the upper Don from Stalingrad to Voronezh, and the southern flank of 4th Panzer Army which had no protection worth mentioning at all. The concentration of the two German armies embedded in the narrow frontage in the centre of a line of abnormal length was, they pointed out, an open invitation even to a strategically untutored adversary to initiate operations with the object of encircling the forces attacking Stalingrad. Paulus also expressed his anxiety regarding the mounting casualties in men and materials being suffered by 6th Army. Since the breakout from the Don bridgeheads on 23 August the army had incurred 38,700 casualties (7,700 killed and 31,000 wounded). Moreover, Zhukov's offensive against Wietersheim's 14th Panzer Corps had stretched its northern flank to the limit, had drawn off significant forces from the divisions preparing to storm Stalingrad, and had diverted the bulk of the air support away from the city to the northern flank.

Firmly adhering to his conviction that the enemy was at the end of his tether, Hitler dismissed the General's misgivings as of no consequence. The resistance being met in the immediate vicinity of Stalingrad, he asserted, was purely a local affair because the Russians were no longer capable of launching a major offensive, and as far as the holding of the flanks was concerned the defences were being strengthened by the arrival of fresh Rumanian divisions. On this account he was sure that no serious danger existed on the flanks, and, anyway, it was vital to concentrate every available man for the assault on Stalingrad which had to be captured as quickly as possible.

Weichs and Paulus left Vinnitsa that evening to prepare for the final assault on the city, still nursing their anxieties, but with the one consoling thought that the whole of the campaign in Russia so far had been based on seemingly impossible improvisations, and that, somehow, the impossible had always been achieved. As Walter Görlitz points out:
'Hitler knew only too well how to make this consoling thought sound plausible and, with his uncanny power of influencing men's minds, he was an adept at instilling confidence.'[15]

Hitler's conviction that no Russian reserves of any consequence existed was buoyed by aerial reconnaissance carried out by Richthofen's Luftflotte IV in the rear areas of the 1,500-mile salient held by Heeresgruppe A and B. But the reconnaissance flights had not penetrated deep enough. Fremde Heere Ost presented a totally different assessment, warning that Soviet reserves did indeed exist. The intelligence gatherers estimated that in the deep rear more than 70 Russian rifle divisions and over 80 armoured formations were in the process of forming up. But, predictably, this unpalatable appreciation was dismissed by Hitler in the same inconsequential manner as he treated the anxieties expressed by von Weichs and Paulus.

The Feldherr had reached the zenith of wishful thinking at a point when he had also reached the zenith of his power. By September, 1942, 400 million people in Europe lay under the yoke of German rule. Hitler's empire stretched from North Africa to the Arctic, from the English Channel to the Black Sea and almost to the Caspian. Between the Pyrenees and the Ukrainian steppes there was no other sovereign state but neutral Switzerland. Even Hitler's allies, Italy, Rumania, Hungary and, to a lesser extent, Finland, had been reduced to little more than German puppets. In the ancient capitals of Europe – in Athens, Rome, Vienna, Brussels, Paris, Prague, Oslo, Copenhagen and Warsaw – freedom and self-determination were stifled by Nazi domination. But the appearance of the map was misleading, for the means to maintain a consolidated grip on this enormously expanded power had been stretched to breaking point.

The first symptom of this was manifested in Caucasia. The Maykop oilfields had been overrun by 9 August, but the oil refineries and tank farms had been set on fire by the Russians, denying the Germans immediate relief from the gathering fuel crisis. Thereafter, progress decelerated rapidly, partly on account of Soviet resistance, partly because the Germans could not adequately supply both Heeresgruppe A and B in their divergent campaigns, but mainly because Heeresgruppe A was too weak to attain its objectives. Hitler had not only stripped the army group of its two Waffen SS motorized divisions (which were transferred to France), but had dispatched the 11th Army, which had originally been earmarked to reinforce the drive into the Caucasus after it overran the Crimea, to the Leningrad front.

The oilfields of Grozny, with an annual production of 2½ million tons of crude, and more importantly the Baku fields on the Caspian coast, with an annual production of 24 million tons, had become unattainable militarily and logistically on account of Hitler splitting his forces to attain both the first objective (Stalingrad) and the ultimate objective (the Caucasian oil) simultaneously.

To preserve his belief in his own infallibility Hitler resorted to blaming his subordinates for the inevitable consequences of the errors he had committed. Furious at the declining pace of the advance into the Caucasus, Hitler cashiered the innocent Field-Marshal List from the command of Heeresgruppe A and did not appoint a successor. Instead he ordered General Ruoff (17th Army) and General Kleist (1st Panzer Army) to submit to him, every other day, situation reports and maps detailed down to battalion level, along with all tactical proposals and requests. In effect Hitler assumed command of Heeresgruppe A, leaving the two generals and their staffs to do the housekeeping. But not even the Führer's genius could achieve the impossible, and the vital oilfields remained beyond his grasp behind the Caucasian mountain range. The divergence of effort and logistics with the limited forces available was proving fatal.

4

THE CRUCIBLE

'To him was given the key to the bottomless pit. And he opened the bottomless pit, and smoke arose out of the pit like the smoke of a great furnace. So the sun and the air were darkened because of the smoke of the pit.'

(Revelation 9:1-2).

THE LINE UP

On the eve of the German attempt to capture Stalingrad, 6th Army and 4th Panzer Army were faced by a total of nine Soviet armies along a 400-mile front. In manpower the nine Russian armies were equal in strength to that fielded by the two German armies. But the Germans had a 30 per cent superiority in artillery and mortars, a 40 per cent superiority in tanks and a 62 per cent superiority in aircraft.

Comparison of Soviet and German Forces
on the 400 mile Front of the Stalingrad Axis:

	Soviet	German
Manpower	590,000	590,000
Artillery and mortars	7,000	10,000
Tanks	600	1,000
Aircraft	389	1,000

Soviet order of battle in the Stalingrad and South-eastern Fronts numbered 65 rifle divisions, 4 cavalry divisions, 7 rifle, 34 tank and 6 motorized brigades, 4 'fortified districts' (used to construct and defend fortified areas, usually consisting of between five to nine combined machine-gun/artillery battalions of some 4,000 men), and the cadres of 5 military schools.

Of the five armies in the Stalingrad Front, two, Twenty-first and Fourth Tank, were holding the northern flow of the Don Bend. On their right the other three armies of this Front, Twenty-fourth, First Guards and Sixty-sixth, were bunched across the 40 miles of the northern neck of the Don-Volga isthmus.

Of the four armies in the South-eastern Front, two, Sixty-second and Sixty-fourth, were holding the thirty-five miles of the improvised defence line running along the outskirts of the city; while the Fifty-seventh and Fifty-first armies were holding the flank south of Stalingrad behind the three salt-water lakes of Sarpa, Tsatsa and Barmantsak, and stretching out into the Kalmuck Steppe.

It was Sixty-second Army, under the command of General Vasili Ivanovich Chuikov (who only assumed command on 12 September), which would bear the full weight of the German fist as it crashed on the city. This army, of some 54,000 men, 900 guns and mortars and 110 tanks, was defending nine-tenths of the city, yet its strength represented only 9 per cent of the total Soviet manpower resources on the Stalingrad axis, 12.85 per cent of the available artillery and 18.33 per cent of the tanks. Sixty-second Army was, in effect, being offered as live bait: the minimum force necessary to prevent the city falling to the Germans, to allow the maximum forces possible to be built up on the flanks, in order to facilitate the means for the massive counter-offensive proposed by Zhukov and Vasilevsky. However, in addition to the 54,000 regular Red Army men, Chuikov also had over 100,000 armed civilians manning the barricades, who would make up for their lack of military training by fighting like demons, as the Germans were soon to learn to their cost.

In comparison with the slender means in regular forces afforded Chuikov to defend Stalingrad, the Germans committed fifty per cent of the twenty-one divisions fielded by 6th Army and 4th Panzer Army to the assault: some 170,000 men, 500 tanks and 3,000 artillery and mortar pieces.

Of the fifteen divisions in 6th Army, four infantry divisions of 11th Corps were holding the line on the northerly flow of the Don Bend opposing the Russian Twenty-first and Fourth Tank Armies. On the immediate right of 11th Corps were the two infantry divisions of 8th Corps, which were holding the neck of the Don-Volga isthmus along with units of the 14th Panzer Corps. Only the 3rd Motorized Division of the latter corps was fully committed to the northern flank, while the units of 60th Motorized and 16th Panzer Divisions were divided between the northern flank and the Russian positions defending Stalingrad on their southern flank.

In the rear only the 22nd Panzer Division was being held back in reserve, leaving the five infantry divisions assigned to Seydlitz-Kurzbach's 51st Corps arrayed along the northern half of the western outskirts of Stalingrad, between Orlovka in the north and the Tsaritsa River running through the centre of the city.

Below the Tsaritsa covering the southern half of Stalingrad were four of the six German divisions in Hoth's 4th Panzer Army (94th Infantry, 29th Motorized and 14th and 24th Panzer). On Hitler's orders these four divisions were transferred to Paulus's command, to allow better co-ordination for the assault on the city.

The remaining two German divisions of Hoth's army (297th and 371st Infantry) were facing the larger part of the Sixty-fourth Army and part of the Fifty-Seventh Army, which were holding the heights in the Beketovka and Krasnoarmeisk area, forming a bridgehead seven miles long and two miles deep on the west bank of the Volga. The Beketovka 'bell', as the Soviet bridgehead became known on account of its bulging church-bell shape, was to prove a constant thorn in the side of 4th Panzer Army, but Hoth did not possess the necessary strength to eliminate it, his main strength having being hived off for the fight for the city.

Lacing up Hoth's southern flank were the four infantry divisions of the Rumanian 6th Corps, which were stretched thin from the south of Lake Sarpa past Lakes Tsatsa and Barmantsak out into the desert of the Kalmuck Steppe. Beyond these was a gaping 250-mile chasm yawning between Heeresgruppe B and the eastern flank of 1st Panzer Army of Heeresgruppe A in the Caucasus. This was one of the symptoms of Hitler's irrational instance of divergent effort to obtain two widely separated objectives with insufficient forces. All that could be spared to protect this 250-mile liability between the two army groups from Soviet incursion was the solitary 16th Motorized Division. Too weak to form any sort of continuous line, the Division could only resort to roving patrols over the vast wastes of the steppe.

RATTENKRIEG

For a full twenty-four hours preceding the attack on Stalingrad, the Soviet defence positions and the already ruined city were subjected to massive air raids and a pulverising bombardment by the 3,000 guns and mortars of the eleven German divisions arrayed along the outskirts.

At 0630 on the morning of 13 September the hail of steel and high explosive pounding the Russian lines reached a crescendo, heralding the onslaught by two 'shock forces' aiming concentric assaults designed to overrun the whole of the southern half of the city.

Three infantry divisions, 71st, 76th and 295th, struck out from the area of Gumrak on a south-easterly axis aimed at the vital central landing stage on the Volga bank, which provided the main artery for Soviet reserves and supplies being fed into the city from the east bank. This thrust was also intended to cut the city and Chuikov's army in two.

Simultaneous with this thrust, the 94th Infantry and 29th Motorized Divisions, backed by the 14th and 24th Panzer Divisions, crashed into the Yelshanka mining suburb in the southern area of the city, advancing on a north-easterly axis with the object of linking up with the spearhead of the other force at the central landing stage.

The German attack was met and disrupted by a heavy artillery and Katyusha rocket barrage laid by Soviet batteries situated on the east bank of the Volga and on the mid-river islands. As there was nowhere in Stalingrad that the heavy guns and howitzers could be deployed, and to relieve the

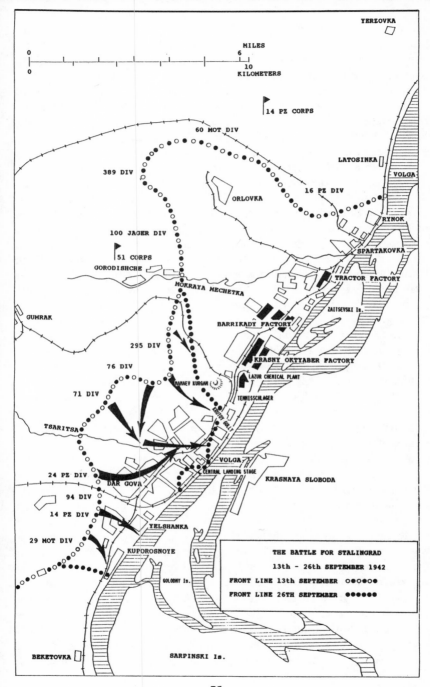

MILES

KILOMETERS

YERZOVKA

14 PZ CORPS

60 MOT DIV

389 DIV

LATOSINKA

VOLGA

16 PZ DIV

ORLOVKA

RYNOK

100 JAGER DIV

SPARTAKOVKA

51 CORPS

TRACTOR FACTORY

GORODISHCHE

MOKRAYA MECHETKA

ZAITSEVSKI Is.

GUMRAK

BARRIKADY FACTORY

295 DIV

KRASNY OKTYABER FACTORY

76 DIV

LAZUR CHEMICAL PLANT

71 DIV

MAMAEV KURGAN

TENNISSCHLAGER

TSARITSA

KRUTOY GULLY

VOLGA

CENTRAL LANDING STAGE

24 PZ DIV

DAR GOVA

KRASNAYA SLOBODA

94 DIV

14 PZ DIV

YELSHANKA

29 MOT DIV

KUPOROSNOYE

THE BATTLE FOR STALINGRAD

GOLODNY Is.

13th - 26th SEPTEMBER 1942

FRONT LINE 13th SEPTEMBER ○●○●●○

FRONT LINE 26th SEPTEMBER ●●●●●●

BEKETOVKA

SARPINSKI Is.

75

pressure on the heavily-burdened cross-river ferries of having to transport thousands of large shells, Sixty-second Army's heavy and medium artillery batteries and the majority of its Katyusha rocket launchers remained on the opposite bank to the city throughout the battle. Aiming their fire at precise co-ordinates worked out by observers in the city itself, these batteries fired an average of 10,000 rounds a day at German positions and troop concentrations. This number did not include the rounds fired by the Katyushas operating from the fringe of the west bank, or the smaller 45mm guns used by the infantry in the city which fired over open-sights.

Apart from minor indentations, the Russian defence line held firm throughout the day and night of the 13th, and it was not until the morning of the 14th that troops of the 76th Infantry Division, spearheaded by tanks, managed to break through in the area of the main hospital. By midday they had captured the main railroad station, and by 1500 they had gained a narrow corridor to the Volga bank. But this was the only lightning thrust through the city that the Germans were destined to achieve. From then on they found themselves embroiled in a costly battle of attrition in which daily advances were measured in yards, as the Russians contested every building in every street with primeval savagery. General Doerr describes the nature of the fighting:

> The time for conducting large-scale operations was gone for ever.... The mile as a measure of distance was replaced by the yard.... For every house, workshop, water-tower, railway embankment, wall, cellar and every pile of ruins, a bitter battle was waged, without equal even in the First World War.... The distance between the enemy's army and ours was as small as it could possibly be. Despite the concentrated activity of aircraft and artillery, it was impossible to break out of the area of close fighting. The Russians surpassed the Germans in their use of the terrain and in camouflage and were more experienced in barricade warfare for individual buildings.[1]

The human battering ram tactics employed by Paulus to capture the city were inept and misguided from the start. Chuikov's defence of Stalingrad was wholly dependent on the supply of ammunition, rations and reinforcements carried on the Volga ferries. To interdict this vital traffic it was necessary to capture all the landing stages and possible landing sites on the west bank. To accomplish this Paulus should have concentrated his main strength at the northern and southern extremities of the city, and incised the Russians away from the river bank by launching simultaneous northern and southern thrusts close to the water's edge. This would ultimately have stranded Chuikov's army in the centre of a cauldron of rubble. Furthermore, every yard of the steep Volga escarpment was vital to the Russian defence system. They had tunnelled into the cliffs to create depots, hospitals, ammunition dumps, fuel stores and even hide-outs for the lorry-borne Katyushas, which would reverse out of their caves, fire a salvo and get back under cover in less than five minutes.

As it was, the west to east direction of the thrusts across the city, even with a diagonal axis, which aimed at reaching the Volga at as many points as possible, resulted in the Germans being unable completely to cut the Volga traffic to Sixty-second Army. The slight curve in the course of the river and the numerous islands which obstructed the stream between the northern and southern suburbs of the long sprawling city made it very difficult for the Germans to enfilade all the ferry crossings even when their guns were installed on various points of the Volga bank, and well-nigh impossible to do so at night when the bulk of the river traffic was on the move.

This fundamental tactical error was compounded by the Luftwaffe effort being dispersed against a wide variety of targets. If, instead of dropping thousands of tons of bombs on to the sea of rubble that was Stalingrad, the bombers had been employed with single-minded persistence in an interdiction role against the Volga traffic, enough of the ferrying craft might have been destroyed to starve the defence into submission.

The nature of the street fighting that unfolded at Stalingrad was something hitherto unknown in German military experience. Baffled by the situation, they reacted, characteristically, by the application of brute force applied in increasingly heavier doses. In comparison the Russians exhibited great skill and versatility in adapting their tactics as the battle wore on.

Within a short time Chuikov had learned to abandon attacks in active-defence by entire units or even sub-units in favour of small, heavily armed storm-groups which proved ideal for carrying out lightning counter-attacks with light machine guns, anti-tank rifles, grenades, bayonets and daggers, on buildings or strong-points captured by the enemy. These groups Chuikov described as 'wily as a snake and irrepressible in action'.

The Russians also perfected the technique of creating 'killing zones' by mining streets and squares and preparing an ambush of camouflaged anti-tank guns and T-34 tanks dug-in and concealed amongst the shattered buildings and piles of rubble, into which the direction of the advancing Germans would be skilfully canalized.

In contrast German tactics were unsophisticated and costly. To capture a street a company of infantry would be preceded by 'packets' of three of four tanks. To combat these formations in the 'killing zones', the Russian troops would hold their fire until the tanks had passed by and the infantry following in their wake had moved into the field of fire. In this way they invariably cut off the infantry from the tanks and destroyed them separately. In this way, too, the German tanks, if not destroyed in the ambush of hidden anti-tank guns and T-34s, would be unable to consolidate the capture of an objective without the infantry and would be forced to retreat. As they back-tracked through the narrow, rubble-strewn streets, the tanks had to face the disadvantage of having their lightly armoured rear decks and engine grilles pierced by anti-tank rifles or grenades thrown down on them from the three or four-storey buildings.

This became such a costly business in lives and tanks that the Germans were forced to reverse their tactics by sending the infantry in first to draw the defenders' fire and thus identify the Russian positions. Once the buildings or strong-points had been revealed the tanks would cover one another while they fired at point-blank range until the buildings collapsed. With tall, substantial structures this could be a protracted business, because armour-piercing shells would invariably pass right through the walls without exploding, creating no more damage than jagged holes two feet in diameter. What was required was high explosive shells, but this would put the German tanks at the mercy of any roaming T-34 or KV that might suddenly appear from around a corner, against which high-explosive shells would be useless. Moreover, the limited elevation of the tank's turrets precluded them from engaging the top storey of tall buildings. For this reason it was found necessary for teams of troops armed with flame-throwers to accompany each attacking formation, so that high buildings could be burned down. However, this was an extremely hazardous occupation, as a single bullet hitting the tank of oil strapped to the back of the flame-thrower operator would turn the man into a human torch. To add to the danger, any *Flammenwerfer*, hated and feared by the Russians for obvious reasons, who fell into enemy hands could expect no mercy, and were put to death in the horrifying manner which their weapons doled out. Special rates of pay were introduced, but as this inducement failed to enlist sufficient volunteers, men from German punishment battalions were pressed into this suicidal service.

Having spent all day clearing a street, starting at the western end and then establishing fire-points at the eastern end, the Germans would suddenly find themselves under fire from the western end again. Eventually they discovered the Russians' trick of knocking communicating holes through the walls between the garrets and attics, 'and running back like rats in the rafters to set up their machine-guns behind some topmost window or broken chimney.'

The battle for the city evolved largely into countless murderous confrontations between small groups or even individual soldiers who would jeer and curse at each other across a street, or while they fought for stairways and rooms in the shattered buildings. Hand-to-hand duels were finished in the smog of smoke and dust from falling plaster and rafters with knives, pickaxes and improvised clubs of wood and twisted steel grasped from the débris. Few prisoners were taken by either side, in what the German infantry nicknamed Rattenkrieg (a war of the rats).

After each miniature battle the streets bore the same appearance: burnt-out tanks surrounded by heaps of dead and dying, upon which swarms of flies descended, overhung by half-shattered walls some with their floor rafters attached but hanging to one side in empty air. And everywhere there was smoke and raging fires and the heavy caustic stench of cordite, charcoal, burned brick and corpses rotting beneath the chaotic mounds of rubble. While overhead German aircraft hung in clusters, sweeping in to rake the streets with their machine guns and cannons and to unload bombs on the already desolate, smashed buildings. Drifting smoke blotted out the sun, and visibility in the crater-strewn city was reduced to no more than a dozen yards in the murk of swirling dust thrown up by toppling walls and crashing buildings, which produced a yellow-grey fog lit only by the flashes of bursting bombs and shells.

The defenders of this fire-blackened shell on the Volga had nowhere to retreat to and were faced with the choice of fighting for survival or being blotted out in the nightmare of rubble and the gaping, burned-out shells of sagging, shattered buildings, where the mind-numbing din of battle never ceased for a moment. Such was the ferocity of the fighting that individual explosions, the grinding and roaring of tanks through the wreckage, the whining of shells in flight, the scream of Stuka sirens and the shriek of falling bombs could not be heard separately in the all-consuming roar of bombing and shelling.

Incredibly, a lot of civilians still lived in the cellars and basements of their ruined homes in some of the most heavily fought-over parts of the city. These were progressively rounded up by the Germans who sent them rearwards on marches which few survived.

At night, 'howling, screeching, bleeding nights', Stalingrad presented an incredible sight. The grotesque shapes of the disembowelled shops, offices, houses and factories were silhouetted by the glow of the innumerable giant fires and huge showers of sparks; the endless flashes of artillery guns; the comet trails of the Katyusha rockets; the constant winking splashes of the reddish-yellow light of small-arms fire and the tracer of heavy machine guns; the searing yellow-green brilliance of parachute flares floating over the city like brilliant chandeliers; the red, green, yellow and white signal flares and rockets sent skywards by the ground forces; the bluish lightning flashes of bombardment.

Under these hellish pyrotechnics, Russian 'storm-groups' and individuals slid through sewers or crawled across precarious bridges formed by the smashed buildings in the ruination that was Stalingrad, to deny rest and to unnerve the battle weary Germans by initiating hundreds of miniature but horrifyingly savage battles in which no mercy was given or expected.

When he launched the assault on 13 September, Paulus confidently envisaged a rapid conquest of the city. In fact he had committed his army to a battle of attrition that would last for 80 days and 80 nights, and would burn out nearly every division he possessed. A German lieutenant lamented that: 'Animals flee this hell; the hardest stones cannot bear it for long; only men endure.'

CARNAGE ON THE ISTHMUS

To relieve the pressure on Chuikov's men in the inferno of Stalingrad, Zhukov launched a new offensive by First Guards, Twenty-fourth and Sixty-sixth Armies against the German 8th Corps and 14th Panzer Corps, which were holding the neck of the Don-Volga isthmus.

The attack had been scheduled to commence on 17 September, but due to the complex pre-attack regrouping and preparation it had to be postponed for twenty-four hours. To improve the chances of a breakthrough, Zhukov caused First Guards to switch sectors with Twenty-fourth Army. Regrouping First Guards (the most powerful of the three armies) on the left flank placed it opposite the two infantry divisions of the German 8th Corps, which presented a weaker front than the neighbouring 14th Panzer Corps. To increase the 'punch' of First Guards, its existing rifle divisions, the strength of which had been heavily depleted in the first offensive, were transferred to Twenty-fourth and Sixty-sixth. In return it was beefed up with fresh reinforcements drawn from Stavka reserve, which brought its strength to nine rifle divisions, three tank corps, three tank brigades, nine artillery regiments, six mortar regiments and eight mortar battalions.

The main point of attack was to be made by First Guards and Twenty-fourth Armies on a narrow front of twenty miles, in the area of the ruined railway sidings (described as point 564 on military maps) on the Stalingrad to Moscow railway line. The aim was to break through the German front and advance on a south-easterly axis towards Gumrak, with the objective of linking up with the northern flank of Chuikov's Sixty-second Army in Stalingrad.

From the start the success of the operation was compromised by the nature of the terrain. The Germans were dug in on commanding elevations which overlooked the flat monotonous steppe, devoid of all cover, over which the Russians had to advance.

At 0530 on the morning of 18 September, after a heavy artillery bombardment, a tank corps, three tank brigades and the infantry of five rifle divisions of First Guards, and two rifle divisions of Twenty-fourth Army, hurled themselves forward against the high ground held by the Germans.

As had happened in the first offensive in this sector, the artillery barrage proved ineffective due to the superficial nature of the reconnaissance raids carried out to determine the enemy's defences. The lightly held forward line had been incorrectly determined as the main zone, with the result that the Russian attack was hurled against a defence system that the artillery had hardly touched, let alone neutralized. In fact most of the shells fired had fallen into vacant areas. For this error thousands of Russian soldiers paid the supreme penalty. The attack was met by a withering fire from German artillery, mortar and heavy machine-gun positions, which were able to pinpoint every move made by the Soviets who were exposed to view for a considerable distance on the flat, low-lying desolate steppe.

To make matters worse the one-mile attack frontage of each division was too narrow. This resulted in a deeply bunched approach with tanks and troops in several echelons, in which only a very small part of the firepower of each division (the lead elements) could be brought to bear during the approach to the German lines. In addition there was no cooperation between the infantry, tanks, artillery and aircraft, each of which operated independently. The tanks went into battle without direct artillery support or air cover, and the infantry, expecting the artillery and tanks to have neutralized the enemy fire system, did not employ their own weapons in an effective manner. Insufficient time for planning the offensive had resulted in questions of cooperation being worked out hastily on the basis of maps. But because of the nature of the steppe, which was deficient in clear reference points, and poor or non-existent signals communication between the different formations, confusion arose and there were even instances of fratricidal clashes between Russian units. Lack of sufficient training for the tank crews in the hastily formed and assembled reserve formations led to lack of manoeuvre in which the tanks would slow down to a crawl or even stop to fire their guns rather than fire while advancing at high speed.

All too quickly the Luftwaffe appeared on the scene, and waves of bombers and Stukas added to the carnage being inflicted on the closely bunched Russians by the saturating fire of the German guns. The battlefield was soon littered with burnt-out or immobilized tanks and heaps of dead infantry.

Despite horrendous losses, the attack gained up to 3,000 yards in places, even reaching the crest of the high ground, but it was stopped dead in its tracks by a violent German counter-attack launched by armour and infantry.

Zhukov attempted to improve the situation by throwing two further tank corps into the affray, but since these formations fielded T-60 and T-70 light tanks they were quickly smashed to pieces by a hail of shells and bombs.

The three armies hammered away at the German positions for a further five agonizing days, but the only breakthrough was achieved by ten tanks of Malinovsky's 66th Army (on the extreme right flank hard against the

Volga bank) which battled their way through 16th Panzer Division's sector into the city during a night attack. But Hube's armour quickly closed in behind them, sealed off the breach, and destroyed all ten tanks.

Although the tactical results were insignificant, the offensive did exert great influence in assisting Chuikov to hold Stalingrad. The Germans suffered heavy losses, were forced to withdraw units from the divisions attacking the city to bolster the defences and had to reduce the Luftwaffe effort over Stalingrad, which was diverted to the northern flank. Colonel H.R. Dingler, who was serving on the staff of the 3rd Motorized Division, describes how hard-pressed the German defence was in repulsing the Soviet attacks:

I do not say too much when I state that during these attacks our position seemed hopeless on more than one occasion. The reinforcements in men and materials we received from home were utterly insufficient. Those men who had no previous battle experience were quite useless in this hard fighting. The losses they suffered from the first day in the fighting line were staggering. We could not 'acclimatize' these people gradually to battle conditions by attaching them to quiet sectors, because there were no such sectors at that time. Nor was it possible to withdraw veterans from the front to give these raw recruits thorough training.

The Russian artillery fire was very heavy indeed. Not only did the Russians shell our forward lines, but their long-range guns fired far into our rear. It may be worthwhile to make a few remarks on our experiences during those anxious days. Our artillery then became one of the most important factors in the defence system. As casualties increased and the strength of our infantry decreased, the main burden of repulsing the Russian attacks had to be borne by the guns. Without our artillery, so well trained and efficient, it would have been impossible to hold out as long as we did against massed attacks, persistently repeated. In principle we only used concentrated artillery fire, and we tried to shoot up the Russian assembly areas before they had time to develop their attacks. It was interesting to note that Russians are very sensitive to artillery fire, if to nothing else.

We learned not to use positions on forward slopes, as they could not be protected against attacks by armour. It must not be forgotten that our main anti-tank defence lay in our armour, and we concentrated all tanks in hollows immediately behind the main line of resistance. From these positions they were able to knock out the Russian tanks as soon as they reached the crest of the height above. At the same time the panzers were able to protect our infantry on the reverse slope from being overrun by Russian Armour.

That our tactics were quite effective is shown by the fact that we counted more than two hundred Russian tanks knocked out during this period of fighting on our divisional front.[2]

The Soviet General Staff study on the battle laments that, 'in the end, this operational success was achieved at the price of great loss of life.'[3] However, the heaps of Russian dead littering the steppe did not die in vain. An analysis of the operation taught the Soviets a great deal about their tactical errors and weaknesses, which they had time to correct during the planning and preparation for the big offensive scheduled for the second week in November.

THE SNARE

By the beginning of October the Germans had succeeded in wresting all of the southern half of Stalingrad from Chuikov's Sixty-second Army which had been compressed into a 12-mile front against the Volga bank with a depth varying from 4,000 to a mere 250 yards. During the murderous grappling in the misshapen ruins of the giant, crumbling city, the Germans had expended 25 million rounds of small arms ammunition, 500,000 anti-tank rounds and 750,000 artillery shells, and incurred 40,000 casualties (killed, wounded and missing). Soviet casualties were double this number, but a carefully measured influx of reinforcements fed into the inferno via the Volga ferries (79,000 in total) actually increased Chuikov's strength slightly (55,000 men, 950 guns, 500 mortars and 80 tanks) to defend what remained of Stalingrad.

The unexpectedly bloody and protracted wrangle for the city had demoralized Paulus, who was growing increasingly concerned at the rate at which his army was bleeding to death in the endless street fighting. When General Rudolf Schmundt, the head of the Army Personnel Office, who was 'filled with a glow of enthusiasm for National Socialist ideology,' visited 6th Army Headquarters, Paulus vented his fears about the lack of resilience on his extended flanks and how his army's strength in the city was fading more rapidly than he could find troops to replace the losses. He predicted that unless the decline was reversed the battle would stretch out indefinitely. The shallowness of the man is evinced by a sudden revival of his flagging spirits, when Schmundt hinted that he was under consideration to replace Jodl as Chief of the OKW Staff. This hint of a career move was enough to inspire Paulus to demand even greater efforts from his battle-weary troops, in order to fulfil Hitler's demand of the 2nd October that Stalingrad must be captured as quickly as possible, on the grounds that it was 'urgently necessary for psychological reasons' in that Communism must be 'deprived of its shrine'.

Paulus was, however, unable to conceive of any alternative solution to the human battering ram tactics that were proving so slow and costly, and he had already brusquely dismissed General von Wietersheim (14th Panzer Corps) and General von Schwedler (4th Corps) from their commands for criticizing his handling of the battle.

During the second week of October, the fighting over the huge desolate corpse of Stalingrad slackened while Paulus reshuffled his divisions and regrouped for the assault on the northern half of the city. His appeal for reinforcement by three infantry divisions produced five engineer battalions, all that OKH could scrape up, which were flown out from Germany. He was able, however, to switch divisions which had been burnt out in the street fighting with relatively fresh divisions from 11th Corps sector on the northern loop of the Don. This was facilitated by the arrival of the 3rd Rumanian Army, which took over part of the line held by 6th Army, slotting in on a 100-mile front between 11th Corps and the Italian 8th Army. At the same time the southern flank of 4th Panzer Army was bolstered by the arrival of the Rumanian 4th Army, which incorporated into its composition the four infantry divisions of the Rumanian 6th Corps already lacing up the southern flank.

Finally, at 0800 on Monday, 14 October, 1942, three infantry divisions (94th, 389th and 100th Jäger), two panzer divisions (14th and 24th) and the five newly arrived engineer battalions, numbering 90,000 men and 300 tanks, with massive air support (3,000 sorties were flown that day), lurched forward in a great wall of steel and fire to overrun the northern industrial complex of Stalingrad. The axis of the advance contained the three giant concrete edifices of the Dzerhezinsky Tractor plant, the Barrikady gun factory and the Krasny Oktyaber plant, ranged one after another for a distance of eleven miles along the Volga bank. To the south of these were the Lazur chemical plant, and what proved to be the deadly meshes of the bomb and shell-cratered railways sidings, which the Germans nicknamed *der Tennisschlager* (the tennis racquet) on account of the looping shape of the railway network.

The Germans fought with frenzied desperation, for in the words of Wilhelm Hoffman, serving in the 267th Regiment of the 94th Infantry Division:

> The days are shortening again, we can definitely sense it. In the mornings the air is quite cool. Are we really going to have to fight through another of those dreadful winters? That's what's behind our efforts. Many of us feel that it is worth anything, any price, if we can get it over before the winter.[4]

The stupendous surge of the most savage and bitter fighting in the whole of the battle, fought over the gaunt and ruined factory district, where the steel ribs of the workshops stuck out amidst enormous mounds of rubble, tangled girders and acres of shattered equipment and thousands of bomb craters and shell holes, is graphically described by Hoffman in his diary:

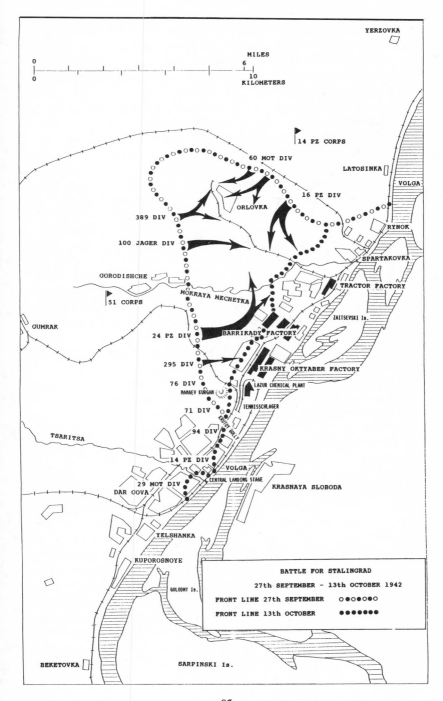

YERZOVKA

MILES
0   6
0   10
KILOMETERS

14 PZ CORPS

60 MOT DIV

LATOSINKA

VOLGA

16 PZ DIV

389 DIV

ORLOVKA

RYNOK

100 JAGER DIV

SPARTAKOVKA

GORODISHCHE

TRACTOR FACTORY

MOKRAYA MECHETKA

51 CORPS

ZAITSEVSKI Is.

GUMRAK

24 PZ DIV

BARRIKADY FACTORY

295 DIV

KRASNY OKTYABER FACTORY

76 DIV

LAZUR CHEMICAL PLANT

MAMAEV KURGAN

71 DIV

TENNISSCHLAGER

94 DIV

KRUTOY GULLY

TSARITSA

14 PZ DIV

VOLGA

29 MOT DIV

CENTRAL LANDING STAGE

DAR GOVA

KRASNAYA SLOBODA

YELSHANKA

KUPOROSNOYE

GOLODNY Is.

BATTLE FOR STALINGRAD

27th SEPTEMBER - 13th OCTOBER 1942

FRONT LINE 27th SEPTEMBER   O●O●O●O

FRONT LINE 13th OCTOBER   ●●●●●●●

BEKETOVKA

SARPINSKI Is.

85

October 14th. It has been fantastic since morning: our aircraft and artillery have been hammering the Russian positions for hours on end; everything in sight is being blotted from the face of the earth...

October 17th. Fighting has been going on continuously for four days, with unprecedented ferocity. During this time our regiment has advanced barely half a mile. The Russian firing is causing us heavy losses. Men and officers alike have become bitter and silent.

October 22nd. Our regiment has failed to break into the factory. We have lost many men; every time you move you have to jump over bodies. You can scarcely breathe in the day time: there is nowhere and no one to remove the bodies, so they are left there to rot. Who would have thought three months ago that instead of the joy of victory we would have to endure such sacrifice and torture, the end of which is nowhere in sight? The soldiers are calling Stalingrad the mass grave of the Wehrmacht. There are very few men left in the companies. We have been told we are soon going to be withdrawn to be brought back up to strength.

October 27th. Our troops have captured the whole of the Barrikady factory, but we cannot break through to the Volga. The Russians are not men, but some kind of cast-iron creatures; they never get tired and are not afraid of fire. We are absolutely exhausted; our regiment now has barely the strength of a company. The Russian artillery at the other side of the Volga won't let you lift your head...

October 28th. Every soldier sees himself as a condemned man. The only hope is to be wounded and taken back to the rear. Have just had the news that our regiment is to be withdrawn to the rear for reinforcements. This is the third time this autumn.

October 30th. We have had no rest. Our battalion was given a few transport drivers and sent to another part of the front, on the northern outskirts of Stalingrad. You can scarcely do battle with a complement of this size. Everyone is depressed. Stalingrad has turned us into beings without feelings — we are tired, exhausted, bitter. If our relatives and families could see us now they would be horrified.[5]

While Wilhelm Hoffman suffered the agonizing realities of Stalingrad, Hitler capitalized on the unrealities. Having returned to Germany from Vinnitsa on 27 September, the Führer addressed the Nazi Party 'old guard' in the Bürgerbrau Beer Cellar in Munich on the evening of 8 November. This was the day when the Anglo-American forces landed in French North Africa, and was only six days after Hitler learned of the defeat of Rommel's Africa Korps by Montgomery at the Battle of El Alamein. Neither of these disturbing events served to temper Hitler's bombast in the speech he made to commemorate the 1923 Putsch or diminish his obsession with Stalingrad — 'the shrine of Communism'.

I wanted to get to the Volga and to do so at a particular point where stands a certain town. By chance it bears the name of Stalin himself. I wanted to take the place, and do you know, modest as we are, we've pulled it off, we've got it really, except for a few enemy positions still holding out. Now people say: "Why don't they finish the job more quickly?" Well, the reason is that I don't want another Verdun. I prefer to do the job with quite small assault groups. Time is of no consequence at all.[6]

The speech was broadcast live on the German radio network, and many of the German soldiers in Stalingrad were able to listen to it. According to Heinz Schröter, one soldier, in a dug out on the northern perimeter of the city, buried his head in his hands and murmured: 'My God, quite small assault groups... if he had only at least reached full corporal!'[7] For men already suffering the first freezing temperatures, frosts, snow and sleet showers of a second merciless Russian winter, Hitler's boast that 'time is of no consequence at all' must have left them dumb with incredulity.

Hitler's boast was made in the knowledge that Paulus was in possession of nine-tenths of the city. But the 'few enemy positions still holding out' — those vital yards along the Volga bank — were the deadly spikes on which the bone-weary troops of 6th Army, their senses numbed with the unending thunder, fire, smoke, dust and countless agonies, were impaled. Chuikov's decimated army, which had been offered as live bait, had held the Germans in its grasp long enough for Stalin to spring his trap.

SOUNDING THE TOCSIN

General Kurt Zeitzler, who had replaced Halder as Chief of the General Staff when the latter was dismissed at the end of September, was horrified when he heard the broadcast of Hitler's speech. 'There was a great danger,' Zeitzler explained, 'that once Hitler had declared his intentions to Germany and the world he would obstinately refuse to modify them, for their fulfilment then became with him a matter of his personal prestige.'[8] In fact the dogmatic nature of the 8 November speech only served to reinforce Hitler's obsessive intention to capture and hold Stalingrad whatever the cost, evinced in a speech he had made some weeks earlier when he declared that: 'Where the German soldier sets foot, there he remains... You may rest assured that nobody will ever drive us away from Stalingrad.'

It fell to Zeitzler to try and convince Hitler that his boasts were in complete variance to the untenable situation to which the German forces on the Stalingrad axis were committed. The rotund, florid, jovial, forty-seven-year-old Zeitzler, who was known throughout the army as 'Thunderball'

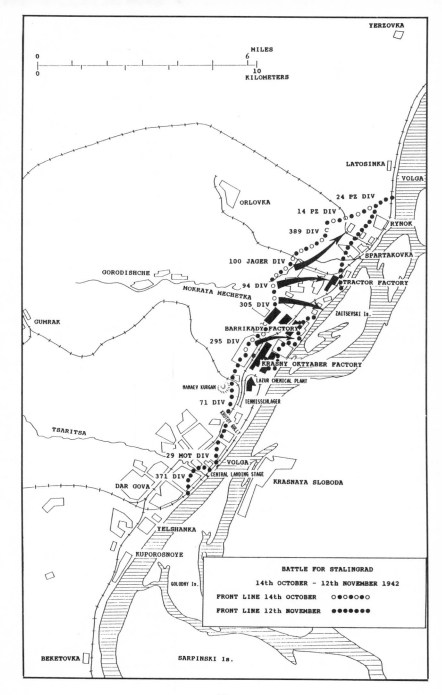

YERZOVKA

MILES
0 ⌐———┴——┴——┴——┴——┴——┴——┤ 6
0 ⌐———┴——┴——┴——┴——┴——┴——┤ 10
KILOMETERS

LATOSINKA

VOLGA

24 PZ DIV

14 PZ DIV

389 DIV

ORLOVKA

RYNOK

100 JAGER DIV

SPARTAKOVKA

GORODISHCHE

94 DIV

TRACTOR FACTORY

MOKRAYA MECHETKA

305 DIV

ZAITSEVSKI Is.

GUMRAK

BARRIKADY FACTORY

295 DIV

KRASNY OKTYABER FACTORY

LAZUR CHEMICAL PLANT

MAMAEV KURGAN

71 DIV

TENNISSCHLAGER

KRUTOY GULLY

TSARITSA

29 MOT DIV

VOLGA

371 DIV

CENTRAL LANDING STAGE

KRASNAYA SLOBODA

DAR GOVA

YELSHANKA

KUPOROSNOYE

GOLODNY Is.

BATTLE FOR STALINGRAD

14th OCTOBER - 12th NOVEMBER 1942

FRONT LINE 14th OCTOBER   o●o●o●o

FRONT LINE 12th NOVEMBER   ●●●●●●●

BEKETOVKA

SARPINSKI Is.

88

because of his bustling dynamic manner in getting things done, had been chosen by Hitler to replace the 'pessimistic' Halder on account of his optimistic attitude. However, Hitler was soon to discover that Zeitzler's optimism was not equatable with his own dismissal of the military realities.

After studying the situation on the Eastern Front, the new Chief of the General Staff presented Hitler with a detailed report, supported by a mass of statistics, which was even more unpalatable than Halder's appreciation. The report concluded with five postulates and consequent demands:

1. Owing to the summer offensive, the territory to be occupied in the East no longer corresponded to the size of the occupying army. In a word, there were too few soldiers for too much ground. Unless this was adjusted, a catastrophe must occur.

2. The most perilous sector of the Eastern Front was undoubtedly the long, thinly-held flank stretching from Stalingrad to the right boundary of Army Group Centre. Furthermore, this sector was held by the weakest and least reliable of our troops, Rumanians, Italians and Hungarians. This created an enormous danger, which must be eliminated.

3. The flow of men, equipment, weapons and ammunition to the Eastern Front was entirely insufficient. Each month losses exceeded replacements. This must have disastrous consequences.

4. The Russians were both better trained and better led in 1942 than they had been in 1941. This fact should be realized and taken into account. Greater caution on our part was essential.

5. This was a detailed point concerning better servicing of the troops, a more skilful utilization of the railways which would ensure greater mobility, and other, largely technical, matters.[9]

To Zeitzler's surprise Hitler did not interrupt or throw a tantrum when these hard facts were presented to him. But it was to no avail. When Zeitzler finished Hitler merely smiled and said: 'You are too pessimistic. Here on the Eastern Front we've been through worse periods than this before... and we've survived. We'll get over our present difficulties too.'

Having thus dismissed Zeitzler's warning, Hitler considered the matter closed. But Zeitzler, alarmed at the inherent dangers of the opportunity being offered to the Soviets on the Stalingrad axis, tried repeatedly, at the daily situation conferences, to convince Hitler of the 'military impossibility' of pursuing his present strategy.

By constant reiteration, he did finally succeed in making Hitler aware of the peril constituted by the weak northern flank running from Stalingrad to Voronezh, but Hitler would not countenance any of the obvious solutions. These were threefold, and were in effect belated rectifications of the errors committed by Hitler in the planning and subsequent divergence of effort in the summer offensive.

The most obvious and effective measure was to withdraw the German armies from Stalingrad and create a shorter, and consequently stronger, front to the west of the Don. This would not only eliminate the endangered flanks, but would also free a large number of divisions to form a strong reserve in the form of a *masse de manoeuvre*.

The second solution was a modification of the first, in that it envisaged holding the present front, including Stalingrad, but on the condition that planning and preparations were made to withdraw to a shorter line to the west at the latest immediately before a Russian counter-attack on the northern flank was deemed imminent. Being a compromise solution, it contained not only all the inherent disadvantages of a compromise, but also a weighty imponderable: would such a withdrawal be physically possible at the critical moment in the harsh climatic conditions of the Russian winter?

The third solution to the impending crisis was to withdraw the unreliable allied armies guarding the German flanks north and south of Stalingrad and replace them with well-equipped German divisions backed by adequate reserves. This was a non-starter because the necessary divisions could only be obtained by a lateral transfer from other sectors of the Eastern Front, which would only result in creating a new crisis on the denuded sectors.

The first solution was the most obvious expediency: obvious to everyone, that is, except Hitler. His insistence that all crises could be weathered by sheer will-power and strategic and tactical rigidity, in conjunction with his obdurate and senseless refusal to surrender any territory whatsoever in planned withdrawals, regardless of circumstances, made this solution totally unacceptable.

As for the second proposal, Hitler, according to Zeitzler, 'refused to countenance it or to order that plans be made accordingly. However, the impression he gave was that he liked it, for the simple reason that it offered him the chance of procrastination. He never made a disagreeable decision, if he could see any way of postponing it until later. He embellished this habitual hesitancy of his by referring to it as a policy of letting the situation mature.'[10]

Faced with Hitler's irrational obstinacy, Zeitzler could only resort to minor expedients in an attempt to bolster the non-German divisions on the northern flow of the Don Bend. These 'bolster tactics' consisted in interspersing a few German anti-tank battalions amongst the Rumanian divisions. These units were intended to stand fast in an attempt to limit the enemy's depth of penetration in the event of a Russian breakthrough. It was hoped that by holding their positions they would also create more favourable conditions for a counter-attack. The danger was that, should the Rumanian troops collapse

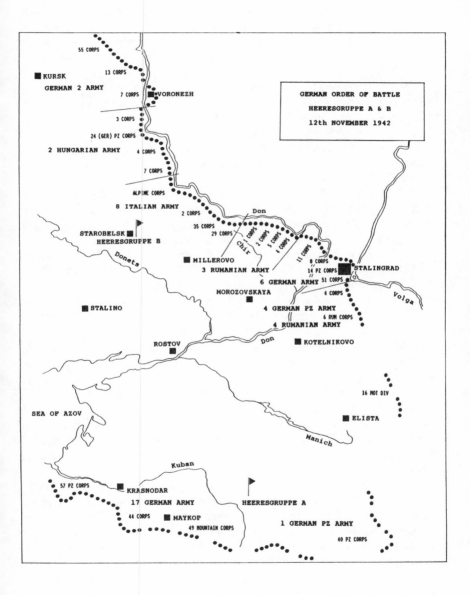

GERMAN ORDER OF BATTLE
HEERESGRUPPE A & B
12th NOVEMBER 1942

55 CORPS
13 CORPS
KURSK
GERMAN 2 ARMY
7 CORPS — VORONEZH
3 CORPS
24 (GER) PZ CORPS
2 HUNGARIAN ARMY
4 CORPS
7 CORPS
ALPINE CORPS
8 ITALIAN ARMY
2 CORPS
Don
35 CORPS
STAROBELSK
29 CORPS
HEERESGRUPPE B
1 CORPS
2 CORPS
5 CORPS
Chir
4 CORPS
Donets
MILLEROVO
11 CORPS
8 CORPS
STALINGRAD
3 RUMANIAN ARMY
14 PZ CORPS
6 GERMAN ARMY 51 CORPS
MOROZOVSKAYA
STALINO
4 CORPS
Volga
4 GERMAN PZ ARMY
6 RUM CORPS
4 RUMANIAN ARMY
ROSTOV
Don
KOTELNIKOVO
16 MOT DIV
SEA OF AZOV
ELISTA
Manich
Kuban
57 PZ CORPS
KRASNODAR
17 GERMAN ARMY
HEERESGRUPPE A
44 CORPS
MAYKOP
1 GERMAN PZ ARMY
49 MOUNTAIN CORPS
40 PZ CORPS

too quickly and a rout develop, the German units would be surrounded and overwhelmed. Zeitzler was under no illusions that the units were too few in number to fundamentally affect the situation, but deemed it necessary to do something with the scant resources available rather than do nothing at all. He also managed to scrape together an operational reserve which was to assemble in the rear of the 3rd Rumanian Army, the most vulnerable sector of the front.

'Panzer Reserve Heim' (it was placed under the command of General Ferdinand Heim) was formed on the Corps Staff of 48th Panzer Corps and a few artillery and anti-tank units withdrawn from Hoth's 4th Panzer Army. But the forces allocated to Heim were a little more than a shadow of what constituted a full-strength Panzer Corps. Its strongest formation was the 22nd Panzer Division, which had been lying inactive behind the Italian 8th Army since mid-September.

This Division had been weakened by the transfer of one of its two Panzer grenadier regiments (140th) to the 2nd Army in the Voronezh area, while its engineer battalion had been called on to take part in the street fighting in Stalingrad. It was weakened further by Russian mice!

While stationed in reserve behind the Italian sector of the front, the tanks of 22nd Panzer's single panzer regiment (204th) had received practically no fuel for training or test-running the engines. Consequently, for a period of two months, the tanks lay entirely immobile in pits dug into the ground under a camouflage of straw and reeds, which also offered protection against frost and snow.

When the order was received to make the lateral move to the new assembly area behind the 3rd Rumanian Army, it was suddenly discovered that only half of the 104 tanks were operational. This halving of the Division's armoured strength had been caused by mice, who, nesting in the straw used to cover the tank pits, had found their way into the immobile tanks in search of food and had nibbled their way through the rubber insulations of the electric wiring. As a result faults developed in the electrical equipment, affecting the ignition, battery-feeds and the turret-training and gun-loading mechanisms.

To make matters worse, on the day the tanks that could be made mobile set off on the 100-mile lateral move, a severe drop in temperature occurred, causing severe icing on the slush-covered roads. As none of the tanks had been equipped with track-sleeves, progress was reduced to a crawl as the tanks skidded and slithered from one side of the icy roads to the other. Shortage of fuel had forced 22nd Panzer to leave without the multifarious vehicles of its tank workshop company, depriving it of the means to carry out the major repairs necessary on the tanks which came to grief on the slippery journey. When the Division finally reached the designated assembly area on 16 November, only 42 tanks (40.38 per cent) of the original total were operational.

The other division which made up 'Panzer Reserve Heim' was the 1st Rumanian Panzer Division, with 108 tanks. However, only 21 were modern German battle tanks, the other 87 being Czech Skoda 38-Ts, whose light scale of armour protection made them as good as obsolete in comparison to Russian T-34s and KV heavies. Moreover, the crews of the Rumanian 1st Panzer were inexperienced, and for the large part still under training.

An armoured reserve of 150 tanks, of which only 63 were fit to engage Russian armour, in addition to a few anti-tank 'bolster' units, amounted to little more than makeshift measures of doubtful value. In fact they constituted more of a danger to the Germans than the enemy, in that they served to satisfy Hitler that sufficient measures had been taken. This made Zeitzler's task of convincing him to the contrary all the more difficult. The exasperated General's constant reiteration of the gravity of the situation, and the dire necessity of implementing one or the other of the two major solutions, henceforth only served to provoke outbursts of rage. The nub of the matter was that Hitler was incapable of thinking in anything other than offensive strategy; where defensive ideas were concerned he was 'talentless to the point of disaster'.

Zeitzler's anxieties were increased by a stream of disturbing situation reports and estimates sent in by Paulus and Hoth, via von Weich's Heeresgruppe B HQ at Starobelsk. The intelligence officers of both 6th Army and 4th Panzer Army were warning that large enemy forces were gathering on both the northern and southern flanks. Interrogation of Russian prisoners and deserters revealed the arrival in these sectors of very high-grade Soviet divisions. This information was borne out by aerial reconnaissance which reported masses of troops and armour moving into the areas opposite the 3rd and 4th Rumanian Armies. Further confirmation was provided by General Dumitrescu, commanding 3rd Rumanian Army, who reported continuous local enemy attacks at company or battalion strength, the scale and nature of which were obviously intended to thoroughly reconnoitre the defence positions and to probe for soft spots.

By the first week of November it had become patently clear to everyone that a major counter-offensive was imminent and that the German dispositions were pregnant with disaster. Zeitzler laments that: 'It was awful to foresee a coming catastrophe and yet to be incapable of preventing it: to see the only remedy disregarded and rejected by the only man with authority to act — in this case Hitler.[11]

THE GATHERING STORM

At the end of September Zhukov and Vasilevsky returned to Moscow after examining all aspects of the northern and southern flanks of the German forces compressed into the tip of the Stalingrad salient. During the resulting detailed discussions with Stalin, Stavka and specialist officers from the Operations Section of the General Staff, regarding the practical problems involved in implementing the *Kontrudar* (counter-blow), the most immediate major decision made was to replace the cumbersome local command structure pertaining to the two Fronts on the Stalingrad axis. As a result the existing South-eastern Front (south of Stalingrad) was re-designated the Stalingrad Front: while the old Stalingrad Front (stretching across the Don-Volga isthmus and the northern side of the Don Bend) was re-designated the Don Front. The unwieldy length of the line held by Don Front inherited from the old configuration, was shortened by its western flank sector being assigned to a newly created South-western Front.

The new Stalingrad Front (holding 280 miles of frontage), under the command of General Yeremenko, encompassed four existing armies in its sector – the mauled and decimated Sixty-second (Chuikov) clinging to its bridgeheads in the fiery ruination of Stalingrad; Sixty-fourth (Shumilov); Fifty-seventh (Tolbukhin); Fifty-first (Trufanov) – and the newly assigned Twenty-eighth Army which took up position on the extreme southern flank in the Kalmuck Steppe.

The Don Front (holding 93 miles of frontage), under the command of General Rokossovsky, was stripped of one of the existing armies in its sector. This was First Guards whose decimated units were withdrawn for rest and re-equipping, while the headquarters staff was transferred to form the nucleus of the new South-western Front staff (the remains of this army was later reactivated as Third Guards). This left Rokossovsky with three armies under his command: Sixty-sixth (Zhadov) with its eastern flank hard against the Volga in the northern Stalingrad suburbs of Rynok and Spartakovka; Twenty-fourth (Galinin), and Sixty-fifth (Batov), formed on the remnants of Fourth Tank Army, which took up a position on the western flank of the Front in the area of Kletskaya on the Don.

The South-western Front (holding 154 miles of frontage), under the command of General Vatutin, comprised three armies: Twenty-first (Chistyakov), adjacent to the Don Front boundary; the powerful Fifth Tank (Romanenko) in the bridgehead on the southern bank of the Don in the area of Serafimovich; and a newly activated reserve army designated First Guards (Lelyushenko) on the western flank of the Front in the area of Pavlovsk.

The final details of the counter-blow, which was code-named 'Uranus', envisaged two thrusts on convergent axes designed to envelope the German 6th and 4th Panzer Army, some 330,000 men, and annihilate them in a huge cauldron battle.

On the northern sector the main blow was to be delivered by a shock group of the South-western Front, consisting of Fifth Tank Army and Twenty-first Army. They were to strike out from bridgeheads north-west of Serafimovich and from the Kletskaya area, with the task of breaking through the front lines of 3rd Rumanian Army and advancing south-eastwards at high speed for Kalach. To protect the shock group from enemy counter-attacks from the west and south-west, the western flank forces of First Guards were to deliver an auxiliary blow on a south-westerly axis.

On the eastern flank of the shock group, the Don Front was to deal two auxiliary blows in the direction of Vertyachiy. These attacks were to be made by Sixty-fifth Army on the western flank, striking south-eastwards from a bridgehead on the southern bank of the Don at Kletskaya; and the Twenty-fourth Army attacking from the area of Kachalinskaya (north bank of the Don) on a south-easterly axis. These two concentric blows were aimed to trap the infantry divisions of the 11th German Corps in a small cauldron on the left bank of the Don Bend, to prevent them falling back on the main German forces at Stalingrad.

On the southern sector the second element of the main blow was to be delivered by a shock group of the Stalingrad Front, consisting of the reinforced Fifty-seventh and Fifty-first Armies. These were to debouch from the defiles between the three salt lakes south of Stalingrad, smash through the front held by the 4th Rumanian Army and advance on a north-westerly axis to link up with the South-western Front forces at Kalach, and close the ring around the two German armies. To protect the northern flank of this shock group, Sixty-fourth Army were to launch a subsidiary thrust from the area of the Beketovka 'bell' bridgehead. This thrust was also designed to seal the southern flank of the cauldron.

In its conception the Kontrudar was based on the German strategic doctrine of Vernichtungsgedanke, which had originally been formulated at the turn of the century by General Graf von Schlieffen. For what was envisaged in strategic terms was decisive manoeuvre in the form of concentric encircling movements, launched from the enemy's flanks with the object of creating an annihilating Kesselschlacten.

To give adequate cover and support to the ground forces, a vast air armada had been built up to ensure the success of 'Uranus'. A total of 1,327 aircraft, disposed in four Air Armies were assigned to the three Fronts. The numbers and types of aircraft fully operational on the day the Kontrudar was launched were as follows:

	17th Air Army	2nd Air Army	16th Air Army	8th Air Army
Fronts.		South-western	Don	Stalingrad
Types:				
Bombers.	46	4	11	29

Ground Attack.	118	57	68	177
Fighters.	147	23	81	235
Reconnaissance.	6	12	2	3
Night Bombers.	71	48	98	91
Totals:	388	144	260	535[12]

The concentration of this mass of aircraft in bases situated on average 100 miles behind the front presented no problems, but the movement of the huge bodies of men, armour, vehicles, horses, and enormous quantities of ammunition and materials into the Front assembly areas was another matter. Apart from trying to disguise the presence of the huge forces gathering on the flanks from enemy observation, the build-up put an enormous strain on the existing lines of communication.

Only one main railway line existed to directly serve both the South-western and Don Fronts. As this was totally inadequate to the needs, 117,000 men of a para-military construction corps worked around the clock to lay 725 miles of track to create six branch lines running from the north towards the Don. Exactly the same situation existed on the Stalingrad Front: one main line which was under constant air attack and surveillance by the Luftwaffe.

To speed up the build-up 'human signallers' were deployed along the tracks, enabling numerous trains to travel in one direction on one track with 12 minute intervals between them. To minimize loss from air attack only small trains of half-a-dozen waggons were employed, one truck carrying light AA guns and/or machine guns. Tanks were carried lashed to railway flat cars, and were hidden under tarpaulins. Twenty-seven thousand lorries were also employed, travelling only at night without headlights. By day all road transport ceased, and the concentration of troops and tanks remained absolutely immobile under skilfully devised camouflage or were hidden in woods and forests.

The extent of the transport problems is illustrated by the vast number of weapons moved up to the Stalingrad Front alone: 500,000 rifles, 80,000 automatic weapons, 17,000 machine guns, 16,000 anti-tank rifles and nearly 6,000 artillery pieces. The build-up on this Front was complicated by having to ferry the vast numbers of troops and materials across the Volga. Because the crossing points were constantly bombed by the Luftwaffe, movement over the river was confined to the hours of darkness up to 15 November. Only in the last three days before the offensive were day crossings made, by which time the Germans no longer enjoyed air superiority over the battlefield: Fliegerkorps VIII's strength having fallen to about 400 operational aircraft of all types. Nine crossing points were fixed (three behind each of the three armies assigned to the attack), employing a total of 59 steamers, 2 icebreakers, 25 tugboats, 3 passenger ferries, 1 ferryboat and 28 barges with a load capacity of 5,100 tons. Despite the difficulties caused by large ice floes on the river, this armada of small boats ferried 135,000 men, 430 tanks, 10,000 motor vehicles, 500 guns, 3,000 horses, 6,000 tons of ammunition and 4,000 tons of food from the east bank to the Stalingrad Front during the final two weeks of the preparatory period.

On the eve of zero-hour of operation 'Uranus', Soviet forces on the Stalingrad axis numbered 1,015,299 men, 1,560 tanks, 4,275 artillery pieces (76mm and above), 11,546 mortars (50mm to 120mm), 440 Katyusha rocket-launchers, 1,041 anti-aircraft guns, 22,258 machine-guns, 169,609 horses, 381 armoured cars and 41,413 motor vehicles. These were disposed in the three Fronts as follows:

	South-western Front	Don Front	Stalingrad Front
Men.	338,631	292,707	383,961
Weapons:			
Rifles.	191,020	159,330	176,957
Sub-machine guns.	27,081	29,902	37,799
Machine-guns:			
Light.	5,143	4,160	5,587
Heavy.	2,424	2,217	2,727
Anti-tank rifles.	6,280	5,733	5,649
Artillery:			
45mm Anti-tank.	740	581	986
76mm Field guns.	974	838	1,185
107mm and above.	487	419	372
Mortars:			
120mm	541	444	624
82mm	1,828	2,010	1,506
50mm	1,932	1,483	1,178
Katyusha rocket-launchers.	148	147	145
Anti-aircraft guns:			
76-85mm	45	53	245
25-37mm	278	133	287
Tanks:			
Heavy (KVs).	145	43	49
Medium (T-34s).	318	67	357
Light.	267	70	244
Armoured cars.	99	38	181
Motor Vehicles.	14,529	12,003	14,881
Tractors.	792	864	1,001
Horses.	69,003	44,915	55,691[13]

Prodigious though the force assembled for the counter-blow undoubtedly was, it represented only 17 per cent of the total manpower being fielded in the Soviet front line armies (6,124,000) in November, 1942; only 22 per cent of the artillery and mortars (72,500); 25 per cent of the Katyusha rocket launchers (1,724); 26 per cent of the tanks and self-propelled guns; and 43 per cent of the total combat aircraft. The decisive nature of Russia's inexhaustible reserves of manpower and her great industrial capacity, which Hitler and the German generals had simply dismissed as of no value when planning the invasion of the Soviet Union, was finally about to make itself felt with devastating effect.

THE BRINK

The Rumanian Armies on which the two main Soviet blows would fall were at a hopeless disadvantage. Defending a frontage of 95 miles opposite the Russian South-western Front were the eight infantry divisions and two cavalry divisions of the 3rd Rumanian Army (General Dumitrescu). From West to East the army's order of battle was: 1st Corps (7th and 11th Infantry Divisions); 2nd Corps (9th and 14th Divisions); 5th Corps (5th and 6th Divisions); 4th Corps (13th and 15th Divisions); with the 1st Cavalry Division on the eastern flank adjacent to the boundary with the German 11th Corps. The 7th Rumanian Cavalry Division was in reserve, some miles in the rear of the 14th Infantry Division.

At full strength the establishment of a Rumanian infantry division was 13,100 men, and a cavalry division 7,600. But all of 3rd Army's formations were below full establishment, and the total strength of the Army was about 100,000 men: less than a third being fielded by the Russians in the South-western Front. Moreover, by German standards the Rumanian troops were inadequately trained, armed and equipped, and the national motivation for involvement in the Russian campaign was lacking. Organized along the lines of a French infantry division of the First World War, and relying heavily on French equipment captured by the Germans in 1940, the Rumanian divisions had only one anti-tank company apiece and these were armed with obsolete, horse-drawn 37mm guns which were little better than pea-shooters against Soviet tanks. The German 'bolster units', armed with far more powerful 75mm anti-tank guns, did little to improve matters because they only strengthened each of the Rumanian divisions with six guns! Ammunition of all kinds along with rations was in short supply, and modern anti-tank and anti-personnel mines were non-existent. A German visitor at the beginning of November noticed that: 'The building of defences was being neglected in favour of large dug-outs for the command posts and shelters for men and animals.'[14]

Identical inadequacies applied to the 4th Rumanian Army (General Constantinescu) on the southern sector, which would bear the brunt of the offensive launched by the Stalingrad Front. With a frontage of 120 miles the Army dispositions from North to South (from the Sarpa Lake out into the Kalmuck Steppe) were: 6th Corps (2nd, 18th, 20th, 1st, and 4th Infantry Divisions) and the 4th Cavalry Corps (5th and 8th Cavalry Divisions). In all some 70,000 men, barely a quarter of the Russian flood poised to pour down upon them. The only reserve was provided by the 29th Motorized Division, which, mauled and decimated in the incessant and murderous street fighting, had been withdrawn from Stalingrad.

The morale of the Rumanian troops, low to begin with, quickly degenerated into apathy and sheer misery with the onset of the Russian winter which numbed the very soul with its agonizing sub-zero temperatures: a torment which was added to the countless agonies already being suffered by the German troops impaled on the spikes of Stalingrad, who found themselves shivering and freezing in the atrocious cold, devoid of adequate clothing.

Unlike the previous winter, protective great-coats, padded jackets, thick woollen socks, balaclavas, gloves and felt-lined boots existed in abundance, but all these items were stuck in base depots far behind the front. With only one single-track railway running from the base areas to the 6th Army rail-head on the Chir River, which was constantly damaged by Russian bombing, and on account of insufficient locomotives and rolling stock, only twelve supply trains a day were getting through. This number, in addition to an abnormally high rate of air-lift by the Luftwaffe, was only sufficient to move up the daily minimum requirement of 750 tons of ammunition, fuel and food to the front, which by necessity took precedence over clothing. 'Thus did it come about that the greater part of 6th Army was compelled to fight its last battle without winter clothing... while in the rear were great warehouses containing everything that the troops in Stalingrad lacked.... Only they went empty-handed, for it was others, a hundred miles behind the front, who wore the fur coats. Forty thousand fur coats, caps and fur-lined boots, and 121,000 greatcoats, along with twenty-five hundredweight of moth powder were stored in Millerovo. 'It's all here,' said the commissariat. 'But not here,' grumbled the private at Stalingrad.'[15]

Freezing, at the pitch of exhaustion, the haggard, dirty, gaunt German troops fought on in the furnace of the wholly ruined city. In his diary, Lieutenant Weiner of the 24th Panzer Division graphically describes the last throes of 6th Army to destroy the remaining Soviet bridgeheads:

> We have fought during fifteen days for a single house, with mortars, grenades, machine-guns and bayonets. Already by the third day fifty-four German corpses are strewn in the cellars, on the landings, and the staircases. The front is a corridor between burnt-out rooms; it is the thin ceiling between two floors. Help comes from neighbouring

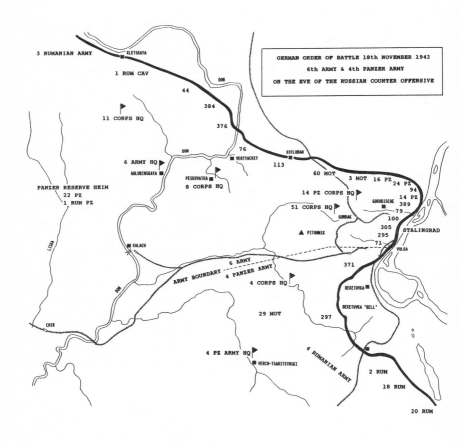

3 RUMANIAN ARMY

KLETSKAYA

1 RUM CAV

DON

44

384

376

11 CORPS HQ

DON

76

KOTLUBAN

VERTYACHIY

113

6 ARMY HQ

60 MOT

3 MOT

16 PZ

24 PZ

GOLUBINSKAYA

94

PESKOVATKA

14 PZ

PANZER RESERVE HEIM
22 PZ
1 RUM PZ

8 CORPS HQ

14 PZ CORPS HQ

GORODISCHE

389

51 CORPS HQ

79

GUMRAK

100

305

PITOMNIK

295

STALINGRAD

71

LISKA

VOLGA

KALACH

6 ARMY

371

ARMY BOUNDARY

4 PANZER ARMY

BEKETOVKA

4 CORPS HQ

BEKETOVKA "BELL"

CHIR

29 MOT

297

DON

4 PZ ARMY HQ

4 RUMANIAN ARMY

VERCH-TSARITSYNSKI

2 RUM

18 RUM

20 RUM

GERMAN ORDER OF BATTLE 18th NOVEMBER 1942

6th ARMY & 4th PANZER ARMY

ON THE EVE OF THE RUSSIAN COUNTER OFFENSIVE

houses by fire escapes and chimneys. There is a ceaseless struggle from noon to night. From storey to storey, we bombarded each other with grenades in the middle of explosions, clouds of dust and smoke, heaps of mortar, floods of blood, fragments of furniture and human beings. Ask any soldier what half an hour of hand-to-hand struggle means in such a fight. And imagine Stalingrad; eighty days and eighty nights of hand-to-hand struggles. The street is no longer measured by metres but by corpses.[16]

Yet this savage misery was but a pale shadow of the terrible, monstrous agony that was about to wrap its grizzly fingers around the throat of the 6th Army.

5

NEMESIS

'And there were noises and thunderings and lightnings; and there
was a great earthquake, such a mighty and great earthquake as had
not occurred since men were on the earth.'

(Revelation 16:18).

THE NORTHERN BLOW

At 1617 on the wintry evening of 18 November, 1942, the commanders
of the armies of the South-western and Don Fronts received the cryptic
message: 'Send a messenger to pick up the fur gloves.' This seemingly
innocuous message had a profound meaning for those who could decipher
its import: 'Infantry attack begins at 0850, 19.11.42.'

On receipt of this alert, the Russian infantry of the divisions assigned to
the first attack echelon of the Kontrudar moved up in the darkness to their
forward jumping-off positions, to lay low and silent on the exposed, bitterly
cold steppe. At midnight snow clouds came in, the temperature dropped to
-6° C, and visibility was reduced to zero in dense freezing fog and driving
snow blizzards which quickly covered the battlefield in a thick white blanket.

Unaware of the sinister movements opposite them, the Rumanian troops
in the 3rd Army sector shivered in their foxholes and dug-outs. Their
forward trenches, bolstered with three to four light earth and timber
pillboxes for each mile of front, were lightly held. The main defence system
of trenches, bunkers and dug-outs lay from half-a-mile to two miles further
back. But even in these relatively better defended areas the Rumanians were
only able to field eight artillery pieces and twenty machine guns to the mile.

Those Rumanian troops not peering into the impenetrable blizzard-filled
fog, ready to repulse another of the constant Russian reconnaissance raids,
sat with their knees drawn up to their chests, backs to the frozen straw-lined
earth of the foxholes and dug-outs, with blankets draped over their heads
and shoulders, enduring the unbearable icy present and fearing the future.
One hundred thousand anonymous soldiers in ninety-five miles of nameless
holes burrowed into the walls of nameless trenches.

At 0720 in the murk of Thursday morning, 19 November, the Russian
artillery officers received the call-sign 'siren', at which all the guns and

mortars which had been settled into their firing pits during the night were loaded and aimed. Ten minutes later, at precisely 0730, the signal to open fire was given by a salvo from the Katyusha rocket-launchers, and the swirling fog was rent by 3,500 brilliant orange and red flashes. For the next one hour and twenty minutes the 'God of War', as Stalin called the artillery, beat its thunderous and terrifying tattoo.

The Soviet gunners found fire correction impossible on account of the fog and driving snow storm, and instead of firing at pre-selected targets the guns had to be aimed and fired at quadrants over the Rumanian positions. The effect was nonetheless devastating. A white-hot wall of flame and steel crept over the defences to a depth of two miles. Pillboxes were torn apart, and dug-outs, bunkers and trenches collapsed, as the steppe was churned up in great pillars of snow and earth. 'Branches, legs, beams, bodies, bits of metal, rifles, clods of earth, platoons, companies, battalions, regiments, were buried under the snow and earth, or hurled high in the air.'[1]

No aircraft took part in the unfolding drama, for both air forces were firmly grounded by the foul weather. The war diary of Luftflotte IV noted that:

Snow and ice have completely prevented air operations, and Fliegerkorps VIII, from its command post at Oblivskaya, can direct only a few single aircraft to the attack. It is impossible to close the Don River bridges by bombing. It is not even possible to gain an insight into the situation by aerial reconnaissance. We can only hope that the Russians will not reach our rail route, our main supply artery... Urgently needed transfers (of air units) are as yet impossible because of the miserable weather. We must have good weather soon, otherwise there is no longer any hope.[2]

At 0850, as the artillery barrage suddenly ceased, four rifle divisions of Fifth Tank Army's first attack echelon crashed into the positions held by the dazed survivors of the 9th and 14th Rumanian Infantry Divisions. At the same time four rifle divisions of Twenty-first Army fell upon the 13th and 15th Rumanian Divisions. Despite the terrible pounding they had suffered, and their pitifully inadequate equipment, the troops of the four Rumanian divisions fought manfully. But by noon they began to crack and then disintegrate when out of the fog loomed swarms of roaring Soviet tanks, with infantry riding on their backs, from the second attack echelons.

By 1400 a rout had developed as the panic-stricken remnants of the four Rumanian Divisions began to fall back in confusion. Through the breach poured the Soviet 1st and 26th Tank Corps and the 8th Cavalry Corps of Fifth Tank Army, and the 4th Tank Corps and the 3rd Guards Cavalry Corps of Twenty-first Army. Smashing their way through the rearguards mounted by the 7th Rumanian Cavalry Division, the German anti-tank 'bolster units' and a few pockets of Rumanian infantry that could be persuaded to turn and fight, the flood of Russian tanks struck out in a south-easterly direction towards Kalach, steering by compass through the blinding fog and driving snow. In their wake came the two cavalry corps at the gallop (a total of 38,646 mounted men, armed to the teeth with rifles, anti-tank rifles, sabres, grenades, sub-machine guns, light and heavy machine guns, and over 800 horse-drawn artillery, anti-tank and mortar pieces). These were followed in turn by the infantry and artillery regiments, consolidating and widening the flanks of the break-through sectors.

By wheeling inwards east and west, infantry from both Soviet armies were able to close in behind the four remaining Rumanian infantry divisions clinging to their defence positions and envelop them in a small cauldron. General Mihail Lascar, commanding the 6th Infantry Division, took command of the encircled group, which was thereafter referred to as the 'Lascar Group'. Although this group continued to resist for five days, it did not alter the fact that 3rd Rumanian Army (which suffered 55,000 casualties) had been completely lifted off its hinges, and a 90-mile gap had been ripped out of the Axis front.

On the Don Front sector, Batov's Sixty-fifth Army also launched an attack that morning against the 1st Rumanian Cavalry Division and the German 44th Infantry Division (of the 11th Corps). The attack was stopped dead in its tracks by the German Division, but, predictably, the Rumanian cavalry (in dismounted formation) wavered and began to fall back.

Apart from the superior fighting qualities and weapons of the German Division, the Soviet attack in this sector was handicapped by an eighty-foot-high chalk cliff, up which Batov's men had to clamber under heavy fire. In his memoirs General Batov describes the difficulties which faced his troops:

We were watching one of the most tense moments of the battle. Let the reader picture the place for himself: deep winding gullies running into a chalky ravine with steep walls 70 to 80 feet high. There was nothing for a hand to catch hold of. Feet slip on the wet chalk.... We could see the soldiers running to the base of the cliff and scrambling upwards. Soon the whole face was dotted with men. They were slipping and falling, supporting each other, creeping stubbornly upwards.... The Front commander (Rokossovsky) spent about two hours at the army's observation post. As he was leaving he said: 'The enemy is putting up an unexpectedly fierce resistance. But remember, you are responsible for the eastern flank of Twenty-first Army.' I took this as a demand for a sharp increase in the shock group's rate of advance.[3]

Apart from protecting Twenty-first Army's flank, Sixty-fifth Army was also assigned the task of striking south-eastwards after effecting a breakthrough, to link up with a second concentric blow delivered by General Galinin's Twenty-fourth Army, with the object of trapping the German 11th Corps in a separate cauldron. But when Galinin's troops launched an attack against the German positions on 22 November, they fared no better than Sixty-fifth Army. However, although the planned encirclement of 11th Corps was not achieved, the failure did not affect the final outcome of the major offensive. Neither were the heavy losses suffered by the two Russian armies in vain, because their attacks prevented the German divisions from launching counter-attacks against the eastern flank of the main Soviet thrust in its drive on Kalach.

With the remnants of the Rumanian 3rd Army streaming over the fog-shrouded, snow-covered steppe in headlong flight towards the Chir River, all that stood between the Soviet flood of 560 tanks and 200,000 assault troops of Fifth Tank and Twenty-first Armies from reaching their objective was 'Panzer Reserve Heim'.

Zeitzler was in the Wolfsschanze command post in Rastenburg, East Prussia, when he received the following signal from von Weichs in Heeresgruppe B HQ, at 0830 on the morning of 19 November: 'Very heavy artillery bombardment of the whole Rumanian front north-west of Stalingrad.' Being in no doubt that the expected Soviet offensive had begun, Zeitzler sent an immediate reply to von Weichs: 'Panzer Corps Heim to be made ready for action immediately. Application has already been made to Hitler for its release from reserve.'

Hitler had instructed that this single reserve was not to be committed to action without his personal approval being first obtained. Therefore, as soon as Zeitzler learned of the Russian bombardment, he sought permission to activate Heim's panzers. But Hitler was not in the Wolfsschanze, he was in the Berghof, his alpine retreat at Berchtesgaden in Bavaria, and it took a lengthy telephone call for Zeitzler to convince the 'military genius' of the seriousness of the situation and persuade him to release 'Panzer Reserve Heim' from OKW reserve and place it under Weichs' control. He would have preferred to postpone this decision,' Zeitzler recorded, and await further reports from the front. It required, as usual, a tremendous effort to convince him that it would then be too late. I regarded my success in securing the release of the Panzer Reserve as a personal triumph, and Army Group B was also delighted.'[4]

The delight of the latter was soon tempered by the flood of contradictory reports from the front which slowly merged into a general picture of a panic rout by the Rumanians, and of Russian tanks appearing deep in the rear. Before the situation became entirely clear, von Weichs ordered Heim's panzers to counter-attack in a north-easterly direction towards Kletskaya — against Twenty-first Army's break-through. But less than an hour after the panzers had set off in this direction, Heim received a counter-order redirecting the attack towards the north-west – against what had emerged on Weichs' situation maps to be a more dangerous breakthrough by Fifth Tank Army's mass of armour in the Blinov area.

Slithering round through 90 degrees, the tanks of 22nd Panzer Division (General von Apell) changed direction, but in so doing it lost contact with General Radu's 1st Rumanian Panzer Division in the atrocious weather and zero visibility. The German signals unit truck assigned to Radu's division did not receive the vital change of direction order, with the result that the Rumanian panzers swept on north-east and ran slap bang into an overwhelming mass of Russian armour, artillery and anti-tank guns, which spelt doom to the lightly-armoured, old fashioned tanks of Radu's division.

Meanwhile 22nd Panzer ran into the huge armoured spearhead of Fifth Tank Army in the area of Peschany. During the division's high-speed dash over the treacherous, icy, snow-covered steppe, without track-sleeves to prevent skidding and slithering, so many tanks came to grief that 22nd Panzer arrived on the battlefield of Peschany with only 20 tanks and a single anti-tank gun battalion. After a brief, confused, but spirited action with the lead Russian T-34s, fought in the blinding fog and the entanglement of the flood of fleeing Rumanians, the division was forced to turn tail and retreat to the south-west to avoid being encircled.

While the Russian forces swept on ever deeper into the German rear towards Kalach, and 'Panzer Reserve Heim' evaporated from the German order of battle, Zeitzler, unaware of the full extent of the disaster unfolding on the steppe, telephoned Hitler again to try and persuade him that the time had come to implement the major solution of withdrawing the German forces from Stalingrad. 'This,' laments Zeitzler, 'only angered Hitler. As usual he clutched at every hopeful straw. He said that we should wait and see what effect the commitment of Panzer Corps Heim would have on the course of the battle. When I told him that the most we could expect from this corps was that it would slow down the Russian penetration, but that it would not stop the enemy's advance, he simply dismissed this appreciation as unduly pessimistic.'[5]

Meanwhile, on von Weichs' situation maps the full gravity of the situation on the steppe was beginning to become terrifyingly clear. Accordingly, at 2200, Weichs dispatched the following signal by radio to Paulus in 6th Army HQ at Golubinskaya:

> The situation developing on the front of the 3rd Rumanian Army dictates radical measures in order to disengage forces quickly, to screen the flank of 6th Army and to assure the protection of supplies in the Likhaya – Chir sector of the railroad. In this connection, I order:
> 1. All offensive operations in Stalingrad to be stopped except for

activity of reconnaissance units whose information is required for organization of defence.

2. 6th Army to detach immediately from its forces two panzer formations, one infantry division, if possible auxiliary motorized unit of 14th Panzer Corps and in addition the strongest anti-tank forces available, to concentrate this group on its left flank and attack towards the north-west and west.[6]

In compliance, Paulus immediately ordered the 14th, 16th and 24th Panzer Divisions to disengage and move westwards across the Don to block the Russian drive into the German rear. Formations from the three divisions began to withdraw from Stalingrad during the same night (19/20 November). But the withdrawal of units actively engaged with the enemy in the murderous street fighting could only be carried out in piecemeal fashion. Further to which, great difficulty was experienced in finding enough fuel for all the tanks and motor vehicles to make the 60 to 80 mile westerly dash, necessary to throw themselves in the path of the Russian spearhead. Thus when the divisions began arriving on the west bank on the morning of 21 November, they did so in weak, scattered, incomplete and disorganized sub-units. A large part of their strength was tied down in repulsing violent counter-attacks by Sixty-second Army in Stalingrad (timed to pin down the Germans forces in the city). None of the grenadier regiments from the three divisions accompanied the armour, and the divisional staffs were forced to round up any man carrying a weapon from the supply and administrative installations which abounded in the Don Bend. However, a hastily assembled collection of lorry drivers, clerks and storemen was a poor substitute for the missing grenadier regiments. The tanks of these units, being scattered over a wide area in small packets, had little chance of stopping the concentrated mass of Russian armour, and ultimately all they succeeded in doing was slowing up the Soviet advance launched from the north by twenty-four hours. Even this small achievement was less their doing than a consequence of the Russian tank formations allowing themselves to be drawn into local engagements contrary to their original orders. In the meantime, while von Weichs was desperately trying to shore up the northern flank, the Russians proceeded to smash in the southern flank.

THE SOUTHERN BLOW

On account of the smaller depth of penetration into the German rear assigned to the Stalingrad Front, the southern blow of the Kontrudar was timed to start twenty-four hours after the northern blow.

The artillery barrage, aimed to smash the defence positions of the 4th Rumanian Army, was scheduled to begin at 0800 on the morning of Friday, 20 November, but General Yeremenko, who had positioned himself in a forward observation post on a hill about 300 feet above the level of the Volga in Fifty-seventh Army's sector, decided to postpone the barrage on account of the dense, freezing fog concealing the snow-covered enemy positions.

When Yeremenko received a call from the Stavka on the V Ch line, demanding to know why the artillery had not opened fire on schedule, he retorted that he was not sitting in his office but in a forward command post and he knew best when to start. It was not until 0930, when the fog lifted slightly to give 200 yards of visibility, that Yeremenko gave thirty minutes' notice to the gunners to prepare to open fire. At 1000 precisely a salvo from the Katyusha rocket-launchers gave the signal, and 1,320 guns and mortars opened fire simultaneously with a thunderous roar and lightning flash of flame.

After the guns had pounded the Rumanian 4th Army positions for 75 minutes, the first attack echelon of Fifty-seventh Army (two rifle divisions and one rifle brigade) attacked from the southern edge of the Beketovka 'bell' and the defile between Lakes Sarpa and Tsatsa against sectors held by the 2nd and 18th Rumanian Infantry Divisions. Within two hours these Divisions began to disintegrate, and the tanks and motorized infantry of the Soviet 13th Mechanized Corps of the second attack echelon began pouring through the gap, littered with smashed guns, vehicles, pill-boxes and heaps of Rumanian dead. Once out onto the snow-covered, wind-swept steppe, 13th Mechanized, driving in two columns, swung northwards.

Further south, three rifle divisions of Fifty-first Army attacked, from the defile between Lakes Tsatsa and Barmantsak, against the positions held by the 1st and 4th Rumanian Infantry Divisions. All organized resistance by these two divisions had collapsed by 1300, and an hour later the three mechanized brigades and two tank regiments of the 4th Mechanized Corps exploited the breakthrough, and struck out in a north-westerly direction for Kalach.

Having to steer by compass through the blinding murk all three brigades converged on to one road, instead of the three routes planned and this slowed down the rate of advance quite considerably. Following through the breach came the 10,284 mounted men of the 4th Cavalry Corps, which struck out to the south-west, pushing the southern flank units of the 4th Rumanian Army back towards the River Aksay.

The Soviet advance in both breakthrough sectors, spearheaded by a total of 397 tanks, was virtually unopposed. Panic and 'tank fright' gripped the disintegrating Rumanian formations. Many of the officers deserted their men and made off in motor vehicles, while most of the troops threw away their weapons without firing a shot and took to their heels, presenting what General Hoth described as 'a fantastic picture of fleeing remnants.'[7] Heinz Schröter recounts that: 'Four or five great columns of men and vehicles had

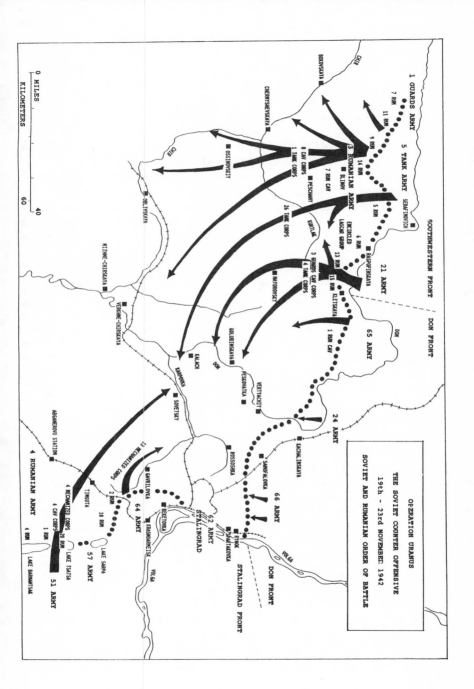

OPERATION URANUS
THE SOVIET COUNTER OFFENSIVE
19th – 23rd NOVEMBER 1942
SOVIET AND RUMANIAN ORDER OF BATTLE

thrown discipline to the wind, and they raced aimlessly along the roads and across the open steppe. No one had a thought to spare for anyone else. The swift overtook the slow, tractors and trucks were driven regardless of the safety of others, and any man who got in their way was simply mown down.'[8] The Rumanian 4th Army suffered some 35,000 casualties (killed, wounded, taken prisoner) during the Russian breakthrough.

After the barrage had ceased in Fifty-seventh Army sector, the guns were limbered up and hurriedly hauled northwards to a new position on the southern edge of the Beketovka 'bell' bridgehead. At 1420 they had opened fire to provide a pre-attack barrage for a subsidiary thrust launched by three rifle divisions and two tank brigades of Shumilov's Sixty-fourth Army.

This attack was designed to protect the northern flank of the 13th and 4th Mechanized Corps on their drive to link up with the forces of the South-western Front advancing from the north. The 20th Rumanian Infantry Division was decimated in this attack, but stiff resistance by the German 297th Infantry Division (4th Corps) slowed Shumilov's advance down to a costly crawl (by the end of the day the depth of penetration was only 3 miles).

The only reserve formation available to parry the blow delivered by the Stalingrad Front was the 29th Motorized Infantry division (General von Leyser), stationed 30 miles south-west of Stalingrad. Acting independently, Hoth (commanding 4th Panzer Army) ordered von Leyser's division to strike against the flank of the Russian break-through.

The 29th Motorized set off south-east hell for leather. The 129th Panzer Battalion roared ahead, in a broad wedge of 55 Mark III and Mark IV tanks. Along the flanks moved the two Panzer Grenadier Regiments in their armoured carriers. Behind them came the artillery. In spite of the fog they drove forward, towards the sound of the guns.

The tank commanders were propped up in the open turret hatches. Visibility was barely 100 yards. Suddenly the fog cleared and immediately ahead, barely 400 yards distant, was the approaching Soviet tank armada of the 13th Mechanized Corps. Tank-hatches were slammed shut. The familiar words of command rang out: 'Turret 12 o'clock — armour-piercing shell — load — 400 yards — numerous enemy tanks — fire in your own time!'

Everywhere there were flashes of lightning and the crash of the 7.5 mm guns. Hits were scored and tanks set on fire. The Soviets were confused...they were milling around among one another, falling back, getting stuck and being knocked out. Presently a new target was revealed. A short distance away, on a railway line, stood two freight trains, disgorging masses of Soviet infantry.... The division's artillery battalions spotted the promising target and started pounding it.'[9]

Despite this initial success, von Leyser's single division was simply not strong enough to stop the advance of a whole Soviet mechanized corps with over 100 tanks in its van. However, in the fog and confusion, 29th Motorized continued to hang over 13th Mechanized Corps's flank, and by constant jabbing attacks slowed down the rate of advance.

This went on until nightfall, when von Weichs ordered Hoth to withdraw 29th Motorized to a defensive position on 6th Army's southern flank. 'Admittedly,' Paul Carell points out, 'orthodox military principles demanded that the flank of an Army threatened by enemy penetrations should be protected − but in this particular instance Heeresgruppe B HQ should have realized that the southern prong of the Soviet drive was not for the moment directed at Stalingrad at all, but at Kalach, with a view to linking up with the northern prong from the Don and closing the big trap behind 6th Army. Weichs's Heeresgruppe HQ has been accused, and not without justification, of having pursued a strategy of piecemeal solutions.... In all probability the staff did not at the time realize the aim of the Russian attacks. Nevertheless a properly functioning reconnaissance could have revealed what was happening within the next few hours.'[10] The upshot was that 29th Motorized fell back into inertia at a critical time, when it could have continued to exert considerable influence on the Russian timetable by repeatedly attacking 13th Mechanized Corps' rapidly extending flank.

During the night the two infantry divisions of 4th Corps, the only German formations left in Hoth's 4th Panzer Army, were detached from Hoth's command and subordinated to 6th Army. All the German forces on the Stalingrad axis were henceforth under Paulus's command, and 4th Panzer Army was reduced in fighting value to nothing more than a leaderless mass of Rumanian troops streaming west and south-west in panic flight across the steppes.

By the morning of Saturday, 21 November, the Russian forces of the Stalingrad Front, on their north-westerly drive, had penetrated 30 miles into the German rear, while the forces of the South-western Front had driven 60 miles across the steppe, and were either smashing or putting to precipitous flight the German rear units and the scattered battle groups of the 14th, 16th and 24th Panzer Divisions, which had been thrown into the affray on the west bank of the Don.

In the path of the Russian advance bearing down on Kalach were army and corps staff HQs, ammunition and supply dumps, motor vehicle and tank repair workshops, hospitals and a host of other support and ancillary units. Officers and men from all of these merged into one south-westward rolling wave of frozen humanity, along with horses and lorries, trying to escape the Soviet tanks.

Suddenly realizing that 6th Army HQ at Golubinskaya (10 miles north-east of Kalach) was directly in the path of the oncoming Russian 4th Tank Corps

(Twenty-first Army), Paulus ordered the transfer of the HQ staff to a recently constructed winter HQ at Nizhne-Chirskaya, forty miles to the south-west, situated at the point where the Chir River ran into the Don, well outside of the developing encirclement of 6th Army.

Paulus and his Chief of Staff, General Arthur Schmidt, flew out of Golubinskaya in two small Fieseler Storch reconnaissance planes at midday, only two hours before Russian tanks appeared on the heights overlooking Golubinskaya. Colonel Adam, 6th Army's senior adjutant, describes the ensuing panic:

> In their feverish desire to save their own lives, the troops abandoned everything that hindered a hasty flight. They threw away weapons and equipment; vehicles fully loaded with ammunition, field kitchens and baggage wagons stood motionless on the road, as men could move faster by unharnessing the horses and riding them. Wild chaos ruled at Verkhne-Chirskaya (on the road to Nizhne-Chirskaya, where there existed one of the few intact bridges over the Don). Soldiers and officers of the 3rd Rumanian Army and German rear services personnel, coming from the north, were added to those from 4th Rumanian Army who were on the run...seized by panic and driven out of their minds by fear, all looked the same. All were hurrying in the direction of Nizhne-Chirskaya.[11]

After studying the situation maps, shortly after his arrival at his new HQ at Nizhne-Chirskaya, Paulus fully realized the deadly peril developing on each of 6th Army's flanks, and he radioed an urgent request to von Weichs in Heeresgruppe B HQ at Starobelsk. He proposed that 6th Army be withdrawn from the Volga and Stalingrad to form a new front more than a hundred miles to the west, on the lower Don and Chir Rivers. With a strong endorsement that this course of action should be effected without delay, von Weichs forwarded Paulus's request to Zeitzler in the Wolfsschanze in East Prussia.

The proposal was identical to the major solution that Zeitzler had long been advocating, and he immediately telephoned Hitler in the Berghof, trying once again to persuade him that the withdrawal of the 6th Army from Stalingrad was the only possible way of avoiding a major catastrophe. He explained that, by turning about, securing the existing front line with rear-guards, and attacking westwards with the greater part of its strength, 6th Army would be able to establish a strong front on a shorter line along the Chir River. This course of action, Zeitzler argued, would not only parry the threat to 6th Army, but could, possibly, inflict a resounding defeat on the Russian columns extended in narrow corridors over the Don steppe. Alternatively, if this solution was not implemented, 'disaster was calculably inevitable, as 6th Army would be cut off and encircled and a great gap would be torn in the front held by Heeresgruppe B.[12]

Predictably, Hitler adamantly refused to sanction this obvious and indeed only solution, purely and simply because of his irrational insistence on not surrendering territory under any circumstance, and the loss of personal prestige that would result from pulling back from Stalingrad. To press home the point at 1525 that afternoon (21 Nov.) he had the following message radioed to Paulus: 'Urgent, Führer Order — Sixth Army will hold positions despite threat of temporary encirclement.... Keep railroad open as long as possible. Special orders regarding air supply will follow.'[13]

During the evening Zeitzler, in another lengthy telephone call to the Berghof, tried once again to make Hitler see sense, but to no avail. 'If we abandon Stalingrad', Hitler retorted, 'we are really abandoning the whole meaning of the campaign in the East.'[14] Joachim Fest concludes from this reply that Hitler 'with his passion for mythologizing, surely felt it as a sign that this city bore the name of one of his great symbolic enemies. Here he wanted to win or go down to his doom.'[15] In such perverse reasoning as this, military reality obviously had no place.

THE PINCERS CLOSE

By the morning of Sunday, 22 November, only 50 miles separated the spearheads of the two Soviet concentric blows. But for the pincers to snap shut it was necessary for the tanks of the Fifth Tank and Twenty-first Armies to cross the Don in the area of Kalach. Although the river was frozen over, the thickness of the ice was not sufficient to bear the weight of a mass of vehicles, particularly tanks. It was, therefore, vital for the Russians to capture an intact bridge.

The lead elements of General Rodin's 26th Tank Corps was the first to reach the heights overlooking the west bank of the Don, opposite Kalach, where the river was some 300 yards wide. Here lay a pontoon bridge, fit for heavy traffic, which German engineers had constructed to replace the bridges the Russians had blown up during August. To seize this vital bridge before the Germans could destroy it with demolition charges, Rodin formed a special squad of two companies from the 14th Motorized Infantry Brigade, supported by five T-34 tanks from the 157th Tank Brigade and some armoured cars from the 15th Reconnaissance Battalion, which was put under the command of Colonel Grigor Fillipov.

The only hope of capturing the bridge intact was by means of a swift *coup de main*. Accordingly Fillipov's detachment raced for the bridge with their headlights blazing, in the hope that the enemy unit guarding the bridge would take them for a German column. Unbeknown to Fillipov, his attempt at subterfuge was aided by the fact that on the heights overlooking the bridge was a German training school for anti-tank warfare, where captured Soviet tanks were used as targets. The proximity of this facility meant that the guard unit was familiar with the sight of captured tanks regularly crossing the bridge in both directions. So it was that, when Fillipov's tanks approached the bridge at 0600 in the murk and driving snow with their lights blazing, the German guard took them for the usual traffic of captured tanks.

The T-34s rolled over the bridge unchallenged. On reaching the east bank they fired a signal rocket beckoning the motorized infantry to follow, which they did, gunning down the German guards in transit.

Not content with capturing the bridge intact, Fillipov then attempted to capture the town of Kalach. This proved over-ambitious for five tanks and two companies of infantry. Elements of the German 71st Infantry Division, including an anti-tank battalion, along with an anti-aircraft battery, were in Kalach, and they pushed Fillipov's force back to the bridge which they tried to recapture. The small Russian force was under heavy pressure until midday, when the main force of Rodin's 26th Tank Corps arrived on the scene, crossed the bridge and swept away all enemy opposition as they drove on to Kalach.

During the night both the 26th and 4th Tank Corps concentrated in the woods north and south of Kalach, to rest and replenish with fuel and ammunition, ready for the final act of the Kontrudar.

While the Russians were pulling off their coup de main at the Kalach bridge, General Martin Fiebig, commanding Fliegerkorps VIII, telephoned General Arthur Schmidt at the Nizhne-Chirskaya HQ. Learning that Hitler had made reference to an air-lift in his radio message to Paulus, Fiebig warned Schmidt that if 6th Army was surrounded by Stalingrad and cut off it would be impossible for the Luftwaffe to supply an army of a quarter of a million men from the air.

An hour later (0800) Luftwaffe General Wolfgang Pickert, commander of the 9th Flak Division, allocated to 6th Army, arrived at the HQ. When Schmidt asked Pickert for his opinion on the situation, the Luftwaffe General replied that all forces should be concentrated as soon as possible and a break-out to the south-west should be made. When Schmidt explained that Hitler had ordered 6th Army to hold its ground and that the Army would have to be supplied by an air-lift, Pickert was flabbergasted. He reiterated Fiebig's warning that such an undertaking was impossible, especially with regard to the prevailing fog, ice and snow storms which could reasonably be expected to worsen.

In the midst of this depressing forecast, and a stream of alarming reports showing that the Russian ring around 6th Army was rapidly being drawn tighter and tighter, Paulus received an order from Hitler to transfer his HQ from Nizhne-Chirskaya to Gumrak, a few miles to the west of Stalingrad.

The reasoning behind this peremptory order was obvious. Hitler was suspicious that Paulus had shifted his HQ from Golubinskaya to the south-west, a position outside the developing encirclement, in order to be better placed to direct a retreat to the west on his own initiative. By ordering him to Gumrak, Hitler was placing Paulus deep within the pocket.

General Hoth, who arrived at Nizhne-Chirskaya later that morning, found Paulus 'irritable and profoundly upset by the humiliating order he had received from Hitler. The features of this military intellectual bore a pained expression and reflected his deep anxiety.'[16]

At 1400, less than twenty-four hours since their arrival at Nizhne-Chirskaya, Paulus and Schmidt once more took to the air in two small Fieseler Storch monoplanes to fly the seventy miles north-east to Gumrak through the fog, driving snow and abysmal visibility, over the mass of the Russian forces piling up behind 6th Army.

The two flights made by Paulus, in twice transferring his HQ, were among the mere 361 sorties flown by aircraft of Fliegerkorps VIII during the critical five-day period 19-23 November. The average of 72 sorties a day, mainly for reconnaissance purposes, were all that were found possible on account of the atrocious weather. This fact alone provided enough empirical evidence of the total impracticality of supplying 6th Army by means of an air-lift. In the same period the vast air armada assembled by the Red Air Force for the Kontrudar managed only 369 sorties.

Realizing that an air-lift had scant chance of adequately supplying his Army's requirements, Paulus dispatched a signal to von Weichs within three hours of his arrival at Gumrak (message timed at 1800). The content was carefully worded to show that in the first instance he intended to obey Hitler's command to stand fast and form a 'hedgehog' defence perimeter, but he qualified this by demanding freedom of action to break out to the south-west should he deem it necessary:

> Army completely encircled. Despite heroic resistance whole of Tsaritsa Valley, railway from Sovetsky to Kalach, the Don bridge at Kalach, high ground on west bank as far as Golubinskaya, Olskinsky and Krainy inclusive now in Russian hands.
>
> Further enemy forces are advancing from the south-east through Businovka northwards and also in great strength from the west. Situation at Surovikino and Chir unknown. Intense patrol activity in Stalingrad and on northern front. Attacks on 4th Corps [Beketovka 'bell' front] repulsed and also attacks on 76th Infantry Division [8th Corps, northern front]. 76th Infantry Division reports small local penetrations.
>
> Army hopes to be able to construct a western front east of the Don along the Golubaya line. Southern front east of the Don still open.

Whether intensive weakening of the northern flank will permit construction of a thin line running Karpovka—Marinovka—Golubinka appears problematical.

The Don now frozen and can be crossed. Fuel supplies almost exhausted. Tanks and heavy weapons will then be immobilized. Ammunition situation critical. Food supplies on hand for six days. The Army intends to hold the area still in its possession between Stalingrad and the Don, and has taken all steps to implement this intention. Success is conditional upon closing the gap on the southern front and on receiving adequate airborne supplies.

Request freedom of action in the event of failure to construct southern defensive position. The situation could then compel the abandonment of Stalingrad and the northern front, and an attack in maximum strength against enemy on southern front between the Don and the Volga with objective of re-establishing contact with 4th Panzer Army. Prospects of a successful attack westwards are unpromising in view of enemy strength and terrain difficulties that sector.[17]

The south-westerly direction of the break-out advocated by Paulus was based on three factors: the minimum distance to the nearest German forces outside of the encirclement; the enemy dispositions; and the nature of the terrain. All of these factors dictated a south-westerly break-out. But it would remain a purely academic exercise unless Hitler could be persuaded as to the wisdom of the proposal. In an attempt to do just that, von Weichs sent the following teletype message within forty-five minutes of the receipt of Paulus's signal:

Despite the exceptional gravity of the decision to be taken, with the far-reaching consequences of which I am well aware, I must report that I regard it as necessary to accept General Paulus's proposal for the withdrawal of 6th Army. My reasons are as follows:

1. The supplying of the twenty divisions that constitute this army is not feasible by air with the air transport available, and in favourable conditions it will only be possible to supply the encircled forces by air with one-tenth of their essential daily requirements.

2. Since the probable future developments do not offer any certainty of rapid penetration of the encircling enemy forces from the outside, the attack to relieve 6th Army cannot, in view of the time required to assemble a relieving force, be mounted before the 10th of December.... The rapid deterioration of 6th Army's situation as regards supplies indicates that these must be exhausted within a few days. Ammunition will soon be expended, since the encircled force is being attacked from all sides.

However, I believe that a breakthrough by 6th Army in a south-westerly direction will result in a favourable development to the situation as a whole.

With the total dissolution of the 3rd Rumanian Army, 6th Army is now the only fighting formation capable of inflicting damage on the enemy. The proposed direction of the attack, opening toward the south-west and then being followed by the northern wing advancing along the railway line from Chir to Morzovskaya, will result in a relaxation of the existing tension in the Svetnoye — Kotelnikovo area. Finally, the remaining combat strength of 6th Army will provide an essential reinforcement for a new defensive front that must now be built and for the preparation of our counter-attack.

I am well aware that this proposed operation will entail heavy losses, particularly in arms and equipment, but these will be far less than those that must ensue if the situation is left to develop, as it must do, in existing conditions, with the inevitable starving out of the encircled army as the certain result.[18]

Hitler's response to Paulus's and Weich's signals was to make immediate preparations to travel to the Wolfsschanze, and to order Zeitzler not to make any major decisions until he arrived in Rastenburg. At 2200, on Sunday, 22 November, Hitler's command train left Berchtesgaden station bound for Leipzig, from where the Führer intended to fly to East Prussia. He was accompanied by Keitel, Jodl and General Hans Jeschonnek, the Luftwaffe Chief of Staff. However, foul weather prevented flying and Hitler and his entourage found themselves confined to the command train for a twenty-four-hour journey across Germany. Every four hours or so the train was halted for brief telephone contact to be established with the Wolfsschanze, so that the grim, up-to-date details could be inked on to Hitler's Stalingrad charts.

During one of the stops made on the morning of Monday, 23 November, Hitler spoke to Zeitzler in person over the telephone. Once again Zeitzler asked permission to order the withdrawal of 6th Army. 'His tone,' Zeitzler relates, 'was icy. He said: "We have found another expedient which Jodl will tell you about. We will talk it over tomorrow".'[19] This expedient, it turned out, was the transfer of a single panzer division from Heeresgruppe A in the Caucasus to the Stalingrad area. Such was the solution to the crisis envisaged on Hitler's command train!

On the morning of Monday, 23 November, while Hitler's train sped north-eastwards across the Reich, the 4th Mechanized Corps of the Stalingrad Front reached Sovetsky, ten miles east-south-east of Kalach, where it became embroiled in a stiff fight with German units. At 1530 a column of tanks advancing through the murk and driving snow from the north-west was sighted by the 36th Brigade of 4th Mechanized Corps (situated on the eastern outskirts of Sovetsky). Unsure if these were German or Russian tanks, General Rodionov, commanding the 36th Mechanized Brigade, despatched an armoured car, displaying a large Russian flag, to investigate. Green flares fired by the lead tanks of the advancing column identified them as Soviet, and at 1400 these tanks of the 45th Tank Brigade (4th Tank Corps), South-western Front linked up with the 36th Brigade (4th Mechanized Corps) of the Stalingrad Front. After only 96 hours of offensive operations, the ring of fire and steel had snapped shut around 6th Army.

THE LOGIC OF NECESSITY

While the armoured forces of the South-western and Stalingrad Fronts were linking up at Kalach, what remained of the German and Rumanian forces on the west bank of the Don were either surrendering, fleeing in panic or carrying out fighting withdrawals.

On the northern front the three infantry divisions of the German 11th Corps (44th, 384th and 376th), along with remnants of the Rumanian 1st Cavalry Division, were ordered by Paulus to withdraw from their exposed position along the northern flow of the Don Bend, to avoid being cut off and surrounded by forces from Batov's Sixty-fifth Army and the 3rd Guards Cavalry Corps of the Twenty-first Army, which were curling round behind 11th Corps's open left flank.

Elements of the 384th Division and two battalions of light artillery from the 44th Division formed a rearguard during 11th Corps' retreat. They held a bridgehead of some nine square miles around three pontoon bridges thrown over the Don near Vertyachiy. The largest bridge, and the only one of the three capable of carrying heavy vehicles, was at Akimovsky. Over this bridge scrambled the entire 376th Division and the fleeing fragments of the 1st Rumanian Cavalry Division, which poured down from the hills to form one great, jostling, hysterical crowd at the western end of the bridge. There was no longer any question of discipline. Every man gave orders, shouting and bullying. The loudest voice, the heaviest lorry won the day. Fighting troops, supply columns, ambulances filled with wounded, units of the Todt Organization, horses, men and vehicles rolled in an unbroken stream across the bridge.

Once across the three bridges, the surviving elements of the four divisions were deployed on the western and southern flanks of the 'hedgehog' circular defence perimeter established by the twenty divisions of 6th Army and the remnants of two Rumanian divisions.

While the 11th Corps was carrying out its chaotic withdrawal, the four Rumanian divisions of the 'Lascar Group', which had been encircled at Raspopinskaya during the Russian break-through on 19 November, surrendered. The Rumanians in this pocket had carried out a spirited defence for five days, but with their ammunition spent, no hope of being supplied from the air as Hitler had promised, and with a guarantee of fair treatment from the Russians, the 27,000 wretched, freezing survivors lay down their arms on the evening of the 23rd and were herded off into captivity. A further 4,000 from this group had fought their way out of the pocket on the previous night, escaping under the cover of darkness and fog to join the flotsam of fearful troops reeling to and fro on the open steppe.

Throughout the evening and night of the 23rd, on both sides of the Don, east and west, a torrent of disorderly Germans and Rumanians, fleeing singly or bunched into columns, scrabbled through the deep snow, either to the bridge over the Don at Nizhne-Chirskaya, or headed eastwards in precipitate flight over the steppe littered with the wreckage of broken divisions and units towards Stalingrad. Cursing, heaving mobs of disorganized units and panic-stricken rear service personnel hurled aside the weak and wounded as they clawed their way out of the clutches of the Soviet tanks.

On the following day the American journalist Henry Shapiro, one of the first foreign correspondents to visit the Stalingrad area, was given a tour of the Don steppe by the Russians. Shapiro recorded that:

Behind the Russian lines there were still thousands of Rumanians just wandering about the steppe, cursing the Germans, and searching desperately for Russian feeding-points. Here they were as well fed as the Russians themselves. Some straggled along to these feeding-points unescorted; or else you would see a column of two or three hundred Rumanians being escorted by just one Russian tommy-gunner. All they wanted was to be formally taken over as prisoners of war.... I talked to hundreds of Rumanian prisoners; they all told the same story: it was not their war; they had been forced into it by Antonescu [dictator of the wartime pro-German Rumanian government]; Russians and Rumanians had never fought against each other before; and the Rumanians had no business to be on the Volga.

A lot of individual stragglers would throw themselves on the mercy of the Russian peasants. I asked some of these peasants why they were feeding them, and they all said: 'They are poor peasants just like us; it isn't their fault. It's Hitler's. Of course, if they were Germans, it would be different. We wouldn't feed them.'

From the area of Serafimovich I drove south-east, nearer to Stalingrad.... The steppe was a fantastic business. The whole goddam steppe was full of dead horses — some were only half-dead, and it was pathetic to see one standing there on three frozen legs, and shaking the remaining one. Ten thousand horses had been killed by the Russians in the breakthrough.

The whole steppe was strewn with these dead· horses, with gun-carriages, wrecked tanks, and guns (some from Skoda, some French, some even English, probably captured at Dunkirk), and no end of corpses – Rumanians and Germans. Every village had its cemetery for the German dead. The civilians were beginning to come back to the villages, which were mostly wrecked.

Kalach was a shambles. Of the whole town only one house was standing; and even it had only three walls.... The German prisoners were nearly all young fellows of nineteen or twenty, and very miserable.... At that time there was thirty to forty degrees of frost; and they wore ordinary coats and blankets round their necks. They had hardly any winter equipment at all.[20]

Late on the afternoon of that fateful Monday the 23rd, Paulus, having learned of the Soviet link-up at Sovetsky, held a council of war with all the 6th Army corps commanders at his HQ at Gumrak: Generals von Seydlitz-Kurzbach of 51st Corps, Erwin Jaenecke of 4th Corps (who had replaced von Schwedler), Walther Heitz of 8th Corps, Karl Strecker of 11th Corps and Hans Hube of 14th Panzer Corps (who had replaced von Wietersheim). The conclusion reached by this galaxy of military talent was the obvious one: the whole of the 6th Army should forthwith fight its way out of the encirclement. This resolution was based on a number of factors:

(a) In the area of the steppes in which the western and southern fronts of the cauldron were forming there were no prepared defensive positions. Moreover, because it was mid-winter there was no wood with which to construct such positions.

(b) It was deemed doubtful whether the creation of an all-round defensive hedgehog was tactically possible.

(c) The available forces were not strong enough to hold, for any lengthy period, a cauldron position of sufficient size to include Pitomnik – the only adequate airfield in the area of the encirclement.

(d) Even when the rear lines of communication were still open and secure, the delivery of supplies had been, latterly, inadequate, and it was obvious that an adequate supply by aircraft alone, as a long-term policy, would be impossible. Lack of adequate supplies would quickly rob the Army of its capability to offer resistance within the near future.

The consensus of opinion was, consequentially, that all available strength should be concentrated forthwith in preparation for a breakout to the south-west. The risks were not underestimated, and the chances of a successful breakout were estimated at ten to one against (probable casualties one in three), on account of lack of fuel and ammunition and the strength of the enemy forces.

A rough plan, worked out at the council of war, envisaged that three days of preparation would be necessary. On the first day the divisions on the northern flank of the pocket would have to draw southwards some five miles to a line running through Baburkin — Gumrak — Gorodishche. On the second day a further withdrawal of another five miles would have to be made, drawing in to the retreat those divisions on the north-western flank and those in the city of Stalingrad, to a line running through Dimitrevka — Pitomnik — Yelshanka (a southern suburb of Stalingrad). On the third day all the divisions would complete the southern withdrawal by concentrating in the south-western 'nose' of the pocket in the Marinovka-Karpovka area. The break out, scheduled for 27 November, would be spearheaded by all available tanks and armoured vehicles, with the mass of the infantry, without artillery preparation, following immediately behind the armoured thrust.

That was the plan minus its one vital factor — Hitler's permission! At 2345 that night, Paulus in another and this time desperate attempt to convince the Führer of the logic and overweening necessity of authorizing 6th Army to break out, dispatched another signal. Paulus addressed the message directly to Hitler:

My Führer! Since the receipt of your wireless message on the evening of the 22nd November, the situation has developed rapidly. It has not proved possible to close the gaps in the west and south-west. Enemy breakthroughs in these sectors are now imminent. Ammunition and fuel are almost exhausted. Countless batteries and anti-tank units have fired all their shells. Timely and adequate receipt of supplies is no longer possible. Within a very short time the army must be wiped out unless an annihilating attack with all available forces is launched at once against the enemy attacking us from the west and south. This necessitates the immediate withdrawal of all the divisions now in Stalingrad and of strong forces from the northern front. The inevitable sequel must be a breakthrough towards the south-west, since such a weakening of the eastern and northern fronts must make those sectors no longer tenable. It cannot be doubted that much valuable equipment will be lost, but the greater part of our valuable fighting strength will be saved as well as a portion, at least, of our equipment and weapons.

I accept full responsibility for the grave contents of this message, though I would inform you that Generals Heitz, von Seydlitz, Strecker, Hube and Jaenecke appreciate the situation in exactly the same terms as I do. I request once again freedom of action.[21]

By the time Paulus dispatched this signal to Hitler, 94 Russian divisions and brigades in 7 Soviet armies had been concentrated in the iron ring around 6th Army. Along the western and southern flanks of the pocket, over 1,000 Russian anti-tank guns alone had been positioned along an arch running from Vertyachiy, through Kalach, bending eastward from below Marinovka to join the Volga just south of Stalingrad. If a break-out was to succeed the sands of time were fast slipping away.

6

DER KESSEL

'...And they worshipped the beast, saying, "Who is like the beast?
Who is able to make war with him?" '

(Revelation 13:4).

THE TRAP

During the night of 23 November a continuous line of defence was created
by the battle-fatigued divisions of 6th Army, to form the perimeter of Kessel
(the cauldron). In its final form the Kessel was thirty miles long, from east
to west, and twenty miles wide from north to south: the outer encirclement
line assuming the sinister and gruesomely symbolic shape of a squashed skull
with its 'nose' protruding to the south-west.

The eastern flank was anchored in the fire-blackened ruination of
Stalingrad itself, while the northern flank was formed on the well-established
positions which had been held by the 8th Corps and 14th Panzer Corps since
the end of August. On both these flanks the troops had some form or other
of pre-prepared or natural shelter from the merciless elements. But on the
newly formed western and southern flanks of the Kessel the troops found
themselves on bare, open steppe exposed to the full blast of the bitterly cold,
howling wind and driving snow storms.

Throughout the freezing night of the 23rd, the bone-weary units on these
two flanks frantically dug-in, or to be more exact blasted holes in the frozen,
rock-hard ground with explosives, to obtain mole-like shelter from the twin
ravages of the Russian artillery and the cutting wind.

In all some 267,000 men (though not the 400,000 first feared by the
German High Command), with over 100 tanks, 1,800 guns, 10,000 assorted
vehicles and 23,000 horses, were trapped, the hard-bitten amongst them
mocking their predicament of being 'the mice in the mousetrap'.

Of the total, 255,000 were German (the best estimate available), the
remaining 12,000 being Rumanians. Elements of 6th Army, numbering some
39,000, had escaped the Soviet pincers by retreating westwards to the Chir
River. A further 34,000 German troops had not been so lucky, being either
killed or captured during the Russian Kontrudar, along with the loss of 457
tanks, 370 artillery pieces, 1,000 machine guns, 1,100 mortars, 1,266

anti-tank guns, 2,500 sub-machine guns, 35,000 rifles, 1 million shells, 5 million rounds of small arms ammunition and 200 motor vehicles. Total German and Rumanian casualties during the five days of the Kontrudar amounted to 124,000 (killed, captured, missing).

The forces sliced away from the main body of the German Army, which now stood isolated on the snow-covered steppe between the frozen Don and Volga Rivers, included five German Corps headquarters and their component 20 divisions, along with the remnants of two Rumanian divisions:

Army Corps HQs: 4th, 8th, 11th, 51st & 14th Panzer.

Infantry Divisions (14): 44th, 71st, 76th, 79th, 94th, 100th Jäger, 113th, 295th, 297th, 305th, 371st, 376th, 384th & 389th.

Motorized Divisions (3): 3rd, 29th & 60th.

Panzer Divisions (3): 14th, 16th & 24th (with only 100 tanks between them).

9th Flak (anti-aircraft) Division (composed of the 37th, 91st & 104th Flak Regiments, with a total of 11 heavy and 19 light AA. batteries).

243rd & 245th Assault Gun Battalions.

2nd and 51st Heavy Mortar Regiments.

648th Army Signals Regiment.

Engineer Battalions (13): 45th, 294th, 336th, 255th, 501st, 605th, 652nd, 672nd, 685th, 912th, 921st, 925th & one unnumbered battalion.

Rumanian Divisions: remnants of the 1st Cavalry Division & 20th Infantry Division.

In addition there were 149 miscellaneous independent units, including Pioneer Battalions, units of Military Police and of the para-military Todt Organization, Field Post Offices, Luftwaffe signal and airfield ground staff, and Army Artillery Battalions. There was also a Croat infantry regiment in the Kessel, which was an integral part of the German 100th Jäger Division.

After the redeployment of a few divisions from the northern and eastern flanks to reinforce the southern and western flanks of the Kessel, and an organizational regrouping of the divisions in the Corps's order of battle, the dispositions assumed the following configuration:

On the northern flank, positioned from east to west, were the 24th Panzer, 16th Panzer and 60th Motorized Divisions (these three divisions now formed the 11th Corps).

At the western end of the northern flank was the 113th Infantry Division, which pivoted its left wing to the west to form the northern end of the western flank. The remainder of the western flank was formed by (from north to south) the 76th, 384th and 44th Infantry Divisions (these four divisions now formed the 8th Corps).

In the south-western 'nose' of the Kessel were the 29th and 3rd Motorized

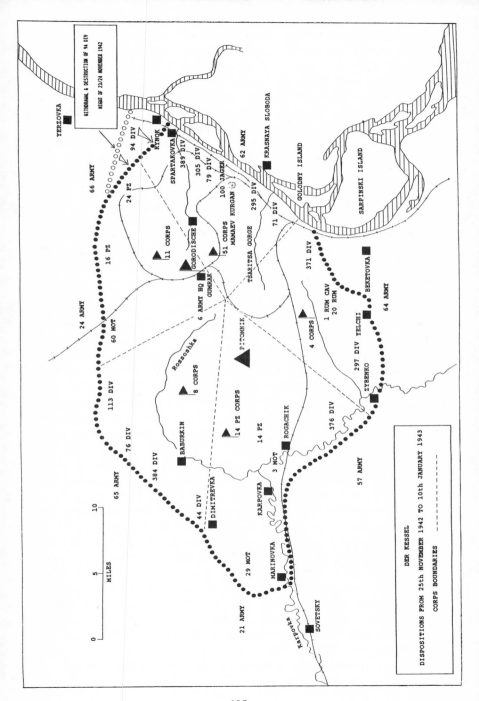

YERZOVKA

WITHDRAWAL & DESTRUCTION OF 94 DIV
NIGHT OF 23/24 NOVEMBER 1942

66 ARMY

24 ARMY

24 PZ

16 PZ

60 MOT

6 ARMY HQ

GUMRAK

11 CORPS

GORODISCHE

51 CORPS

SPARTAKOVKA

389 DIV

305 DIV

79 DIV

100 JAGER

MAMAEV KURGAN

295 DIV

TSARITSA GORGE

71 DIV

62 ARMY

KRASNAYA SLOBODA

GOLODNY ISLAND

SARPINSKI ISLAND

94 DIV

RYNOK

113 DIV

76 DIV

65 ARMY

384 DIV

BABURKIN

8 CORPS

Rossoshka

14 PZ CORPS

PITOMNIK

4 CORPS

371 DIV

1 RUM CAV
20 RUM

BEKETOVKA

64 ARMY

YELCHI

297 DIV

ZYBENKO

376 DIV

ROGACHIK

14 PZ

3 MOT

KARPOVKA

44 DIV

DIMITREVKA

29 MOT

MARINOVKA

57 ARMY

21 ARMY

Karpovka

SOVETSKY

0   5   10

MILES

DER KESSEL

DISPOSITIONS FROM 25th NOVEMBER 1942 TO 10th JANUARY 1943

CORPS BOUNDARIES - - - - - - - - - -

125

Divisions, flanked on their right by the 376th Infantry Division (these three divisions along with the 14th Panzer Division, held back in the rear of the 'nose' as a mobile reserve, now formed the 14th Panzer Corps).

The remainder of the southern flank, on the right of the 376th Division, was held by the 297th Infantry Division, the 20th Rumanian Division (reinforced by the remnants of the 1st Rumanian Cavalry Division), and the 371st Division (these three divisions formed the 4th Corps).

The remaining seven divisions (positioned from south to north), 71st, 295th Infantry, 100th Jäger, 79th, 305th, 389th and 94th Infantry, formed the eastern flank amongst the ruins of Stalingrad (these divisions formed the 51st Corps).

The headquarters staff of one of the twenty German divisions, the 384th, had become separated during the retreat across the Don, and had managed to escape westwards to the Chir River. Consequently the combat units of 384th, being devoid of their command structure, and having been all but decimated by the time they formed up on the western flank of the Kessel, were divided between the 76th and 44th Divisions.

Although bare and largely devoid of cover against the elements, the topography of the area over which the Kessel had formed did have advantageous defensive features. These are described in the Soviet General Staff appreciation of the battle:

The terrain in the area of the encirclement... had an area of about 1,450 square kilometres (900 square miles).... For the most part it was bare, without vegetation; rolling, with a gradual and gentle transition from one undulation to the next steppe; cut up by deep ravines, running from the west toward the east. The open terrain makes orientation and masking difficult for the troops. In the winter time, orientation in this locality is still more complicated by the presence of snow cover. The terrain gradually rises from the west toward the east and has many elevations; the crests and ridges are, for the greater part, plateaux with a barely perceptible convexity.

The elevations and their crests enabled the Germans to use the flat trajectory of the infantry fire and small-calibre artillery in a very effective manner and they also gave the defence a great advantage in observing both the battlefield and the depths of the dispositions of the attacker. Observation was possible to an average distance of 5 to 6 kilometres (some 3 to 4 miles). The possession of the dominating heights and of the inhabited localities by the Germans made it easier for them to organize defences, to conduct fire, and to take anti-tank measures. The frequent occurrence of elevations alternating with ravines in the possible directions for the action of tanks and infantry made it possible for the Germans to organize deep defences and centres of resistance, coordinated with a system of flanking fire by machine guns, sub-machine guns and anti-tank guns.

The character of the terrain made it possible for the enemy to make extensive use of oblique fire and flank fire at close and average ranges and from reverse slopes. Placing fire positions on the reverse slopes subjected the attacking rifle troops wedging into the defences to the whole firepower of the defence. Thus the rifle troops could not, due to the absence of reference points, correctly designate the targets for the artillery and mortars supporting it. Here, the manoeuvrability and actions of the tanks could be carried out only against the crests of the elevations, in comparatively narrow corridors between the ravines, easily covered by fire or anti-tank artillery, engineer entanglements and minefields.

The enemy's possession of fortified lines along the east bank of the Rossoshka and Chervlenaia rivers, a number of fortified, inhabited localities (Gorodishche, Gumrak, Karpovka, Alekseevka, etc.), and of the Stalingrad fortified area helped the enemy to a certain extent in organizing its defence in the ring of encirclement. During the autumn battles, even before encirclement, the enemy was able to fortify himself strongly in the northern, eastern and south-eastern sectors of the ring. In the subsequent battles, he was able to hold the sectors and from them offer strong, organized resistance.

In addition to this, after the great autumn-summer battles, on the battlefield in the north in the area of Orlovka and Kuzmichi, both our own knocked-out tanks and those of the Germans were left on the battlefield, and the Germans used them as armoured fire positions.

The inhabited localities in this area are few in number and located chiefly along the ring of encirclement and within it, close to the banks of the rivers and streams. Hence, the majority of the inhabited localities were in the hands of the encircled enemy. Our units had at their disposal only a few inhabited localities, the majority of which were burned or destroyed in the preceding battles.[1]

During the course of the very night the Kessel was forming (23 November), one of the German infantry divisions was wiped from the order of battle. The most fervent of the five German Corps Commanders in advocating a breakout was General Walther von Seydlitz-Kurzbach (51st Corps). During the council of war held at Gumrak on the afternoon of the 23rd, Seydlitz had attempted to persuade Paulus to disregard the Führer's 'stand fast' order, and by ordering a breakout on his own responsibility present Hitler with a fait accompli. Paulus refused, so Seydlitz, in an attempt to force the issue, resorted to a desperate subterfuge.

In the misguided belief that his action would precipitate a general retreat from Stalingrad and the northern front, Seydlitz ordered the 94th Infantry Division, which was holding the pivotal position between the eastern and northern flanks in the area of Yersovka north of Stalingrad, to destroy all equipment not required for the breakout, including medium and heavy artillery and the ammunition dumps, and to begin a withdrawal. Seydlitz set the troops an example by burning everything he possessed save only the uniform he was standing in.

Accompanied by spectacular, flaring explosions, the troops of the 94th abandoned their deep-dug winter bunkers, trenches and foxholes, and began to withdraw southward over open ground to a line running between Orlovka and Rynok.

Pursued by three rifle divisions of the Soviet Sixty-sixth Army, and struck in the right flank by units of Chuikov's Sixty-second Army, the 94th Division was cut to ribbons and quickly overrun. The gap in the perimeter defence was plugged by the flank units of the 24th Panzer and the 389th Infantry Divisions, the pitifully few survivors of the 94th being incorporated into the former. This sacrifice of an entire division, some 10,000 men, failed to precipitate the south-westerly push which Seydlitz believed to be the sole salvation of 6th Army, and only served to strengthen the Russian stranglehold.

A TIGER BY THE TAIL

The withdrawal and destruction of the German 94th Infantry Division facilitated a link-up between Sixty-sixth Army units with the northernmost of the three bridgeheads in Stalingrad. These were being held by the savagely mauled units of Chuikov's Sixty-second Army, which were pressed into their 800-yard-deep positions amongst the rubble on the western bank of the Volga, over a total length of some 12 miles.

Between 13 September and 13 November, the multifarious craft employed as ferries had made a total of 35,000 runs into Stalingrad from the east bank, transporting 122,418 reinforcements, 627 lorries and 4,323 tons of assorted military supplies. But after 13 November, the ferrying of supplies and reinforcements across the river dwindled to a few sporadic loads, on account of the drifting ice which made the navigation of the river impossibly dangerous even for the hardiest Volga boatman.

This situation lasted until 16 December, when the surface of the Volga finally froze solid, and 'bridges' formed out of rows of planks laid on the ice allowed the flow of supplies to resume. During the intervening period

Soviet aircraft had tried hard to replenish the 40,000 Soviet troops cut off in Stalingrad by dropping bales of food and ammunition. But, due to the narrowness of the bridgeheads, the bales invariably fell either into the river or behind German lines, while a percentage of the few which landed on target burst on hitting the ground damaging the ammunition.

Worst of all, the period of drifting ice prevented the evacuation of the wounded, the majority of whom lay freezing and soaking among the ruins in the sleet and snow-storms.

Chuikov recounts the heroism of a woman called Tamara Shmakova, who braved the enemy small arms and artillery fire to carry seriously wounded Red Army men from the forward positions to the relative safety of the Volga bank:

> She would crawl up to the wounded man on all fours, would lie down next to him and bind his wounds. Having discovered how badly wounded he was, she would then decide what to do with him. If the man was too badly wounded to be left on the battlefield, she would take steps to evacuate him straightaway. To remove a man from the battlefield two men, with or without stretchers, are normally needed. But more often than not Tamara coped alone. What she did was to crawl under the wounded man, and, straining every muscle, would carry on her back a living load sometimes one and a half times or twice her own weight. But when a wounded man could not be lifted, she would spread out her ground-sheet, roll the wounded man on to it and, again on all fours, drag the heavy burden behind her. Tamara Shmakova saved many lives.[2]

To pin down as many of the German divisions as possible in the fire-blackened shell of Stalingrad, Chuikov's troops, using their last ounce of strength, began round the clock counter-attacks from the day the Kontrudar was launched. The Soviet journalist Vysokoostrovsky described the fighting in an article in the *Red Star* newspaper:

> The whole character of the fighting inside Stalingrad has sharply changed. Having suffered severely on other sectors of the front, the enemy has been obliged, at Stalingrad, to go over to the defensive. Clinging on to the factory buildings, the Germans are still hoping to keep the positions they previously captured, and are defending themselves stubbornly. Through open spaces, through the garden cities of the Workers Settlements, through the platforms and workshops of the shattered factory buildings, the front-line positions wind their way, forming a curious ribbon. The trenches on the two sides of the front almost touch each other at some points; buildings and the remnants of buildings are wrapped in barbed wire, which also crosses streets and paths. Anyone little acquainted with the set-up would find it difficult

to say what's what. The Germans have built here a hard defence line, with substantial depth: here is a solid system of fortifications along the whole length of the front line; here are several rows of barbed wire, pillboxes, wood-and-earth works, mined areas, and buildings turned into strongpoints.

There are similar fortifications behind the front line, with numerous firing-points for cross and flank fire. But there is no great German activity these days. They are sitting underground, and their fire is thin and sporadic. At night they light up their front lines with flares. Yet the German defences come to life when we attack, and they always try very hard to recapture any positions they have lost. The fighting is usually limited to tiny areas, but here the fighting is bloody, and is conducted ferociously with tommy guns, grenades, light mortars, machine guns and sometimes bayonets and knives.

Our frequent artillery barrages cause them great losses. If, in the past, the German Command did not worry about losses, they do now, with their forces thinned out. They have built a lot of shelters and warming-points; and often they use smoke-screens.

We also live mostly underground, and secret passages to the German positions are dug by our reconnaissance parties, who then blow up some of these positions from below. Then, over the wreckage thus formed, our infantry break through into the depth of the enemy lines. Hard and persistent work is being done by our storm groups, who thus smash some of the links in the German chain of defences, and dislocate the Germans' well-coordinated firing system. The gaps thus formed enable our men to undertake more active operations on a larger scale, and step by step the enemy defences are being broken up.[3]

In contrast to the German High Command which, initially, grossly overestimated the number of troops encircled, the Russians hopelessly underestimated the extent of their achievement. Front reconnaissance units, basing their calculations and estimates on prisoner statements concerning the losses in their formations, reckoned that between 80,000 - 90,000 men had been trapped, roughly a third of the actual number.

On this basis, Stalin, when he learned that the Soviet pincers had closed, ordered Vasilevsky over the V Ch line to 'reduce' the encircled German forces off the march with the seven Soviet armies which were forming the ring around 6th Army. Accordingly, during the night of the 23rd, Vasilevsky prepared a formal directive to the Front Commanders.

Twenty-first Army, reinforced by the 26th Tank Corps (from the Fifth Tank Army), which was positioned on the western flank of the Kessel, was to attack eastwards. Sixty-fifth, Twenty-fourth and Sixty-sixth Armies, on the northern flank were to attack on a southerly axis; while Sixty-fourth and

8. General Georgi Konstantinovich Zhukov, Deputy Supreme Commander of the Red Army, who, with General Vasilevsky, formulated the plan to encircle the German forces at Stalingrad.

9. General Alexander Mikahilovich Vasilevsky, Chief of the Soviet General Staff, co-architect with Zhukov of the Russian counter-offensive.

10. A German machine-gun post to the south of Stalingrad. The curve
in the course of the Volga River made it very difficult for the Germans
to enfilade all the Russian ferry crossings, even when their guns were
installed on various points of the river bank .

11. The Russians soon learned to abandon attacks by entire units during the street fighting. They favoured small, heavily armed 'storm groups' which proved ideal for carrying out lightning counter-attacks in the ruins of the city ,

12. During the fighting in Stalingrad, the Russians perfected the technique of creating 'killing zones'. These were prepared by digging-in and concealing ant-tank guns and T-34 tanks among the shattered buildings.

13. The battle for the city evolved largely into countless murderous confrontations between small groups of soldiers.

Fifty-seventh Armies were to bite into the cauldron from the south. All these attacks were to be directed at Gumrak, with the object of chopping up the German formations into small groups. During the operation Chuikov's Sixty-second Army was to keep up the pressure on the seven German divisions in Stalingrad by constant attacks with storm groups.

After a week of bloody fighting, which failed to crack the perimeter defence of the Kessel, it became unpalatably plain that the triumphant Red Army had caught a tiger by the tail, and that a force far more formidable than initially appreciated had been walled in by the Soviet armies.

The reason for the error in reckoning became apparent after a German transport plane was forced down behind Russian lines on its outward flight from the Kessel. The aircraft was carrying mail sacks containing some 1,200 letters written by German troops, and when Soviet intelligence officers checked the names against formations, they realized that the 'guard units' identified by the front reconnaissance units were in fact nothing less than full-scale German infantry divisions.

Stalin, along with the Stavka officers, now realized that the encircled 6th Army, which the revised reckoning now overestimated as in excess of 300,000 men, could only be broken up by sledgehammer blows requiring large-scale reinforcements. To this end Stalin ordered Vasilevsky, Rokossovsky and Yeremenko to prepare a new plan of operations, code-named *Koltso* (Ring), which was to be ready not later than 18 December. In the meantime he ordered the most powerful army in Stavka Reserve, which had been forming in the Tambov — Morshansk area since 23 October, to be activated and dispatched to the northern flank of the Kessel. Activated as the Second Guards Army, this formation, being comprised of veterans from Guard units which had been withdrawn from the front for rest and refitting, was one of the most formidable in the Red Army at that time. To transport Second Guards to its unloading point to the north-west of Stalingrad required 165 trains.

The Russian armies surrounding 6th Army formed the 'inner' line of the encirclement. The forces of the 'outer' line, consisting of the First Guards and Fifth Tank Armies (minus 26th Tank Corps), suspended offensive operations and set about building up a firm front on the eastern banks of the Chir and Krivaya rivers, and on a line facing south-west, running along the Rostov to Stalingrad railway to cover the Oblivskaya — Surovikino — Rychkovsky sector, to hold off German attacks from the west and south-west. Not that immediate attacks were likely, as in these sectors the German line was being held by weak, hastily scraped together ad hoc forces.

The creation of this 'line', which was 120 miles long, was due largely to Colonel Walther Wenck, the Chief of Staff of the 57th Panzer Corps (engaged in heavy fighting for Tuapse on the Caucasus front), who had been ordered to fly to Morozovskaya, situated to the west of the Chir River, on 21 November.

Wenck gives the following account of the situation he was presented with when he arrived at the HQ of the wrecked Rumanian 3rd Army (situated at Morozovskaya) on the evening of the 21st:

I reported to Colonel-General Dumitrescu (commanding 3rd Rumanian Army). Through his interpreter, Lieutenant Iwansen, I was acquainted with the situation. It looked pretty desperate. On the following morning (22 November: the fourth day of the *Kontrudar*) I took off in a Fieseler Storch to fly out to the front in the Chir bend. Of the Rumanian formations there was not much left. Somewhere west of Kletskaya, on the Don, units of General Lascar's brave group were still holding out. The remainder of our allies were in headlong flight. With the means at our disposal we were unable to stop this retreat. I therefore had to rely on the remnants of 'Panzer Reserve Heim', on ad hoc units of the Luftwaffe, on such rearward units of the encircled 6th Army as were being formed into combat groups by energetic officers, and on men from 6th Army and 4th Panzer Army gradually returning from leave. To begin with, the forces along the Don — Chir arc, over a sector of several hundred miles, consisted merely of the groups under the command of Lieutenant-General Spang, Colonel Stahel, Captain Sauerbruch and Colonel Adam, of *ad hoc* formations from rearward services and 6th Army workshop personnel, as well as of tank crews and panzer companies without tanks, and of a few engineer and flak units.... I was unable to make contact with Heim's Panzer Corps until Lieutenant-General Heim had fought his way through to the southern bank of the Chir with 22nd Panzer Division. The Heeresgruppe responsible for us, at first, was Heeresgruppe B under Colonel-General Freiherr von Weichs. However, I frequently received my orders and directives direct from General Zeitzler, the Chief of the Army General Staff, since Weichs's Heeresgruppe was more than busy with its own affairs and probably could not form a detailed picture of my sector anyway.

My main task, to start with, was to set up blocking units under energetic officers, which would hold the long front along the Don and Chir along both sides of the already existing Combat Groups Adam, Stahel and Sprang, in cooperation with Luftwaffe formations of Fliegerkorps VIII — at least on a reconnaissance basis. As for my own staff, I literally picked them up on the road. The same was true of motor-cycles, staff cars and communications equipment — in short, all those things which are necessary for running even the smallest headquarters. The old NCOs with experience of the Eastern Front were quite invaluable in all this: they adapted themselves quickly and could be used for any task.

I had no communication lines of my own. Fortunately, I was able to make use of the communications in the supply area of 6th Army, as well as of the Luftwaffe network. Only after countless conversations over those connections was I able gradually to form a picture of the situation in our sector, where the German blocking formations were engaged and where some Rumanian units were still to be found. I myself set out every day with a few companies to form a personal impression and to make what decisions were needed on the spot — such as where elastic resistance was permissible or where a line had to be held absolutely.

The only reserves which we could count on in our penetration area was the stream of men returning from leave. These were equipped from Heeresgruppe stores, from workshops, or quite simply with 'found' material.

In order to collect the groups of stragglers who had lost their units and their leaders after the Russian breakthrough, and to weld these men from three armies into new units, we had to resort sometimes to the most out-of-the-way and drastic measures.

I remember, for instance, persuading the commander of a Wehrmacht propaganda company in Morozovskaya to organize film shows at traffic junctions. The men attracted by these events were then rounded up, reorganized and re-equipped. Mostly they did well in action.

On one occasion a Field Security sergeant came to me and reported his discovery of an almost abandoned 'fuel-dump belonging to no one' by the side of a main road. We did not need any juice ourselves, but we urgently needed vehicles for transporting our newly formed units. I therefore ordered signposts to be put up everywhere along the roads in the rearward areas, lettered 'To the fuel-issuing point'. These brought us any number of fuel-starved drivers with their lorries, staff cars, and all kinds of vehicles. At the dump we had special squads waiting under energetic officers. The vehicles which arrived were given the fuel they wanted, but they were very thoroughly screened as to their own functions. As a result of this screening we secured so many vehicles complete with crews — men who were merely driving about the countryside trying to get away from the front — that our worst transport problems were solved.

With such makeshift contrivances new formations were created. Although they were officially known as ad hoc units, they did in fact represent the core of the new 6th Army raised later. Under the leadership of experienced officers and NCOs these formations acquitted themselves superbly during those critical months. It was the courage and steadfastness of these motley units that saved the situation on the Chir, halted the Soviet breakthroughs, and barred the road to Rostov.[4]

Between Nizhne-Chirskaya, which marked the southern extremity of the Russian 'outer' line on the Chir River, and Kotelnikovo, where the Soviet Fifty-first and Twenty-eighth Armies were consolidating an 'outer' line, there was a yawning gap which neither side had sufficient forces to plug.

In this sector the Germans had managed to form a covering line, by employing the kind of drastic measures resorted to by Wenck on the Chir. Colonel Hans Doerr, Chief of the German liaison staff with the shattered Rumanian 4th Army, had built up a thin front with ad hoc units scraped together from retreating Rumanian units, Cossack auxiliaries, German flak units, rearward services of the 4th Panzer Army, and a combat unit under Major Sauvant from the 14th Panzer Division. To the south of these was the 16th Motorized Division, which had pulled back from its advanced and extended position on the Kalmuck Steppe.

Even if the necessary forces had been available, Stalin had no desire to exploit the thirty-mile gap between the 'outer' lines. Indeed it suited Soviet strategic design to hold all the German forces on the 'outer' lines of the encirclement in their present positions, so that they, along with the whole of Heeresgruppe A fighting in the Caucasus, could be netted in a planned mammoth outer sweep which was to smash through the Italian 8th Army, and was to be aimed directly at Rostov.

The prospects inherent in this new operation, code-named 'Saturn', were dazzling and loaded with intimations of decisive strategic success. Not only would 'Saturn' smash in the whole of the German southern wing, it would also open the road to the Dnieper and with it access once more to the coalmines and power stations of the Donbas and the eastern Ukraine. But the success of 'Saturn' depended on the rapid reduction of the encircled 6th Army, in order to free the large Russian forces investing the Kessel for the new offensive.

DUEL IN THE WOLFSSCHANZE

During the evening of Monday, 23 November, Hitler's command train made the last of its periodic stops to maintain contact with Zeitzler in the Wolfsschanze. Over the telephone Jodl informed Zeitzler that Hitler would see him at noon on the following day in order to discuss the situation at Stalingrad. Zeitzler retorted that this would be too late, but Jodl insisted that an earlier appointment would not be possible because Hitler would be tired after his long journey. 'This,' Zeitzler remarks incredulously, 'was at a time when the whole front was ablaze and hundreds of brave soldiers were dying with each hour that passed!'[5]

Seething with indignation, the Chief of Staff ignored Jodl's instructions, and at midnight, when Hitler finally arrived at the East Prussian HQ, Zeitzler was not only waiting for him but insisted on seeing him immediately. Hitler and his entourage were furious at Zeitzler's temerity, but when the insistent General was finally ushered into Hitler's office he was greeted with an outstretched hand and a beaming smile 'deliberately radiating confidence and hope.'[6] Zeitzler records that:

> Hitler shook me by the hand and said: 'I thank you. You have done all that could be done. I myself would not have been able to do more, had I been here.' Then since I took care that my expression remained grave, he allowed a certain note of pathos to creep into his voice. He went on: 'Don't let yourself be upset. We must show firmness of character in misfortune. We must remember Frederick the Great.' No doubt he wished to encourage me. Perhaps he hoped that if he could inspire in me 'firmness of character' of which he spoke, I should then abandon my 'defeatist' arguments in favour of withdrawing 6th Army. Also, he probably wished me to admire his own steadfastness in the face of misfortune. It seems that Hitler quite failed to realize that in time of extreme danger and crisis such play-acting is not only useless but can have an exactly contrary effect to the one desired.[7]

Zeitzler began his report on the situation by presenting the message in which Paulus had made a desperate appeal for freedom of action to break out. It had been dispatched from the Kessel at 2345, only fifteen minutes before Hitler arrived at the Wolfsschanze. When Zeitzler added his weight to Paulus's appeal it provoked a temper tantrum, in which Hitler thundered about the solution which he, Jodl and Keitel had worked out during the long train journey across the Reich: namely the transfer of a single panzer division from the Caucasus.

Zeitzler was prepared for this ludicrous panacea, and he pointed out that on account of transport difficulties the earliest that this division could be expected to arrive on the Stalingrad axis would be at least a fortnight. Even then one division, which was far below full strength, would be patently incapable of influencing events. Furthermore, Zeitzler contended, it was doubtful whether it would prove possible to commit this division to battle as a unit. In view of the gravity of the situation, its component parts would, in all probability, have to be committed piecemeal as and when they detrained. Hitler retorted that in that case he would order two divisions to be transferred from the Caucasus.

Exasperated, Zeitzler remonstrated that not even this expediency could redeem the situation, and that the only solution was for 6th Army to break out from the encirclement and attack south-westwards to help build the new front. At this point Hitler lost all self-control and crashing his fist down on the table, shouted, 'I won't leave the Volga! I won't go back from the Volga!'

Refusing to be intimidated, Zeitzler continued to argue vehemently that to leave 6th Army in the Kessel was a crime, as the entire army must inevitably perish. Finally, after several hours of intense argument, Zeitzler began to make some progress in bringing the by now exhausted Hitler around to his point of view that only a break-out offered any possibility of transforming a hopeless situation into a tactical success. However, when Zeitzler presented him with a pre-prepared break-out order, Hitler prevaricated, declaring himself so exhausted as to be incapable of signing it.

Clutching at straws, Zeitzler, the moment Hitler retired, immediately telephoned General Sodenstern, Heeresgruppe B's Chief of Staff, intimating that an order for a break-out would be transmitted to Heeresgruppe B between 0700 and 0800 that morning. On his own authority Weichs issued preliminary orders to 6th Army, so that as soon as Hitler's authorization was received the operation might begin without delay.

Expectation ran high both at Starobelsk and in the Kessel. But they were doomed to disappointment, for when Zeitzler re-presented the break-out order to Hitler on the morning of the 24th, he refused to sign it, saying that he had changed his mind. In accordance with his obsession and boast that 'where the German soldier sets foot, there he remains, and nobody will ever drive us away from Stalingrad,' the Führer then proceeded to drive the nails into 6th Army's coffin by sending a signal to Paulus under the classification of a *Führerbefehl* — the highest and strictest category of command decree.

At his HQ at Gumrak, Paulus, standing in the entrance of the signallers' dug-out, read the fatal message bit by bit as it was decoded and handed to him personally:

The 6th Army has been temporarily encircled by Russian forces. I intend to assemble the Army in the area (here followed a more precise definition of the area of the *Kessel*, between the northern suburb of Stalingrad, through Point 137, Marinovka and Zybenko to a point just south of Stalingrad on the Volga bank). The Army may rest assured that I will do everything in my power to see that it is kept adequately supplied in the meantime and relieved as soon as possible. I am familiar with the courageous performance of the 6th Army and of its Commander-in-Chief, and I am convinced it will do its duty.[8]

The receipt of this message (timed at 0830, 24 November) now made it impossible for Paulus to implement a break-out without acting in flagrant contradiction of the will of the 'all highest'. As, by temperament, Paulus was incapable of such rank insubordination, the Führerbefehl effectively doomed 6th Army, which was being sacrificed on the altar of the overweening considerations of Hitler's personal prestige and inconceivable military amateurism.

FESTUNG STALINGRAD

Having re-asserted his will by means of the Führerbefehl directive, Hitler began Tuesday, 24 November in a relatively affable mood. Indeed, when he announced to Zeitzler that henceforth the encircled forces would be known as the troops of *Festung* (fortress) Stalingrad, 'he was positively beaming with delight'.[9] Thus with the stroke of a pen an encirclement on a bare, snow-swept steppe was elevated to a fortress.

By bestowing this bombastic but meaningless title of Festung on 6th Army's predicament, Hitler seriously believed that he could deceive the Russians into regarding the Kessel as a fortified area with defensive works capable of repulsing an assault; that the morale of the German troops would be lifted by their belief that they were now within a fortress, which could withstand a long siege and spare them from heavy casualties; and that the German population would be duped.as to the realities of the situation by recalling historical precedents of fortresses heroically defended in the past and, ultimately, heroically relieved.

To believe that anyone would be taken in by this ruse was the height of serendipity, but according to Zeitzler, Hitler even expected his enthusiastic approval of his invention. But Zeitzler was at pains to point out that the historical fortresses to which Hitler alluded were the product of long preparatory work, and that, after a fortification had been built, it would have to be stocked with large quantities of supplies, ammunition and food. Stalingrad was neither fortified nor supplied, and on the greater part of the perimeter line the troops were forced to burrow into the frozen earth in conditions of raging blizzards and freezing temperatures, on a desolate steppe devoid of building materials.

By disagreeing with Hitler over this trivial matter of nomenclature, Zeitzler provoked yet another round of bitter quarrelling, the main point of contention being Zeitzler's repeated and impassioned attempts to secure Hitler's authorization for a break-out. However, during the course of the morning, after having studied the detailed situation maps in the Wolfsschanze, Hitler found a scapegoat, not only on whom to vent his frustration and anger, but to lay the blame for the whole Stalingrad debacle. Concluding that the catastrophe was attributable to 'Panzer Reserve Heim', which had failed to stop the Russian break-through on 3rd Rumanian Army sector, Hitler turned to Field-Marshal Keitel, who was responsible for disciplinary procedure within the army, and shouted, 'Send for the Corps Commander [General Heim] at once, tear off his epaulettes, and throw him into jail. It's all his fault!'

In an 'Order of the Day' directive which was communicated to all senior army officers on 5 December, Hitler attempted to exorcise himself of all the responsibility for the disaster on the Stalingrad axis by laying all the blame on Heim:

The failure by Panzer Reserve Heim was alone responsible for the fact that the 3rd Rumanian Army was broken through on both wings. This has resulted in a catastrophe of immense proportions, the ultimate consequences of which cannot even now be foreseen. In view of the extremely grave consequences that have followed this disaster, namely the loss of a large number of units and an immense amount of war material and the encirclement of the 6th Army, the conduct by the Corps Commander, Lieutenant-General Heim, must be regarded as not merely grossly careless, but as a crime of negligence hitherto unparalleled in the course of this war. In addition, the moral effect will have serious repercussions on the German war effort. I am determined that the conditions which prevailed during the Battle of the Marne in 1914, and which German military and historical research has not, after twenty-five years, yet succeeded in explaining, shall in no circumstances be allowed to reappear in the new army. In view of the disastrous consequences that have resulted from the failure of this General I have decided:

1. That he shall be immediately dismissed from the Army.

2. That while awaiting final elucidation of the failure of this German officer, no further decisions will be made concerning the ultimate action which, in accordance with military tradition in such cases, may have to be taken against him.'[10]

Despite Zeitzler's protestations that the two under-strength panzer divisions which constituted Panzer Reserve Heim had simply been too weak to stop the Russian flood, and that only a large force of many full-strength divisions, manned by veteran troops with first-class equipment, could have done this, Hitler would not rescind his decision.

Consequently, the unfortunate Heim was called to the Wolfsschanze where Keitel stripped him of his General's epaulettes and decorations and dismissed him from the army. He was then flown to Berlin to be incarcerated in the Moabit Prison.

So that the truth of the matter could not leak out Heim was kept totally incommunicado in solitary confinement for five months, being denied the privilege of visitors or communication by letter. He was neither charged nor interrogated, nor was the affair ever brought before a military tribunal, for this would have revealed where the blame for the Stalingrad fiasco really lay.

Finally, at the end of April, 1943, without explanation, he was transferred to the military hospital at Zehlendorf and three months later was released, reinstated and placed on the retired list. A year later, in August, 1944, Lieutenant-General Heim (Retired) was 'rehabilitated' and once again given a front-line command, as commandant of the beleaguered Channel port of Boulogne. Much to Hitler's chagrin Heim surrendered the port to the Allies without much ado, causing Hitler to vow that he would not give other army 'delinquents' a second chance in future.

To fuel Hitler's rage on the morning of 24 November, he was also made aware of the unauthorized withdrawal of the 94th Division during the previous night. The destruction of this Division had been witnessed by a Luftwaffe signals section in the Kessel, which had sent a report on the incident to the Luftwaffe Liaison Officer at the Wolfsschanze, who in turn brought it to Hitler's attention.

Infuriated, Hitler sent a radio signal direct to Paulus: 'Demand immediate report why front north of Stalingrad was pulled back.' After making inquiries and establishing what had happened, Paulus magnanimously decided not to denounce Seydlitz to Hitler, and he accepted responsibility by leaving the demand for an explanation unanswered. This was to have an incongruous repercussion.

Believing that Paulus, by his silence, was culpable for the patent infringement of military discipline, Hitler dispatched another curt radio signal later the same day:

'The Führer wishes that, because of its decisive importance for the 6th Army, the eastern and northern fronts of Festung Stalingrad up to the strong-point south of Kotluban, are to be placed under the command of one military commander. This commander will be responsible to the Führer that this fortified area is held at any price. The Führer, therefore, has charged the General Commanding 51st Corps, General von Seydlitz-Kurzbach, with this responsibility. This order does not affect the overall responsibility of the Army Commander for the conduct of the operations of his Army.[11]

The slighted Paulus personally handed this order to Seydlitz at the latter's 51st Corps headquarters, which was also situated at Gumrak, and asked him what he proposed to do about it? Seydlitz replied that in the circumstances he had no option but to obey.

What Hitler hoped to gain from this piece of crude Machiavellianism was obviously a 'divide and rule' situation. Effectively he had appointed Seydlitz as a kind of supervisor to ensure that Paulus did not act unilaterally in ordering a break-out. The irony of it was that he chose the culpable party to bridle the innocent.

Throughout the remainder of the 24th November, the duel between Zeitzler and the Führer continued unabated. Hitler always had a tendency to regard any new weapon as a 'miracle-weapon', and this naive theory he now applied to the first of the new Tiger tanks that were coming off the production line. These 54-ton monsters, armed with an 88mm gun, and protected by 100mm-thick armour plate, were more than a match for the Russian T-34 medium tanks and KV heavies. But Hitler's belief that a single battalion of Tigers (all that was immediately available) could succeed in breaking through the Russian encirclement to relieve 6th Army was another flight of sheer fantasy.

Zeitzler records that 'He was all afire for this plan, which indeed seemed to intoxicate him. He probably did actually believe that the employment of this single battalion of Tigers [some 45 tanks] could alter the whole course of the battle overnight. With glowing eyes and voice raised, Hitler attempted to inspire me with his own enthusiasm. He seemed to desire my approval for this plan of his.'[12]

When Zeitzler burst this bubble, by pointing out that although a single battalion of Tigers might conceivably succeed in breaking through the Russian lines and establishing contact with 6th Army, it could not possibly keep a corridor open, Hitler grew more and more angry. In conclusion Zeitzler stated that, 'Since the proposed operation to relieve 6th Army cannot succeed, it is essential that orders be issued for that army to carry out a fighting withdrawal. This must be done at once: the last possible moment has arrived!'[13] At this Hitler shouted, 'Sixth Army will stay where it is. It is the garrison of a fortress, and the duty of fortress troops is to withstand sieges. If necessary they will hold out all winter, and I shall relieve them by a spring offensive.'[14]

Zeitzler shouted back that this was sheer fantasy, that Stalingrad was not a fortress, and that there was no way of keeping 6th Army supplied. In a paroxysm of rage Hitler yelled, 'Reichsmarschall Goering has assured me that he can keep the army supplied by air. I will not leave the Volga!'[15]

Zeitzler seized on this reference to an air-lift to employ a different approach. Reasoning that further argument on strategic considerations was pointless, and that Hitler always tended to be impressed by statistics, he set out to prove that logistically it would be impossible to keep the army supplied from the air.

Zeitzler had already ordered the relevant data to be prepared by his operations department and the Army Quartermaster-General's office. The conclusions were set out in a series of statistical tables broken down by the type of supplies required. These showed that, allowing for the supplies already within the Kessel, 6th Army needed an air-lift capable of delivering some 600 tons per day, and that the absolute minimum on which 6th Army could hope to survive — in circumstances of great privation, and by making use of such expedients as slaughtering and eating the army's horses — was 300 metric tons. However, this minimum figure would have to be met every day, regardless of such external factors as weather conditions, which were unlikely to be favourable. From the facts clearly marshalled in the tables of figures, it was concluded that, taking into account an assumed number of days on which aircraft would be unable to operate, at least 500 tons of supplies would have to be flown in to the Kessel for every day which the weather did permit flying. Zeitzler records that:

I succeeded in arousing Hitler's interest in the figures which I laid before him, and he permitted me to complete the explanations necessary to understand the full meaning of the statistical data. I ended my statement with the words: 'Having examined the facts in detail, the conclusion is inescapable: it is not possible to keep the Sixth Army supplied by air.' Hitler's manner became icy. He said, 'The Reichsmarschall has assured me that it is possible.' I repeated that it was not. Hitler then said, 'Very well. He shall tell you himself.' He sent for the Commander-in-Chief of the Luftwaffe and asked, 'Goering, can you keep the Sixth Army supplied by air?' Goering raised his right arm and said, with solemn confidence, 'My Führer! I assure you that the Luftwaffe can keep the Sixth Army supplied.' Hitler cast a triumphant glance at me, but I simply said: 'The Luftwaffe certainly cannot.'

The Reichsmarschall scowled and said, 'You are not in a position to give an opinion on that subject.' I turned towards Hitler and asked: 'My Führer! May I ask the Reichsmarschall a question?' He replied that I could. 'Herr Reichsmarschall,' I said. 'Do you know what tonnage has to be flown in every day?' Goering was evidently embarrassed by this and frowned. He said, 'I don't, but my staff officers do.' I then said, 'Allowing for all the stocks at present with Sixth Army, allowing for absolute minimum needs and for the taking of all possible emergency measures, the Sixth Army will require delivery of three hundred tons per day. But since not every day is suitable for flying, as I myself learned at the front last winter, this means that about five hundred tons will have to be carried to Sixth Army on each and every flying day if the irreducible minimum average is to be maintained.'

Goering replied, 'I can do that.' I now lost my temper and said, 'My Führer! That is a lie.'

An icy silence descended on the three of us. Goering was white with fury. Hitler glanced from one to the other of us in apparent perplexity and surprise. At last he said to me: 'The Reichsmarschall has made his report to me, which I have no choice but to believe. I therefore abide by my original decision.' I now said, 'I should like to make another request.' Hitler asked what it was, and I said, 'May I submit a daily report to you giving the exact tonnage of supplies flown in to the Sixth Army during the previous twenty-four hours?'

Goering objected, saying that this was no concern of mine, but Hitler overruled him and I was granted permission to submit this daily report. And with that, the conference ended.[16]

Zeitzler's opinion regarding the impracticality of supplying 6th Army from the air was shared by his counterpart in the Luftwaffe, the Air Force's Chief of the General Staff, General Hans Jeschonnek and his Adjutant, Colonel Werner Leuchtenberg. In addition the Luftwaffe commanders at the front, von Richthofen (Luftflotte IV), Fiebig (Fliegerkorps VIII), and Pickert (9th Flak Division in the Kessel), all protested against the madness of the proposal.

It is debatable whether Goering realized the full implications of what he was promising. Luftwaffe General Bruno Lorzer, a close associate of the Reichsmarschall, was of the opinion that Goering was subjected to a great deal of pressure from Hitler to pronounce the air-lift feasible, because it was his only hope of avoiding a withdrawal and the resultant loss of face. In an attempt to restore his tattered image in Hitler's eyes, Goering probably felt he could not refuse the 'request' to avoid laying himself open to further condemnation due to the Luftwaffe's failure to prevent the Allied air-raids on the Reich. Jeschonnek, too, after his initial expression of doubt, refrained from arguing against the Führer's wishes, and his concept of unswerving obedience prevented him from following the dictates of common sense.

It was thanks, in large measure, to Goering's vanity and Jeschonnek's docility that the Luftwaffe was given an impossible task and Zeitzler lost his battle to save the quarter of a million men trapped in the Kessel.

THE FÜHRER'S WILL PREVAILS

Hitler's decision to make General Seydlitz-Kurzbach responsible for the northern and eastern flanks of the Kessel, in the belief that he would check any intention of Paulus to unilaterally order a break-out, was a futile miscalculation. On the morning of Wednesday, 25 November, less than twenty-four hours after Seydlitz received the Führer's order, he submitted a memorandum to Paulus urging that he should indeed act unilaterally by ordering an immediate break-out:

The Army is faced with a clear alternative: break through to the south-west in the general direction of Kotelnikovo or face annihilation within a few days.... This decision involves the abandonment of considerable quantities of material, but on the other hand it holds out the prospect of smashing the southern prong of the enemy's encirclement, of saving a large part of the Army and its equipment from disaster and preserving it for the continuation of operations. In this way part of the enemy's forces will continue to be tied down, whereas if the Army is annihilated in its hedgehog position all tying down of enemy forces ceases. Outwardly such an action could be represented in a way avoiding serious damage to morale: following the complete destruction of the enemy's armaments centre of Stalingrad the Army has again detached itself from the Volga, smashing an enemy grouping in doing so. The prospects of a successful breakthrough are the better since past engagements have shown the enemy's infantry to have little power of resistance in open ground....

Unless the Army High Command immediately rescinds its order to hold out in a hedgehog position it becomes our inescapable duty before our own conscience, our duty to the army and to the German people, to seize that freedom of action that we are being denied by the present order, and to take the opportunity which still exists at this moment to avert catastrophe by making the attack ourselves. The complete annihilation of 250,000 fighting men and their entire equipment is at stake. There is no other choice.[17]

This highly emotional and polemically coloured appeal for outright disobedience of Hitler's orders carried no conviction with the ever-obedient Paulus, even when the remaining four Corps Commanders put their weight behind Seydlitz's appeal. General Heitz argued that 'it would be better to survive a break-out with five divisions than perish in the Kessel with twenty'. General Strecker urged him to 'take the course of the Lion,' a reference to General Karl Litzmann who, in November, 1914, had made a daring break-out against orders when encircled by Russian forces. Finally General Jaenecke commented that 'Reichenau wouldn't have hesitated to break out without orders'. To which Paulus replied gravely, 'I'm no Reichenau'. Despite all these appeals Paulus decided to stand fast. He reasoned that:

What we need in the way of supplies has been stated in unambiguous terms. It is now up to the Supreme Command to calculate by means of staff study whether these large quantities can be delivered, how, and then to issue the necessary orders. So far as 6th Army is concerned, all we can do is to report what exactly it is that the encircled troops need: it is not up to us to say how those needs can and will be met. That depends on the availability of transport space, the state of the railways, the condition of the airfields, stocks of supplies already accumulated, the weather, enemy activity and last but not least the stability of the rest of the German front. In view of the general situation, a withdrawal by 6th Army would appear the more useful course to follow, but I cannot make such a decision from 6th Army Headquarters, since it presumes an inability on the part of the Supreme Command to meet 6th Army's requirements concerning the delivery of supplies and the breaking of the encirclement from without, and we lack the facts on which to base such a presumption.[18]

In short Paulus was declaring undeviating loyalty to the Führer. An unquestioning general of the 'orders-are-orders' type, who was not given to independent and decisive decision-making where major strategic issues were concerned, this abdication to Hitler's will was completely in keeping with Paulus' character. He was also a career man who was obviously not prepared to share General Heim's fate which would be the inevitable consequence of taking unilateral action.

In contrast, Seydlitz, the most senior of the five Corps Commanders in the Kessel, was impulsive and self-willed, and infraction was in keeping with his family tradition. One of his ancestors, General Friedrich Wilhelm von Seydlitz, had won the Battle of Zorndorf (1758) in the Seven Years' War by disobeying the orders of Frederick the Great. Later, Major General Florian von Seydlitz had taken part in the unauthorized negotiations with the Russians during the Napoleonic Wars, which led to a Russo-Prussian truce and eventually resulted in the Prussian defection from Napoleon in 1813.

Paulus had declared himself to be no Reichenau, neither was he a Seydlitz, for if he had been possessed with the strength of character and the incisive military competence of either, he would not have hesitated to do what the situation and the fate of a quarter of a million men demanded – an immediate break-out from the Kessel!

7

HOPE DEFERRED

'And the smoke of their torment ascends for ever and ever; and
they have no rest day or night, who worship the beast and his
image, and whoever receives the mark of his name.'

(Revelation 14:11).

THE AIR-LIFT LIFTS OFF

The responsibility for supplying 6th Army by means of an air-lift fell upon
von Richthofen's Luftflotte IV, which was already stretched to the limit
attempting to provide air support for both Heeresgruppe B and
Heeresgruppe A fighting in the Caucasus. To direct the air-lift operations,
Richthofen appointed General Martin Fiebig (commanding Fliegerkorps
VIII): he was faced with an impossible situation.

To deliver 500 tons of supplies per day to 6th Army would necessitate 375
Ju-52 transport planes, each carrying a payload of two tons, taking off each
day and actually landing in the Kessel. Since in the prevailing weather
conditions, only a 30 to 35 per cent degree of operational readiness could
be relied on, a total of 1,050 Ju-52s would be needed.

The madness of the demand becomes fully apparent in view of the fact
that the entire Luftwaffe air transport force in November, 1942, amounted
to only 750 Ju-52s, and these were scattered all over Europe and North
Africa. Indeed, when Fiebig took command of the operation he had a mere
47 Ju-52s on hand. Consequently, between 25 and 29 November, the first
five days of the air-lift, an average of only 53.8 tons of supplies a day was
flown into the Kessel. The total of 269 tons for this five-day period amounted
to only 10.76 per cent of the minimum tonnage necessary to sustain 6th
Army, and was achieved at the cost of 17 Ju-52s shot down by enemy fighters
and flak.

Paucity of transport planes was only one aspect of Fiebig's problems. On
27 November he noted in his diary that: 'Weather atrocious. We are trying
to fly, but it's impossible. Here at "Tazi" [Tatsinskaya airfield] one
snowstorm succeeds another. Situation desperate.'[1] Nonetheless, a dozen
Ju-52s did brave the elements on that day and, despite the danger of icing
up, managed to fly the 132 miles from Tatsinskaya to Pitomnik airfield in

the centre of the Kessel. The result of this near suicidal mission was the delivery of 24 cubic metres of fuel, a literal drop in the ocean in comparison to 6th Army's requirements.

Made aware that the available Ju-52s were incommensurate to the allotted task, Goering ordered the Luftwaffe Staff to requisition every available Ju-52 from the training units, and from the transport units of staffs and ministries throughout Germany and occupied Europe. As a result of these ruthless measures, a total of 500 Ju-52s were commandeered for the air-lift, but it was a month or more before they all arrived in the forward bases, and they were in a variety of conditions, ranging from the brand-new, which still needed running in (some even lacked guns and radios), to the clapped out.

By the beginning of December Fiebig had 320 transports under his command, but this number was still only 30 per cent of the required number, and von Richthofen was forced to divert the large number of He-111 and Ju-86 medium bombers, with a cargo capacity of 11½ tons, based at Morozovskaya from their bombing role and commit them to the air-lift. In addition Goering also eventually requisitioned seven FW-200 Condors (long-range reconnaissance planes), but their first sortie to the Kessel did not take place until 9 January. They were followed a few days later by two giant Ju-290s, capable of carrying 10 tons of cargo, along with several Ju-90s (long-range reconnaissance) and seven of the prototype He-177 long-range bombers. The three latter types proved, for various reasons, to be totally unsuitable as transports in this particular situation; both Ju-290s were quickly put out of action and all seven He-177s crashed in flames during the one and only mission they flew to Stalingrad.

By the end of the air-lift a total of 850 aircraft had taken part in the operation, but Fiebig never had more than 500 machines under his command at any one time, less than half the requisite number. Moreover, their serviceability dropped on occasions to as low as 25 per cent owing to the savage weather conditions.

Three main airfields were employed for the air-lift. At Tatsinskaya, 132 miles (60 minutes flying time) from Pitomnik, was based the large number of Ju-52 transports, under the command of Colonel Forster. At Morozovskaya, 105 miles (50 minutes flying time) from Pitomnik, were based the He-111s and Ju-86 medium bombers, under the command of Colonel Ernst Kühl, while the long-range reconnaissance and bomber aircraft were based at Stalino, 200 miles (80 minutes flying time) from Pitomnik, under the command of Major Willers.

The ground organization services and the technical facilities at these three airfields were woefully inadequate for the demands of a large-scale air-lift. The personnel were housed in improvised barracks, bunkers and even mud huts, which offered scant protection from the ravages of the Russian winter.

Aircraft hangers were non-existent, and on all three fields the aircraft had to be serviced in the open. For the mechanics, working without cover in icy snow-storms, their fingers frozen stiff, every engine change became a torture. If they dared to remove their gloves to make intricate adjustments, their fingers froze to the metal, with the result that essential maintenance was left undone and the degree of operational readiness never rose above 40 per cent (some 200 aircraft at any one time).

To add to the problems, not all the hastily activated units were capable of meeting the demands of such an arduous mission as the Stalingrad air-lift. On account of the immediacy of the situation, there was no time for the air-crews to become acclimatized to the sub-zero temperatures and harsh conditions. The majority of them were young and inexperienced, and the long and dangerous approach to the Kessel and the return flights over enemy territory, in the face of swarms of Soviet fighters and heavy flak, having to land on insufficiently prepared air strips which were deep in snow, pitted with bomb craters and scattered with wrecked aircraft, the unloading of supplies and re-loading with wounded in the Kessel under constant artillery fire and bombing attacks and the ever-present danger of icing, ignition trouble, defective carburettors, wireless equipment that constantly broke down, and guns that jammed in the bitter cold all combined to make the situation a veritable nightmare.

In addition, there was the depression that must have affected the young air-crews at the sight of the doomed, half-starved troops in the Kessel, and of the thousands of wounded, many of whom had to be left behind because there was not sufficient space available to fly them out. But above all it was the atrocious, bitterly cold weather that proved to be the insuperable enemy. Icing up whilst in flight, abysmal visibility, and the resulting accidents caused more casualties than enemy action. 'Nevertheless, the air crews displayed a dash and gallantry as in no previous operation. Never before in the history of aviation had men set out with such disdain of death and such firm resolution as for the air-lift to Stalingrad.'[2]

On the rare occasions when the weather was good and the cloud ceiling high, the supply units flew in squadrons, or in groups of five aircraft, with a fighter escort of four to six Me-109s. When the weather was bad, which was the norm, and visibility was poor and the cloud ceiling low, only those crews fully experienced in instrument flight flew in groups, the remainder flew singly or at most in groups of two.

Up to the 1st of December Soviet aircraft threw the main weight of their attack against the German positions on the perimeter of the Kessel. From then on the interdiction of the German air-lift became the main mission. This was undertaken by the 8th and 16th Air Armies, the former operating in the area to the south and south-west of the Kessel, the latter operating to

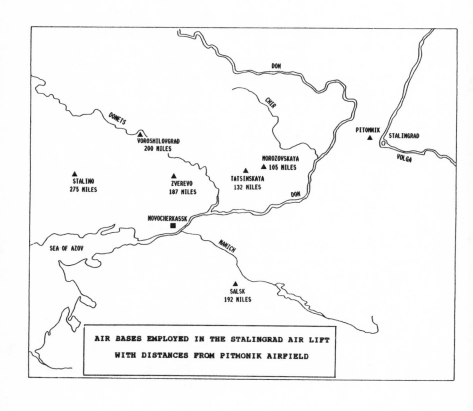

DON

CHIR

DONETS

VOROSHILOVGRAD
200 MILES

PITOMNIK
STALINGRAD

VOLGA

MOROZOVSKAYA
105 MILES

STALINO
275 MILES

ZVEREVO
187 MILES

TATSINSKAYA
132 MILES

DON

NOVOCHERKASSK

MANICH

SEA OF AZOV

SALSK
192 MILES

AIR BASES EMPLOYED IN THE STALINGRAD AIR LIFT
WITH DISTANCES FROM PITMONIK AIRFIELD

the north and north-west. During December these two Air Armies (comprised of some 800 aircraft) flew 4,147 sorties against the German transports, as opposed to 1,838 sorties against the enemy defence positions.

Apart from the losses suffered from the ubiquitous Soviet fighters and flak guns, constant bombing and fighter strafing attacks on the German airfields outside and within the Kessel also took a high toll of the transports, especially when the attacks came during take-off or landing, or when the transports were being loaded or unloaded. These harassing attacks considerably disrupted the supply missions and on occasions brought them to a complete standstill. Even the relatively strong German anti-aircraft batteries surrounding Pitomnik, and the covering patrols flown by German fighters over the airfield, were incapable of deterring these attacks.

The fighter patrols over Pitomnik were mounted by a group of fourteen Messerschmitt Bf-109s, which managed to maintain almost constant patrols of three or four aircraft at a time, this despite the fact that the pilots were subjected to the great nervous strain of being in almost constant action, and were in an exhausted physical condition caused by the unbearable cold and lack of food.

The unloading of the transports at Pitomnik was carried out by the survivors of the 104th Anti-Aircraft Regiment, under the command of Colonel Rosenfeld. The remainder of this Regiment had been split asunder during the Russian Kontrudar, and only one decimated battalion had managed to retreat into the Kessel. These one hundred freezing men, who sheltered in dug-outs on the edge of the airfield, not only unloaded the supplies but also kept careful inventories of every single item of food, ammunition and fuel, and supervised the flying out of the wounded who accumulated in blue hospital tents near the runway.

In fact there were five airfields in the Kessel, but only the one at Pitomnik was adequate to handle a large amount of air traffic. The primitive strips at Basargino (5 miles south of Pitomnik), Gumrak, Karpovka and Stalingradski (4 miles to the east of Gumrak), had been used on odd occasions as landing fields prior to the encirclement of 6th Army, but they were not adequate to the heavy demands of a large air-lift. This became apparent during the early stages of the operation, when half of the twenty Ju-52s which attempted landings on these fields crashed, despite being piloted by the best and most experienced crews.

Despite the myriad difficulties, the air traffic control facilities met the unusually high demands of the operation and functioned perfectly well until the very end. For navigation, and guiding approaches and take-offs, the air-crews were aided by three strong radio beacons – one within the Kessel, one at Tatsinskaya and one at Tsimlyanskiy (some 50 miles to the south-east of Tatsinskaya). There were also weaker radio beacons at Basargino,

Pitomnik and Morozovskaya, backed up by two-man radio direction finding stations at the two latter locations. In addition, a flight safety wave-length, operating on long and short-wave frequencies, was broadcast from Tatsinskaya.

The strong radio beacons were always clearly audible to the air-crews, but the weaker beacons were rendered useless for most of the operation by Russian jamming. Unfortunately, not all the aircraft participating in the air-lift could take advantage of these navigation aids, as there were so many different types and vintages that they did not all possess the modern radio equipment necessary.

The task of meteorologists in the air-lift was both vitally important and extremely difficult. Weather predictions, particularly those pertaining to the Kessel, were a determining factor in establishing take-off schedules and in planning the course of each day's missions. But because the Volga is a meteorological frontier, marking the boundary where the continental and maritime air masses meet, weather conditions changed rapidly and unpredictably, and this created almost insoluble problems for both the operations staff and the air-crews.

On numerous occasions pre-flight briefings indicated good weather over Pitomnik, but when the aircraft reached the Kessel they encountered either low-lying clouds, fog, snowstorms or all three. The same was true of the return trips: finding the bases too obscured by bad weather to risk a landing, the transports would be forced to fly on to airfields far to the west. As a result, these aircraft would be rendered unavailable for the air-lift for one or more days until they could, weather permitting, return to their assigned bases.

The frantic requisitioning of transport aircraft almost doubled the average tonnage of supplies flown into the Kessel during the first eleven days of December, over and above the average of 53.8 tons delivered during the first five days of the operation. However, the total of 1,167 tons flown in during the period 30 November to the 11 December (an average of 97.25 tons per day) was still only 19.4 per cent of the minimum tonnage necessary to sustain 6th Army. By 11 December, the cumulative deficit already amounted to 7,064 tons, the equivalent of 14 days' delivery of the required minimum of 500 tons. Goering's assurance to Hitler that the Luftwaffe could deliver was already proving to be a completely empty boast.

By the seventeenth day of the encirclement (11 December), the physical condition of the troops in the Kessel had manifestly deteriorated. In the severe climatic conditions prevailing, a minimum of 2,500 calories per man per day was necessary to maintain fighting strength. For a ration strength of 250,000 men this equalled 282 tons of food per day. As a daily average of only 84.47 tons had been flown into the Kessel during the first seventeen days of the encirclement, and as approximately half of this tonnage constituted fuel and ammunition (a minimum of 75 tons and 100 tons respectively were required for purely defensive purposes) the daily deficit in the food delivery alone amounted to some 240 tons. When the Soviet pincers snapped shut on 23 November 6th Army had six days' full rations for each man trapped in the encirclement, but as this stock was only being replenished by 14.9 per cent of the minimum requirement, the scale of rations issued to the weary, frozen troops was reduced to 1,500 calories on 26 November, and again to 1,000 calories on 8 December. Even this starvation level of nutrition was only made possible by the decision to slaughter the majority of the horses for meat. In total there were some 23,000 horses in the Kessel (7,300 troop horses and 15,700 pack and transport horses). If they were all slaughtered it would completely immobilize the artillery of the infantry divisions, which was, for the large part, horse-drawn. As a compromise solution it was decided to preserve the 7,300 troop horses in order that at least a portion of the heavy weapons and divisional artillery could remain mobile, although this would depend on the future supply of 22 tons of fodder per day (3 kilos per horse).

As a result of an inadequate diet, the bitter inescapable cold, and the drying up to a trickle of mail from loved ones at home, the majority of the troops fell victim to melancholic forebodings and an acute decline in morale set in. On 11 December 6th Army War Diary noted the first victims of death from malnutrition and exposure, along with the fact that the fuel stocks held by each of the five Corps were negligible, amounting to barely 0.1 per cent of normal daily consumption.

On this same day General Fiebig, in company with Major Kurt Stollberger (Chief Quartermaster of Fliegerkorps VIII), flew into the Kessel. They were received by the bitter reproaches of Paulus that 6th Army could 'neither exist nor fight' on the paltry amount of supplies being delivered by the Luftwaffe. Fiebig retorted by referring to the warning he had given over the telephone on 23 November, that it would be impossible to supply 6th Army from the air. Indeed the very reason he had flown into the Kessel was to declare categorically to Paulus, in person, that the long-term provision of 6th Army from the air was an impossibility, and would remain so even if the strength of the transport force at his disposal were multiplied.

When Zeitzler repeated this same categoric warning to Hitler at the Wolfsschanze, backed up by the actual tonnage figures that had so far been flown into the Kessel, the only response was the Führer's reiteration of the excuses that Goering was making for the obvious failure of the air lift: 'The Reichsmarschall is preparing a better organization. The Reichsmarschall is bringing up more planes. The Reichsmarschall has given me his word.' Each empty excuse was a toll of the bell for 6th Army. The only remaining hope now rested on a relief force that was gathering at Kotelnikovo, 60 miles to the south-west of the Kessel. It was a tenuous hope.

THE ADVENT OF VON MANSTEIN

While hoping that Goering would somehow or other cajole a miracle out of the Luftwaffe, Hitler called upon the military brilliance of Field-Marshal Erich von Manstein (who was serving on the northern sector of the Eastern Front) to reverse the situation on the Stalingrad axis by performing a miracle of superior generalship. Ordered 'to bring the enemy attacks to a standstill and recapture the positions previously occupied by us,' Manstein and his staff arrived at Novocherkassk, situated on the lower Don twenty-five miles north-east of Rostov, on 26 November, 1942. Here Manstein assumed command of a newly created army group – Heeresgruppe Don – positioned between Heeresgruppe A and B, which encompassed in its structure 6th, 4th Panzer and the 3rd Rumanian Armies, along with the 48th Panzer Corps (formed on the staff and remnants of 'Panzer Reserve Heim').

But the grandiose titles of 'Armies' and 'Corps', which appeared on Manstein's situation maps, were a pure fiction. The 4th Panzer Army consisted of nothing more than ad hoc units of service and communication troops, the remnants of four infantry and two weak cavalry divisions from the wrecked 4th Rumanian Army; the shattered 3rd Rumanian Army had only two infantry divisions to its name; 48th Panzer Corps, under the command of General von Knobelsdorff, was formed out of what little remained of the mauled 22nd Panzer Division and a ragged mixture of hastily formed 'emergency' units which lacked cohesion and weapons, particularly tanks. As for 6th Army, Manstein was unable to exercise any operational control over it, because it was immobilized by Hitler's categoric order that it must stand fast in Festung Stalingrad. In effect Manstein could not 'command' 6th Army, merely give it assistance. Outside of the Kessel the best force that Manstein possessed was the 16th Motorized Division, but this could not be withdrawn from its defensive position on the Kalmuck Steppe because it was covering the rear of Heeresgruppe A.

On the day Manstein arrived at Novocherkassk, one of 6th Army's staff officers flew out of the Kessel, bearing a hand-written letter from Paulus in which the general gave an appreciation of his position:

... the airlift of the last three days has brought only a fraction of the calculated minimum requirement. In the very next few days lack of supplies can lead to a crisis of the utmost gravity. I still believe, however, that 6th Army can hold out for a time. On the other hand – even if anything like a corridor is cut through to me – it is still not possible to tell whether the daily increasing weakness of the army, combined with the lack of accommodation and wood for constructional and heating purposes, will allow the area around Stalingrad to be held for any length of time.

As I am being daily bombarded with numerous understandable inquiries about the future, I should be grateful if I could be provided with more information than hitherto in order to increase the confidence of my men.

Allow me to say, Herr Feldmarschall, that I regard your leadership as a guarantee that everything possible is being done to assist 6th Army. For their own part, my commanders and gallant troops will join me in doing everything to justify your trust.[3]

The reason for the delivery of this letter was that, because 6th Army had only a single thousand-watt transmitter to maintain contact with both the Wolfsschanze and Heeresgruppe B HQ, Manstein had to rely to a large degree on reports from Paulus in longhand, delivered 'by hand of officer,' because the single transmitter was so overloaded with work. This unsatisfactory situation existed until 19 December, when a direct link was finally established. In the meantime General Schulz, Manstein's Chief of Staff, and Colonel Busse, his Chief of Operations, had to fly into the Kessel at different times to establish a closer contact with Paulus, and to brief him in detail on Manstein's plans for raising the siege.

In addition to Paulus's appreciation of 26 November, Manstein also received a personal report from General Pickert (commanding the 9th Flak Division), who flew out of the Kessel for the express purpose of acquainting the Field-Marshal with the 6th Army's supply position. According to Pickert, the army had enough rations − albeit on short issue − for twelve days. Ammunition stocks were at 10 − 20 per cent of the normal scale, which corresponded to the amount which would be expended in one day's intensive fighting!

On the strength of these appreciations, and after studying the situation in detail, Manstein concluded that the task confronting Heeresgruppe Don was a two-sided one:

The chief feature, and the one on which everything depended, was the relief and rescue of 6th Army. Apart from being a priority in the humane sense, this was also vital from the operational point of view, first and foremost because there could be hardly any hope of restoring the situation on the southern wing of the Eastern Front − or, indeed, in the eastern theatre as a whole − unless the forces of 6th Army were preserved.

The other side of the task − and this had to be borne in mind throughout − was the already existing danger that the entire southern wing of the German armies would be destroyed. If this were allowed to happen, it would most probably be the end of the struggle in the east and consequently lose us the war. Should the Russians succeed in tearing through the flimsy screen – for the moment consisting mainly of Rumanian remnants and German B-echelon troops and emergency units – which, leaving aside the so-called Festung Stalingrad – constituted the sole protection of the whole operational area between the rear of Heeresgruppe A and the still-existing Don front, not only would 6th Army's position become hopeless, but that of Heeresgruppe A, as well, would become more than critical.[4]

Despite the mortal threat hanging over the whole of the southern wing of the front, Manstein decided that Heeresgruppe Don must first and foremost, 'to the very limit of its powers and resources,' attempt to relieve 6th Army, rather than establish a firm defensive front. With the promise of reinforcements amounting to four panzer divisions, four infantry divisions and three Luftwaffe field divisions, Manstein believed that 'the forces indicated... might conceivably suffice to make temporary contact with 6th Army, and restore to it freedom of movement.'[5] To this end he submitted the following proposals to Hitler for his sanction (which were in effect a modified form of the proposals already expressed by Zeitzler):

1. 6th Army must break out from Stalingrad and meet the forces advancing to its relief. The loss of 6th Army's heavy weapons and equipment must be accepted.

2. The mass of Heeresgruppe A must be withdrawn from the Caucasus to a position behind the Lower Don, where a bridgehead at Rostov must be formed and held by a reinforced 4th Panzer Army and 3rd Rumanian Army for as long as possible. This bridgehead is not to be given up unless the attack to relieve Stalingrad fails to reach its objective.

3. After a successful break-out by 6th Army, a defensive front must be created along the Donets or in the Mius position or to the north (roughly the line from which Heeresgruppe South had launched the 1942 summer offensive).

4. The whole Eastern Front must be rationalized with the object of shortening the front.

Predictably, Hitler rejected these proposals out of hand. He preferred to ignore all the factual considerations in favour of his 'hold or bust' policy by ordering Manstein to cut a corridor to 6th Army, through which to replenish its fuel and ammunition stocks, with the sole intention of allowing 6th Army not only to maintain its grip on Stalingrad but also, in the jargon of static warfare, 'to re-occupy the positions held prior to the Russian counter-offensive'.

For the operation to relieve 6th Army, code-named Wintergewitter ('Winter Storm'), Manstein decided to create two separate forces from the reinforcements in the process of being transferred from the Caucasus, France and other sectors of the Eastern Front.

On the Chir River front Armeeabteilung (army detachment) Hollidt (named after its Commanding Officer, General Karl Hollidt) was to assemble. It was to consist of the 62nd, 294th and 336th Infantry Divisions, the 7th and 8th Luftwaffe Field Divisions, and the 48th Panzer Corps – composed of the existing, but shattered, 22nd Panzer Division and the full strength 11th Panzer Division.

In the area of Kotelnikovo, and within the framework of 4th Panzer Army, Armeegruppe Hoth (named after the existing commander of 4th Panzer Army) was to assemble. It was to consist of the 57th Panzer Corps, under the command of General Kirchner, which had only one existing panzer division (the badly mauled 23rd) to its name, but which was to be reinforced by the up-to-strength 6th Panzer Division, which entrained in France on 24 November, and the below-strength 17th Panzer Division which was refitting at Orel.

While these forces were en route to their assembly areas, Manstein worked on the planning of Wintergewitter, which was finalized by the 1st December. Although the assembly area of Armeeabteilung Hollidt was in the area of a bridgehead across the Chir at Nizhne-Chirskaya, which was only twenty-five miles distant from Marinovka on the south-western edge of the Kessel, Manstein decided that the main thrust would be delivered by Armeegruppe Hoth from the Kotelnikovo area, on the axis of the Kotelnikovo – Stalingrad railway line, even though this was some sixty miles south-west of the Kessel. The reasoning on which this decision was based was that there were indications of heavy Russian reserve forces concentrating on the west bank of the Don, and Manstein suspected that the Russians were preparing to counter any relief attacks debouching from the Nizhne-Chirskaya bridgehead (being the shortest route to the Kessel, it was the most obvious). Armeeabteilung Hollidt was, therefore, to be relegated in the early stages of Wintergewitter to a diversionary show of force, designed to draw off the Soviet mobile reserves from the north-easterly thrust to be made by Armeegruppe Hoth. However, if and when Hoth's columns drew level with the bridgehead at Nizhne-Chirskaya, the 48th Panzer Corps was to attempt an easterly drive on Kalach with the object of offering Paulus an alternative route for a possible extrication of 6th Army from the Kessel. For, in spite of Hitler's strictures, Manstein planned that if the relief forces could get within close proximity of the Kessel, Paulus, on receipt of the code word *Donnerschlag* (Thunderclap), was to carry out an ostensibly limited break-out to the south-west or west to link up and assist the advancing relief forces. However, Manstein was working on the assumption that the concentration of sufficient forces at any given point necessary to rupture the perimeter of perimeter of the Kessel from the interior, would so weaken the eastern or northern flanks of the Kessel that they would be forced to retire under Soviet pressure, and the resulting momentum created by the withdrawal of one or the other of these flanks would precipitate a full-scale break-out en masse which Hitler could not countermand and would have no choice but to accept. In short, Manstein hoped to present Hitler with a *fait accompli*.

Within three days of finalizing his plans for Wintergewitter, the success of the operation was compromised by a crisis which flared up on the Chir River. On 4 December the Russian and Fifth Tank Army began a series of attacks along the whole of the Chir front, striking without respite at one point after another. By 7 December, when this army was reinforced on its southern flank by a newly activated reserve army − the Fifth Shock Army − with a strength of 71,000 men, 252 tanks and 804 guns and mortars, it became clear to Manstein that the Russians were mounting their strength in earnest against the Chir front, both as a spoiling attack against the concentration of Armeeabteilung Hollidt and with the more ambitious purpose of capturing the airfields at Tatsinskaya and Morozovskaya − the main bases serving the Stalingrad airlift.

Unbeknown to Manstein, the Soviet pressure on the Chir front was also mounted as a preliminary requisite for Operation Saturn − the planned mammoth outer sweep, aimed at Rostov, designed to encircle the whole of the German southern wing in a 'Super Stalingrad'. The aims were outlined in Vasilevsky's initial proposals to Stalin regarding the launching of Saturn:

> Most immediate aim of the operation to be the destruction of Operational Group 'Hollidt'... Fifth Tank Army must be committed... to the destruction of enemy forces in the area of Chernyshevskaya − Tormosin − Morozovskaya to obtain a more definite isolation in the south-west of enemy forces encircled in Stalingrad, with a view to developing its offensive further towards Tatsinskaya in order to exit on the line of the Northern Donets.[6]

The effect of these attacks was that the three infantry divisions, two Luftwaffe field divisions, and the 11th Panzer Division, which had been assigned to Armeeabteilung Hollidt, became dissipated along the whole length of the Chir, rather than concentrated into the planned striking force. General Hollidt had no other choice but to commit the divisions as they detrained, in his efforts to stop the Chir front from disintegrating under the unrelenting Soviet pressure.

During these efforts the strength of 11th Panzer Division (General Balck) was cut by a half in little more than a week, as it had to be employed as a veritable 'fire-brigade', dashing from one crisis point to another to intervene every time the Russians punched a hole in the thin screen spread along the Chir. By 12 December, after constantly moving by night and fighting by day for over a week, 11th Panzer was finally ground to a standstill, and was compelled to dig in at Nizhne Kalinovsky to become a part of the static line of defence. Tanks and vehicles broke down for want of maintenance, and the exhausted tank crews had hardly the strength left to lift shells into the gun breeches.

As for the newly formed 7th and 8th Luftwaffe Field Divisions, within days of being committed to action on the Chir front they were – in the words of General Balck – 'gone, finished, in spite of good mechanical equipment. Their training left everything to be desired, and they had no experienced leaders. They were a creation of Hermann Goering, a creation which had no sound military foundation – the rank and file paid with their lives for this absurdity.'[7]

With Armeeabteilung Hollidt fully committed to the defence of the Chir, the success of Wintergewitter, not auspicious from the start, now rested entirely on Armeegruppe Hoth.

THE LAUNCH OF WINTERGEWITTER

Manstein had scheduled 'Winter Storm' to begin on 8 December, but General Hoth was suffering agonizing delays in his efforts to concentrate the main relief force at Kotelnikovo. By 11 December only two of the three panzer divisions allotted to the attack had reached their assembly areas. The errant division (17th Panzer) had been waylaid by Hitler while *en route* from Orel. He ordered it to detrain behind the left wing of Heeresgruppe Don, because he feared a large-scale Russian offensive was impending in that area (which indeed there was – Operation Saturn). But Hitler could not have it both ways: the success of Wintergewitter and security against an attack on the left wing of Heeresgruppe Don which, if it did materialize, 17th Panzer, being under-strength, would not be strong enough to prevent in any case.

Despite Manstein's protestations that the success of the relief operation would be compromised by diverting 17th Panzer, Hitler opted for the security he hoped to achieve by the retention of the panzer division behind the junction of Armeeabteilung Hollidt (Army Group Don) and the 8th Italian Army (Army Group B). As for Manstein's misgivings, Hitler attempted to allay them by pointing out that Soviet divisions were always smaller and weaker than they first appeared to be, and that the Soviet command had in all probability been thrown off balance by its own success!

During the afternoon situation conference at the Wolfsschanze on 11 December Zeitzler also tried to persuade Hitler to release 17th Panzer for Wintergewitter. Once again Hitler refused, citing the threat which appeared to be building up on the left flank of Manstein's Army Group to be the imperative. During this conference he restated his position on Stalingrad, saying, 'I have reached one conclusion, Zeitzler. We cannot under any circumstances give that up (pointing to Stalingrad on a chart). We will not retake it if we do. We know what that means... if we give up that [Stalingrad] we sacrifice the whole sense of this campaign. To imagine that I will get there again next time is insanity.'[8]

Despite being deprived of 17th Panzer, Manstein, on the evening of 11 December, despairing of being able to make Hitler see sense, decided that a further postponement of Wintergewitter could not be tolerated on account of the daily deterioration of the supply situation in the Kessel. Paulus had reported that ammunition stocks would soon be entirely exhausted, and that any meaningful scale of rations would run out by 19 December. Moreover, Soviet armour had been detected moving in opposite Armeegruppe Hoth, which Manstein feared presaged a large build-up of enemy forces on the planned axis of the relief attempt.

The attack by Armeegruppe Hoth, timed to start at dawn on Saturday, 12 December, was to be spearheaded by General Kirchner's 57th Panzer Corps, comprising the full strength 6th Panzer Division, with 160 tanks and 40 self-propelled guns, and the mauled 23rd Panzer Division with only 30 tanks in running order. Protecting the panzer corps's left flank was the 6th Rumanian Army Corps, made up of the remnants of three Rumanian infantry divisions whose combined strength barely amounted to the effective strength of one full division, while the right (or eastern) flank was covered by the 7th Rumanian Army Corps, with a strength of one infantry division and two weak cavalry divisions.

Opposing Hoth was the Russian Fifty-first Army, which had been reduced to about half its strength since the Kontrudar. Three of its tank brigades had been transferred to the Chir front, and most of its artillery was being used on the perimeter of the Kessel. This left Fifty-first Army with four rifle and four cavalry divisions, with one tank and one motorized brigade forward and one tank and one rifle brigade in reserve. These forces were covering 100 miles of front, and were insufficient to provide a defence in depth.

The nature of the steppe over which Hoth's forces would have to travel sixty miles to link up with 6th Army favoured the defending forces. The ground was hard, iced over with a covering of snow. At first sight it appeared completely flat, without ground elevation or cover of any kind. But, in fact, it was criss-crossed by the beds of rivers and brooks, gullies and ravines (balkas), the majority of which ran in an east-west direction, with a few running in a north-south direction.

Two rivers crossed the line of Hoth's advance – the Aksay (18 miles north of Kotelnikovo) and the Mishkova (31 miles north of Kotelnikovo and some 35 miles from the southern perimeter of the Kessel). Narrow and shallow, both rivers could be forded over almost their entire course, but, due to the steepness of their banks, they proved difficult to cross in many stretches.

At the time of Wintergewitter both rivers were frozen over and had lost their importance as natural anti-tank barriers. However, they proved to be good defence lines. In the balkas groups of Russian infantry lay hidden, sometimes up to a battalion in strength and with a full complement of heavy weapons. Russian cavalry units also hid their horses in the balkas during the day, riding out at night to harass the flanks of the German columns with mortar and machine-gun fire. In addition the balkas were filled with deep snow and these served to slow the advance of the tanks and transport vehicles, frequently making progress impossible in places.

The artillery bombardment of the Russian positions by 266 field guns, which heralded the launch of Wintergewitter, began at 0515 on the morning of Saturday, 12 December, 1942. When the barrage lifted the 6th and 23rd Panzer Divisions rolled forward and broke through the Russian 126th and 302nd Rifle Divisions with relative ease. Ten miles behind the carapace of tanks was the 'soft tail' of 800 lorries, tractors and buses carrying 3,000 tons of supplies for the beleaguered 6th Army.

The two divisions made good, though not spectacular, progress against light opposition, and by 0800 on the following morning (13 December), having captured an intact bridge at Zalivskiy, German tanks began crossing the Aksay River.

Despite this auspicious beginning, at noon on the 13th, Manstein informed Hitler that without the 17th Panzer Division, 57th Panzer Corps would not be able to sustain enough momentum to carry it all the way through to the Kessel. Wrongly advised by Fremde Heere Ost that there was a growing impression that the Russians were merely simulating an offensive build-up on Heeresgruppe Don's left flank, Hitler, enthused by Hoth's progress, agreed to release 17th Panzer. This Division, which only possessed 44 tanks, detrained and took up position on the left flank of 6th Panzer on the morning of 17 December, by which time, as Manstein had feared, Wintergewitter had lost its momentum, having become bogged down in heavy fighting with two Soviet mechanized corps and two tank brigades around Verkhne-Kumsky, half-way between the Aksay and Mishkova Rivers. Moreover, by now the continuation of the relief operation had become a gigantic gamble on account of the Russians launching Operation Saturn — a massive offensive on the Middle Don, some 250 miles to the north-west of Armeegruppe Hoth.

THE LAUNCH OF SATURN

As early as 23 November, the day the Soviet pincers closed around 6th Army, Stalin had instructed General Vasilevsky, the Chief of the Soviet General Staff, to work up a plan for an offensive by General Vatutin's South-western Front and the left wing of General Golikov's Voronezh Front, which was to be aimed through Millerovo at Rostov, with the aim of encircling the whole of the German southern wing, including Heeresgruppe A in the Caucasus.

The plan, code-named Operation Saturn, was submitted by Vasilevsky on 2 December, but its success depended on the inclusion of the armies which were tied down investing 6th Army. A reduction of 6th Army – Operation Koltso (Ring) – was scheduled to start on 18 December, as a prerequisite for Saturn, but the launching of Wintergewitter forced Stalin to alter his plans.

On the morning of 12 December Vasilevsky telephoned Stalin on the V Ch line, immediately after he was made aware of the German relief attack, requesting that the Second Guards Army, which had been sent to the northern flank of the Kessel (under Don Front command) to take part in Koltso, be transferred to Yeremenko's Stalingrad Front to block Hoth's relief attack by taking position on the Mishkova River. Stalin refused an immediate reply, snapping bad-temperedly at Vasilevsky that the question would have to be thrashed out in a session of the State Defence Committee (GKO), of which Stalin himself was chairman. Stalin was incensed because the transfer of Second Guards to the Mishkova would necessitate a postponement of Koltso.

Soviet plans for both Saturn and Koltso now passed through a thirty-six-hour storm, which had been stirred up by the onset of Wintergewitter, in which the strategic plans vitally affecting both operations had to be re-formulated. It was not until 0500 on the morning of 13 December that Stalin finally passed Vasilevsky the authorization to move Second Guards from the Don Front to the Mishkova River. Consequently, at 2250 on the following day, the formal order for the postponement of Koltso was duly sent to Yeremenko (whose Stalingrad Front was investing the southern and eastern flanks of the Kessel) and Rokossovsky (whose Don Front was investing the western and northern flanks):

Rokossovsky and Yeremenko are ordered to continue the systematic harassment of the encircled enemy troops by air and ground attacks, denying the enemy any breathing space by night or by day, pulling the encirclement ring ever tighter and nipping off any attempt by the encircled troops to break out of the ring.... The main task of our southern forces is to defeat the enemy group at Kotelnikovo, using the troops of General Trufanov (Fifty-first Army) and General Malinovsky (Second Guards Army), to capture Kotelnikovo in the immediate future and to dig in there.[9]

The postponement of Koltso also affected Saturn, and, during the night of 14 December, Golikov and Vatutin, the Voronezh and South-western Front commanders, who were in turn under the command of Stavka 'co-ordinator' General Voronov, received a re-formulated plan of the operation. Despite the fact that the armies besieging 6th Army could not now be considered for employment in Saturn, Stalin decided to bring forward the launch date of the operation, which was made possible by reducing its scale and strategic objective. By shifting the direction of the attack south-eastwards rather than southwards (towards Rostov), *Bol'shoi Saturn* ('Big Saturn') was transformed into *Malyi Saturn* ('Small Saturn'), which was to be aimed at the rear of Manstein's forces trying to fight their way into the Kessel, to encircle the whole of Heeresgruppe Don (Bol'shoi Saturn had been aimed to encircle Heeresgruppe A as well). In the new directive, dated 13 December, Stalin laid out the basis for the revised decision:

First: Operation Saturn aimed at Kamensk – Rostov was conceived when the overall situation was in our favour, when the Germans had no more reserves in the Bokovsk – Morozovskaya – Nizhne-Chirskaya area, when the Fifth Tank Army had made successful attacks in the direction of Morozovskaya, and when it appeared that an attack from the north would be supported at the same time by an offensive from the east aimed at Likhaya. Under these circumstances it was proposed that the Second Guards Army (after the reduction of 6th Army had been achieved) should be swung into the area of Kalach and used to develop a successful advance in the direction of Rostov – Taganrog.

Second: Recently, however, the situation has not developed in our favour. Romanenko (Fifth Tank Army) and Lelyushenko (Third Guards Army) have been unable to cross the Chir and cannot advance; while from the west a number of enemy infantry divisions and tank formations have appeared, which are containing the Soviet forces (on the Chir front). Consequently, an attack from the north would not meet with direct support from the east by Romanenko's Fifth Tank Army, as a consequence of which an offensive in the direction of Kamensk – Rostov would meet with no success. I have to say that Second Guards Army can no longer be used for Operation Saturn since it is operating on another front (against Armeegruppe Hoth).

Third: In view of all this, it is essential to revise Operation Saturn. The revision lies in the fact that the main blow will be aimed not at the south, but towards the south-east in the direction of Nizhne Astakhov, to exit at Morozovskaya in order to take the enemy grouping at Bokovsk – Morozovskaya in a pincer movement, to break into his rear and to destroy these forces with a simultaneous blow from the east with the forces of Romanenko (Fifth Tank) and Lelyushenko (Third Guards) and from the north-west with the forces of General Kuznetsov (First Guards) and mobile formations subordinated to his command. General Golikov (Voronezh Front) has as his assignment to help Kuznetsov to liquidate the Italians (8th Army), and get to the River

Boguchat, in the area of Kramenkov, to set up a major covering force against possible enemy attacks from the west.

Fourth: The break-through will proceed in those sectors which were projected under Operation Saturn. After the break-through, the blow will be turned to the south-east in the direction of Nizhne Astakhov – Morozovskaya, breaking into the rear of the enemy forces facing Romanenko and Lelyushenko. The operation will begin on 16 December, and has the code-name Malyi Saturn.'[10]

'Small Saturn' opened at 0800 on the thick foggy morning of 16 December, when Soviet artillery – 'the God of War' – pounded the enemy positions for a full ninety minutes along 200 miles of front running from Novaya Kalitva in the north to Nizhne-Chirskaya in the south. Along this front the Russians had amassed 425,000 men, 1,030 tanks and almost 5,000 artillery pieces and mortars (81mm and above in calibre). These forces were disposed in four armies. Reading from north to south these were Sixth Army (General Kharitonov) and First Guards Army (General Kuznetsov) on the southern wing of Golikov's Voronezh Front; and the Third Guards Army (General Lelyushenko) and the Fifth Tank Army (General Romanenko) of Vatutin's South-western Front.

The main blow was delivered by Sixth, First Guards and Third Guards Armies, which fell upon General Gariboldi's 8th Italian Army, which, with 216,000 men in eleven divisions, was defending a front of some 130 miles. The only reserves in the rear of the Italian front were the German 298th Infantry Division, two battalions of the 62nd Infantry Division, and a mobile reserve provided by the 27th Panzer Division, a weak unit in the process of being re-equipped with repaired and reconditioned tanks from workshops at Millerovo. (Within two days of being committed to action this division was reduced to eight tanks.)

For three days the Italians put up a savage resistance, but on 19 December the centre and southern wing of the 8th Army finally cracked, and the Italians took to their heels in precipitous flight across the fog-shrouded, snowy steppe, leaving their northern wing dangling in the air. With them fled the two Rumanian divisions positioned between the Italian 8th Army and Armeeabteilung Hollidt.

Through the 100-mile gap which they had torn out of the Axis front, the three Soviet armies began a south-easterly drive: Sixth Army advancing on Millerovo, First Guards on Tatsinskaya, and Third Guards on Morozovskaya. The axis of the advance was aimed along the rear of Armeeabteilung Hollidt, which was itself in the process of being unhinged from its position on the Chir by the relentless attacks of Romanenko's Fifth Tank Army. Unless the Germans could plug the gap, the way was open for the Russians to encircle the Hollidt group, overrun the two main air bases

14. At night—'howling, screeching, bleeding nights'—Stalingrad presented an incredible sight. The grotesque shapes of the disembowelled shops, offices, houses and factories were silhouetted by the glow of innumerable giant fires.

15. A German 50mm PAK 3A anti-tank gun. During the first month of the murderous grappling in the ruins of the giant, crumbling city, the Germans expended 25 million rounds of small arms ammunition, 500,000 anti-tank rounds and 750,000 artillery shells.

16. German infantry, supported by an assault gun mounted on a Mark III tank chassis, advance through the deady meshes of the bomb and shell cratered railway sidings of *Der Tennisschlager* .

17. The ruins of the Barrikady gun factory. The most savage fighting for the city occurred in the factory district in the north of the city .

18. Paulus surveying Russian positions through periscope binoculars. On his right is General Seydlitz-Kurzbach. By the first week of November it had become patently clear to everyone that a major Russian offensive was imminent.

19. At 0730 on the morning of 19 November, 1942, a salvo fired by Katyusha rocket-launchers signalled the start of a thunderous bombardment of the Rumanian positions by 3,500 guns and mortars.

20. In the wake of the tanks which smashed through the Rumanian positions on 19 November, 38,646 mounted men of two Russian Cavalry Corps exploited the breakthrough and charged across the snow-covered steppe.

21. In the Kessel the German troops found themselves encircled on a bare steppe exposed to the merciless Russian winter. A German soldier is shown piling blocks of frozen snow around the engine of his lorry to protect it from the icy wind.

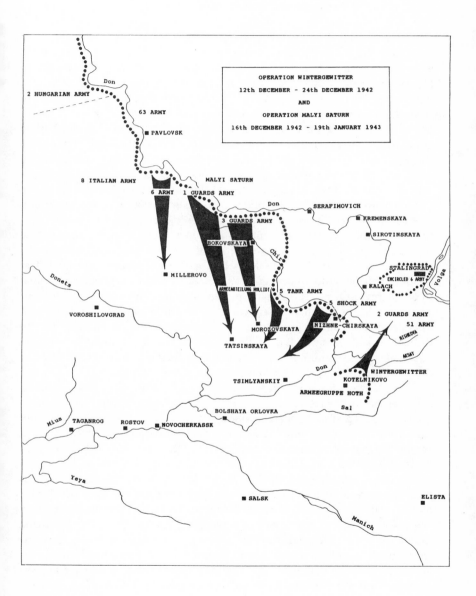

OPERATION WINTERGEWITTER
12th DECEMBER - 24th DECEMBER 1942
AND
OPERATION MALYI SATURN
16th DECEMBER 1942 - 19th JANUARY 1943

employed in the Stalingrad air-lift, and, once across the Lower Don, drive
into the rear of Armeegruppe Hoth's relief attack.

END OF A HOPE

Despite the danger of continuing to press forward with Wintergewitter
while the north-eastern flank of Heeresgruppe Don was disintegrating,
Manstein decided that the relief of 6th Army must remain the first
imperative. He reasoned that if 57th Panzer Corps could prise open the ring
around Stalingrad and release the divisions of 6th Army, the whole situation
might be saved, on the assumption that the Russians' efforts on the Middle
Don would weaken if they believed that the main prize, 6th Army, was
slipping from their grasp. Everything now depended on Paulus concentrating
the mass of his army at a single point of the siege perimeter and blasting a
way through the Russian ring of steel to link up with Hoth's tanks.

To ensure that Paulus fully understood his intention of bringing about a
breakout *en masse*, Manstein ordered his intelligence chief, Major Eismann,
to fly into the Kessel to present the plan in person. Eismann drove from
Heeresgruppe Don's HQ at Novocherkassk to the airfield at Morozovskaya,
and flew from there into the Kessel in a Fieseler Storch. He landed at
Gumrak at 0750 on the morning of 19 December and was immediately taken
to 6th Army HQ, where Eismann presented Manstein's case for a breakout
en masse with as much persuasiveness as he could muster. Although 'not
unimpressed', Paulus proceeded to emphasize 'the magnitude of the
difficulties and risks which the task outlined to him would imply'.[11] Paulus's
misgivings were amplified by General Arthur Schmidt, 6th Army's Chief of
Staff, who ultimately decided the outcome of the conference.

Schmidt was an ardent Nazi and a forceful personality, who exercised
considerable influence on Paulus, playing the part of 'Party conscience',
always standing at the General's elbow. 'It is quite impossible to break out
just now,' Schmidt told Eismann. Such a solution would be 'an
acknowledgement of disaster. Sixth Army,' he claimed, 'will still be in
position at Easter. All you people have to do is supply it better.'[12]

The conference dragged on all day, and during the afternoon an egregious
meal was served during which Eismann tried once more to convince Paulus
and his staff that a complete withdrawal from Stalingrad was necessary 'from
the point of view of operations as a whole'.[13] As for the air-lift, Eismann
pointed out that, although the Army Group was doing everything possible
to maintain supplies, it was not to blame when the weather brought the
air-lift to a virtual standstill, nor was it in a position to produce transport
machines out of a hat. But Eismann's remonstrances had no effect whatever
on Schmidt, and Paulus remained unconvinced. Indeed, during the course
of the day Paulus's attitude hardened, for he finally dismissed Eismann with

the assertion that a complete withdrawal was 'a sheer impossibility', and that in any case the evacuation of Festung Stalingrad was forbidden by the Führerbefehl.

When Eismann returned to Novocherkassk late on the afternoon of 19 December and reported on the outcome of the conference Manstein toyed with the idea of dismissing both Paulus and Schmidt and replacing them with members of his own staff or with corps commanders from within the Kessel. But time was short and anyway 'it would have been hopeless to try to obtain Hitler's approval for such a change, since it would have affected the very men who recommended holding out at Stalingrad'.[14]

During the course of that same day the vanguard of 6th Panzer Division reached the Mishkova River, a mere 35 miles from the southern perimeter of the Kessel. However, the effort had exhausted the three divisions of 57th Panzer Corps, which now mustered only 100 tanks between them, and they were now faced by General Malinovsky's powerful Second Guards Army which was deploying on the northern banks of the Mishkova. For these reasons Manstein informed Hitler that, because of mounting losses and ever stiffening enemy resistance, he doubted that 57th Panzer Corps could get through to 6th Army, and certainly could not open a permanent corridor to the Kessel. The only solution, he ventured, was the obvious one of ordering 6th Army to break out en masse, gradually pulling back its northern and eastern flanks as it pushed southwards towards the relief force. Manstein set out his views fully in a teletype message to Zeitzler in the Wolfsschanze 'for immediate submission to the Führer':

'The situation... has developed in such a manner that a relief of the Sixth Army cannot be expected in the foreseeable future.

Because of the shortage of available aircraft as well as the inclement weather, the supply and maintenance of the army by means of an air-lift are not possible — as was proven during the four weeks since the encirclement. The 57th Panzer Corps alone cannot clear a corridor to the Sixth Army and can far less keep such a corridor open. I now believe that a sortie by the Sixth Army towards the south-west is the last possibility, to save at least the mass of the Army's soldiers and still mobile weapons.

The immediate objective of the sortie will be the establishment of contact with 57th Panzer Corps in the approximate position of the Mishkova River. This can only be accomplished by the Army fighting its way free toward the south-west, and gradually shifting the entire Army in such a manner that section by section of the fortified area in the north is given up as ground is gained in the south-west. It is imperative that, in the course of this operation, the air supply of the Army is ensured.

It is imperative that the break-out is no longer delayed in case the 57th Panzer Corps remains stalled on, or north, of the Mishkova River, as this would exclude the possibility of a simultaneous attack by the forces within and outside of the Kessel. Moreover, prior to assembling for the attack, the Sixth Army will need several days for regrouping and refuelling.

Provisions in the Kessel will last until 22 December. The men already show symptoms of debilitation.... According to an Army report, the mass of horses cannot be used because they are starved or else have been eaten.'[15]

By 1730 that evening, not having received a reply from the Wolfsschanze, Manstein decided that he would have to act unilaterally to save 6th Army. First of all he decided to confirm the comments Paulus had purportedly made to Eismann earlier that same day. Manstein now had the means to contact Paulus direct. During the course of the day a decimeter-wave telecommunication system had been installed at Gumrak, along with the erection of a 120-foot-high antenna beacon near the south-western perimeter of the Kessel. Messages, reproduced on teleprinters, which the enemy could not monitor, could now be passed direct between Manstein's HQ at Novocherkassk and Paulus's HQ at Gumrak 225 miles to the north-west.

At 1750 on the evening of 19 December, the clickety-clack of the teleprinter in the operations bunker at Gumrak began recording the first message from Manstein:

+++ Are you gentlemen present?

+++ Yes, sir.

+++ Please comment briefly on Eismann's report. (Paulus formulated his comments concisely).

+++ Case 1: Break-out from Kessel towards Businovka (to the south) in order to link up with Hoth is only possible with tanks. We are short of infantry forces which are necessary for the defence of Stalingrad and will be needed to protect the long new flanks (created by the break-out). In addition, if this alternative is implemented, all the armoured reserves hitherto used in clearing up enemy penetrations of the defence perimeter will be used in the break-out and will have to quit the Kessel.

Case 2: Break-out without link-up with Hoth is possible only in extreme emergency. This would result in heavy losses of material. Prerequisite is preliminary flying-in of sufficient food and fuel to improve condition of troops. If Hoth could establish temporary link-up and bring in towing vehicles this alternative would be easier to carry out. Infantry divisions are almost immobilized at the moment and we are getting more so every day as horses are slaughtered to feed men.

Case 3: In view of the present situation, further defence of Stalingrad Kessel depends on sufficient reinforcements and supplies being flown in. At the present rate of supply it will not be possible to hold the Kessel much longer.

[A moment later a question from Manstein came ticking through]:

+++ What would be the earliest date on which you could form up for Case 2 – the complete withdrawal from the Kessel?

+++ Preparatory period three to four days.

+++ How much fuel and provisions are needed? Objective Mishkova.

+++ One and a half times the normal fuel supply rate; let Chief Quartermaster Heeresgruppe Don calculate it. Reduced rations for about 10 days for 270,000 men.[16]

Clearly, Paulus had turned *volte-face* and was now telling Manstein that a break-out *en masse* – a complete withdrawal from Stalingrad – was the only viable alternative: a complete contradiction of what he had told Eismann earlier that same day! It was just as well, because without having had time to consider Paulus's latest appreciation, Manstein told Paulus to stand by to receive an order, which came clicking over the teleprinter in so short a space of time that it had obviously been pre-prepared:

+++ Order! To Sixth Army.

(1). Armeegruppe Hoth has defeated the enemy in the Verkhne-Kumsky area and the 57th Panzer Corps has reached the Mishkova sector. An attack has been initiated against a strong enemy group in the Kamenka area and north of it. Heavy fighting is to be expected there. The situation on the Chir front does not permit the advance of forces west of the Don towards Stalingrad. The Don bridge at Nizhne-Chirskaya is in enemy hands.

(2). Sixth Army will assemble as soon as possible for Operation Wintergewitter (the attempt to link up with the approaching relief force while continuing to hold Stalingrad). The object is to establish contact with 57th Panzer Corps, in order to get the convoy of supplies into the Kessel.

(3). Developments (the inability of the relief force to advance any further than the Mishkova) may necessitate an extension of paragraph 2 to a break-out by the entire Sixth Army with the objective of joining 57th Panzer Corps on the Mishkova River. Code word *Donnerschlag* (break-out *en masse* and relinquish Stalingrad). In that case the main task will again be the quickest possible establishment of contact, by means of tanks, with 57th Panzer Corps with a view to getting the convoy through. The Sixth Army would then advance toward the Mishkova River, covering its flanks while the Kessel is evacuated section by section.

Under certain circumstances it may become necessary to immediately follow up Operation Wintergewitter (link up) with Operation Donnerschlag (complete withdrawal from the Kessel). On the whole the Army will have to make do with current air supplies without major build-up of stores. The airfield at Pitomnik must be held for as long as possible.

All arms and artillery that can be moved... but also such weapons and equipment that are difficult to replace... must be concentrated in the south-western part of the Kessel as soon as possible.

(4). Prepare for item No. 3 (complete break-out) which becomes effective only upon specific order Donnerschlag.

(5). Report date and time of attack as under item No. 2 (Wintergewitter).[17]

Manstein's order was subtly worded to pay lip-service to Wintergewitter while the real intention was innocuously tucked away in paragraph 3: 'Under certain circumstances it may become necessary to immediately follow up Operation Wintergewitter with Operation Donnerschlag', the import being that the concentration of sufficient forces on the south-western flank of the Kessel to implement Wintergewitter, the link-up with Hoth, would so weaken the other flanks that they would collapse and a complete withdrawal (Donnerschlag) would be forced upon Paulus, which Hitler would be powerless to countermand. As Paulus was now apparently in agreement with this point of view, in that he had declared Donnerschlag to be the only viable alternative, all that was necessary to spark off 6th Army's long overdue bid for freedom was for 57th Panzer Corps to force through the convoy of vital supplies to restore the beleaguered army's mobility.

However, half-an-hour after the dispatch of Manstein's order, the Nazi die-hard Arthur Schmidt made a further report over the teleprinter link which proved to be the first of a number of reservations which led Manstein to doubt that Paulus had any real intention of breaking out *en masse* without Hitler's permission:

Today's combat activities have contained the mass of our tanks and part of the infantry forces (from concentrating for the break-out) in defensive action.... Much fuel and ammunition was used up from our reserves intended for the thrust (to link up with Hoth).... Only when these forces have ceased to be tied down in defensive fighting can a break-out be launched. Earliest date 22 December.[18]

Early on the following morning Paulus began a tour of the crisis points of the Kessel. Throughout the day (20 December) heavy fighting took place in many sectors, as the Soviets began to tighten the pressure on 6th Army. That afternoon Schmidt made another discouraging report over the teleprinter link:

As a result of losses during the past few days manpower situation on the western flank and in Stalingrad exceedingly tight. Penetrations can be cleared up only by drawing upon the forces earmarked for Wintergewitter. In the event of major penetrations, let alone breakthroughs, our Army reserves, in particular the tanks, have to be employed if the Kessel is to be held.... We request that we are not ordered to form up (for the break-out) until it is certain that Hoth's relief force reaches the area around Businovka (a mere 10 miles south of the Kessel).... The situation would be somewhat different if it were certain that Wintergewitter would be immediately followed by Donnerschlag. In this case we might put up with local penetrations on the other flanks, provided they do not endanger the retreat of the Army as a whole. We would then be much stronger for the breakthrough toward the south, because we could concentrate numerous local reserves from all fronts in the south.[19]

Here was the nub of the matter: the complete evacuation of the Kessel could only be brought about by the instigation of Wintergewitter, which in turn depended for its implementation on the 57th Panzer Corps forcing a corridor through to 6th Army. But as long as Hoth's tanks remained pinned down on the Mishkova by the Second Guards and the reformed and reinforced Fifty-first Armies, Wintergewitter and consequently Donnerschlag were dead letters. This vicious circle could only be broken if permission for Donnerschlag was obtained from Hitler.

During the evening of Tuesday, 22 December, Zeitzler actually thought he had finally obtained this vital permission from the Führer. Zeitzler records that:

I believed that I had brought Hitler round to my way of thinking, for he said: 'Very well then, draft a message for Paulus asking him how far he can get if he is ordered to break out.'

I sighed with relief and, lest Hitler should change his mind, immediately drafted the signal in Hitler's presence, which I then gave him to sign. He read it, picked up a pencil, and inserted the words: the condition being that you continue to hold the line of the Volga. This clearly altered the whole purpose and nature of the proposed operation. On occasions such as this I sometimes felt that I was being driven insane. In any case, the message was sent off, and Paulus's reply came back almost at once. I forget the exact figure he gave, but I believe it was twenty or twenty-five miles – at any rate, a shorter distance than that which separated him from Hoth's vanguards (35 miles as the crow flies).

At the next day's afternoon conference (23 December), which was attended by a large group of officers, Hitler said: 'I have sent a radio message to Paulus asking him how far he could get, if ordered to break out. He has replied, saying that his troops could advance only twenty or twenty-five miles. So there is no purpose in ordering such an operation.'.... Hitler would not give way. In vain did I describe to him conditions inside the so-called fortress: the despair of the starving soldiers, their loss of confidence in the Supreme Command, the wounded expiring for lack of proper attention while thousands froze to death. He remained as impervious to arguments of this sort as to those others which I have advanced.[20]

On that same Wednesday afternoon Manstein spoke to Hitler over a direct telephone line linking Novocherkassk with the Wolfsschanze in Rastenburg, in a desperate effort to persuade Hitler where Zeitzler had failed. 'I fail to see what you are driving at,' was Hitler's cynical response. 'Paulus has only enough gasoline for fifteen to twenty miles at the most. He says himself that he can't break out at present.'

This was the final toll of the bell for the starving, bleeding, freezing men of 6th Army. The insane, nightmarish situation had now arisen whereby Paulus pleaded that whatever the technical requirements he was bound by an order of the Führer, while the Führer refused to rescind his order on the grounds that Paulus was raising technical objections!

On 22 December Hoth made his final effort to link up with 6th Army, hurling over sixty tanks against one regiment of the 24th Guards Rifle Division on the eastern flank of Malinovsky's Second Guards Army in the area of Vasilevka on the north bank of the Mishkova. This Soviet regiment consisted largely of ex-sailors from the Pacific Fleet drafted into the army who, to show their contempt for the bitter cold, cast off their padded jackets and fought in the sub-zero temperatures in their naval vests! By nightfall the battlefield was littered with burnt-out or immobilized German tanks, and Malinovsky was able to report to Stalin that: 'Today we finally halted the formidable enemy attack. Now we'll go over to the offensive ourselves.'

Any hope that Hoth still entertained of reaching 6th Army died on the following day (23 December) when Manstein was forced to transfer the 6th Panzer Division from the 57th Panzer Corps to the lower Chir, to prop up the southern flank of Armeegruppe Hollidt. To avoid encirclement by the three Russian armies advancing across its rear, Armeegruppe Hollidt had begun a hectic 90-mile retreat from the Chir all the way back to the Donets, 130 miles distant from the western flank of the Kessel.

The two panzer divisions and their flanking Rumanian divisions, which remained on the Mishkova, were by now completely burnt out. As a result of 13 days of heavy fighting (12-24 December) the relief force had suffered

8,000 casualties (killed and wounded), and had lost 160 tanks and 177 field-guns and mortars, while the 23rd and 17th Panzer Divisions were reduced to a mere 28 tanks between them.

The condition of the survivors was such that they were incapable of mounting an effective defence, let alone any further offensive action. Freezing in temperatures of minus 30° centigrade on open steppe devoid of cover, unable to sleep because their exposed positions were continually bombed around the clock and swept by hurricanes of fire laid down by 1,500 guns and mortars, short of fuel, food and ammunition, unable to bury their dead in the rock-hard frozen earth, the remnants of the relief force were not only exhausted but frozen into apathy by the pitiless cold which visibly sapped their remaining strength.

In such reduced straits the German and Rumanian troops were simply swept from the Mishkova, and back over the Aksay, when the Russian Second Guards, Fifty-first and the flank forces of the Fifth Shock Armies (a total of 149,000 men and 635 tanks) began their counter-offensive at 0800 on the morning of Christmas Eve, 1942. Within three days the Germans were forced all the way back to their start lines at Kotelnikovo. During the rout the Rumanian forces, which had lost all will to go on fighting, disintegrated and completely disappeared from the order of battle. Walter Kerr, who passed through Kotelnikovo a few days after it was captured by the triumphant Red Army recalls that:

In the centre of the town there was a small park, a block square, that had been turned into a German cemetery. On one side of the square there were neat graves outlined in brick, at the head of each a wooden cross on which were burned the name of a soldier, his date of birth, his date of death, his rank and serial number. The days of death were all in October and early November.

On another side of the square mounds of freshly turned earth covered hastily prepared graves. There were no lines of brick around them and the crosses were rudely fashioned. The days of death were late November and early December.

And then there was a gaping hole in which a soldier was being buried as the Russians entered the town. There were no bricks. There was no cross. No dirt covered his body. I saw him lying there. His feet were bare. His clothing had been removed except for a suit of woollen underwear that was sprinkled with snow that had fallen that morning.

There are many paths of glory. One of them stopped in Kotelnikovo at the end of a hopeless effort to rescue 6th Army.[21]

The retreat did not stop until what remained of Armeegruppe Hoth had been pressed back over the River Sal, sixty miles beyond Kotelnikovo, and some 125 miles from the Kessel. During the retreat the Germans lost another

8,000 men, killed, wounded or taken prisoner, bringing the total cost of Wintergewitter to more than 16,000 men — slightly more than half the number of the original force which launched the relief attack on the 12 December.

During the four days of fighting on the Mishkova the troops of 6th Army on the southern perimeter of the Kessel had been able to see the flashes of the guns and the coloured flares and signal rockets lighting up the night sky thirty-five miles to the south, and hear, when the wind was in the right direction, the rumble of gun-fire and explosions. Distant sights and sounds laden with the hope of salvation — hope that began to wither on Christmas Eve as the troops of the beleaguered army watched night after night as the flashes in the sky receded further and further away until finally they were seen no more. Troops on the western flank of the Kessel had also watched the hellish pyrotechnics of war lighting up the night sky on the lower Chir, only twenty-five miles distant, but the sky had also grown dark in that direction as Armeeabteilung Hollidt began to retreat westwards towards the Donets River — a darkness that spelled doom for 6th Army.

8

THE AGONY

'...and a foul and loathsome sore came upon the men who had the
mark of the beast and those who worshipped his image.'

(Revelation 16:2)

THE SLOUGH OF DESPOND

At midnight on Christmas Eve the night sky over the Kessel was suddenly
rent apart by the simultaneous explosions of thousands of multi-coloured
flares, which were fired by every unit trapped in Festung Stalingrad. This
brilliant display, saluting the Holy Season, lasted for several minutes, as the
white, green, red and orange flares drifted to earth, lighting up the
snow-covered steppe with their garish hues. The thoughts of the German
troops who watched this dazzling display are represented in the letters which
some wrote home. Karl Binder, the Deputy Chief Quartermaster of the 305th
Infantry Division, which was enmeshed in the ruins of the industrial district
of northern Stalingrad, wrote to his wife that:

During the past weeks all of us have begun to think about the end of
everything. The insignificance of everyday life pales against this, and
we have never been more grateful for the Christmas Gospel than in
these hours of hardship. Deep in one's heart one lives with the idea
of Christmas, the meaning of Christmas. It is a feast of love, salvation
and pity on mankind. We have nothing else here but the thought of
Christmas. It must and will tide us over grievous hours.... However
hard it may be, we shall do our utmost to master fate and try everything
in our power to defeat the sub-humanity that is wildly attacking us.
Nothing can shake our belief in victory, for we must win, if Germany
wants to live....

I have not received any mail from you for some time... there is a
terrible longing for some dear words from home at Christmas, but there
are more important things at present. We are men who know how to
bear everything. The main thing is that you and the children are all
right. Don't worry about me; nothing can happen to me any longer.
Today I have made my peace with God....

I give you all my love and a thousand kisses – I love you to my last breath. Affectionate kisses for the children. Be dear children and remember your father.[1]

In a letter to his parents a Catholic Army Chaplain wrote:

On the evening before the Holy Day, in a hut which was still fairly intact, eleven soldiers celebrated in quiet worship. It was not easy to find them in the herd of the doubting, hopeless, and disappointed. But those I found came happily and with a glad and open heart. It was a strange congregation which assembled to celebrate the birthday of the Christ-child. There are many altars in the wide world, but surely none poorer than ours here. Yesterday the box still held anti-aircraft shells; today my hand spread over it the field-grey tunic of a comrade whose eyes I closed last Friday in this very room. I wrote to his wife a letter of consolation. May God protect her.

I read my boys the Christmas story according to the Gospel of Luke, chapter 2, verses 1-17; gave them hard black bread as the holy sacrifice and sacrament of the altar, the true body of our Lord Jesus Christ, and entreated the Lord to have pity on them and to give them grace. I did not say anything about the fifth commandment (Thou shalt not kill). The men sat on footstools and looked up to me from large eyes in their starved faces. They were all young, except one, who was 51. I am very happy that I was permitted to console their hearts and give them courage. When it was over, we shook each other's hands, took down addresses, and promised to look up relatives and tell them about our Christmas Eve celebration in 1942, in case one of us should return home alive.

May God hold his hands over you, dear parents, for now the evening is at hand, and we will do well to set our house in order. We will go into the evening and the night calmly, if it is the will of the Lord of the world. But we do not look into a night without end. We give our life back into the hands of God; may He be merciful when the hour has come.[2]

In a letter to his wife and daughter a soldier wrote:

Just now the master sergeant told me that I cannot go home for Christmas. I told him that he has to keep his promise, and he sent me to the captain. The captain told me that others had wanted to go on leave for Christmas too, and that they too had promised it to their relatives without being able to keep the promise. And so it wasn't his fault that we couldn't go. We should be glad that we were still alive, the captain said, and the long trip wouldn't be good in the cold winter anyhow.

Dear Maria, you must not be angry now because I cannot come on leave. I often think of our house and our little Luise. I wonder if she can laugh already. Do you have a beautiful Christmas tree? We are supposed to get one also, if we don't move into other quarters. But I don't want to write too much about things here, otherwise you'll cry. I'll enclose a picture; I have bread in it; it is already three months old and was taken in Kharkov by a friend... Sometimes I am afraid we will not see each other again. Heiner from Krefeld told me that a man must not write this; it only frightens his relatives. But what if it's true!

Maria, dear Maria, I have only been beating around the bush. The master sergeant said that this would be the last mail because no more planes are leaving. I can't bring myself to lie. And now, nothing will probably ever come of my leave. If I could only see you just once more; how awful that is! When you light the candles, think of your husband in Stalingrad.[3]

Throughout the night of the 24/25 December the Russian artillery batteries surrounding the Kessel remained ominously quiet. All that was heard from the enemy lines was the monotonous voice relayed over Russian loudspeakers, which repeated over and over again with a mechanical regularity: 'Every seven seconds a German soldier dies in Russia. Stalingrad − mass grave.' After seven seconds were ticked off the announcement was repeated. The heartbeat of the encircled twenty-two divisions took its tempo from this ticking: henceforward they beat together.

In the early hours of Christmas Day a violent blizzard broke over the Kessel. Visibility dropped to less than ten yards as the snow was hurled across the steppe by fifty-mile-an-hour gusts. Then, suddenly, at 0500, to add to this onslaught of nature, thousands of Katyusha rockets and artillery shells screamed down on the German positions held by the 16th Panzer and the 60th Motorized Divisions on the north-eastern section of the Kessel. As the frozen ground heaved and trembled under the cannonade, swarms of Russian tanks and infantry loomed up in the swirling mists of snow. The attack was sudden and violent and the Russians, aided by the appalling visibility, were able to penetrate up to two miles in places. Opposing infantry fired at shadows indiscriminately in the blinding storm. German artillery batteries quickly ran out of ammunition and the gunners blew up their guns with the last shells before retreating to a second line of resistance. But the line held, although the Kessel reverberated to the clatter and roar of small arms and artillery fire until late in the afternoon, when the Russian attacks suddenly petered out, and all that was heard once more was the howling of the piercing wind and the endless, monotonous intoning of the loudspeakers: 'Every seven seconds a German soldier dies in Russia. Stalingrad − mass grave.' On

Christmas Day, 1942, 1,280 German soldiers died in the Kessel — one every sixty-seven seconds.

At 1735 General Schulz, Manstein's Chief of Staff, contacted General Schmidt at 6th Army HQ over the teleprinter:

+++Here General Schulz. Is General Schmidt there?

+++Yes sir, General Schmidt here.

+++Good evening Schmidt. We hope Christmas was not too bad for you and the entire army. All day today Armeegruppe Hoth was compelled to ward off heavy attacks by superior enemy infantry and armoured forces... Major casualties were inflicted on the enemy, but there were also considerable casualties on our side. Although bridgeheads in the Aksay section were compressed, the section itself could be held. According to reconnaissance results the enemy has assembled yet another armoured corps in the area and south-east of the Aksay... There can be no doubt that the enemy has concentrated major forces in the space between the Kessel and Armeegruppe Hoth.

...We have not yet received a decision from the Supreme Command of the Army (Hitler) regarding our proposals for further operations with the objective of relieving the Sixth Army. General von Richthofen told the Field-Marshal (Manstein) today that, if the weather should improve, he will be able, during the next few days, to supply the Sixth Army with 120 tons of supplies daily, and later on with 200 tons daily (the minimum requirement was 500 tons a day)... I wished, in particular today, I could give you better news... What is the situation on your side?

Schmidt dictated the stark facts to the operator, who typed them into the teleprinter:

+++Today we suffered fierce attacks against fronts of 16th Panzer Division and 60th Motorized Division which temporarily led to penetrations of between 1 and 2 kilometres in depth. On the whole the counter-attack was successful, but the Russians are still holding Hill 139.7 (an important commanding height in the area). We hope to regain it early tomorrow... The army's provisions and fuel have decreased dangerously. In view of an icy east wind and very low temperatures, we need a considerable increase of rations, otherwise we will have numerous men on the sick list from exhaustion and frostbite. We cannot manage with an air supply of 120 tons daily. Measures must therefore be taken to increase our supply rapidly or else you might just as well forget about Sixth army right away. Is Armeegruppe Hoth still in the Mishkova sector?

+++Armeegruppe Hoth holds the Aksay sector with small bridgeheads north of the river.

+++According to information we received today, some of the aircraft which were intended for our supply were again ordered to fly combat missions. In the opinion of the Commander-in-Chief (Paulus) this is very unwise. Please do not regard our supply situation too optimistically. We suggest that the Luftwaffe should rather supply us with bread than drop a few and not always effective bombs... I have nothing else.

+++Believe me, your supply situation is our greatest concern. I shall immediately and again report to the Field-Marshal on the situation and he is in constant contact with Richthofen and the Supreme Command of the Army, with the aim of increasing your supplies. We are aware of your desperate situation and shall do our very best to improve it. I have nothing else. Please give my regards to the Commander-in-Chief. Until tomorrow.

+++I have nothing else either, greetings − ending.[4]

Thus did the commanding officers of 6th Army learn that Hoth's relief attack had failed, a fact that quickly spread down through the ranks until every soldier in every unit, the length and breadth of the Kessel, was faced with the nightmare realization that Festung Stalingrad was probably going to become their grave. In a letter home one soldier wrote:

I was horrified when I saw the map. We are entirely alone, without help from outside. Hitler has left us in the lurch... Our position is to the north of the city. The men of my battery have some inkling of it too, but they don't know it as clearly as I do. So this is what the end looks like. Hannes and I will not surrender; yesterday, after our infantry had retaken a position, I saw four of our men who had been taken prisoner by the Russians [a reference to atrocities]. No, we shall not go into captivity. When Stalingrad has fallen, you'll hear and read about it. And then you'll know that I shall not come back.[5]

To round off the misery of Christmas Day, the men of the doomed army who had tuned into the radio broadcast from Germany on their short-wave sets were treated to the insult of Propaganda Minister Joseph Goebbels' 'Ring Broadcast'. After Goebbels had announced the name of a conquered city a chorus of male singers − supposedly German soldiers at that particular location − would sing a Christmas Carol or a popular song of the period. The whole thing was a sheer fabrication, as the choirs were all safely ensconced in broadcasting studios in Germany. When Goebbels announced Stalingrad and a rendition of '*Stille Nacht, Heilege Nacht*' floated over the air waves, the troops inside the Kessel, particularly those enduring the hell in the fire-blackened ruins of the city itself, could only stare at each other in horrified disbelief.

Christmas Day, 1942, was the thirty-third day of the encirclement of 6th

Army. During that period the Army had suffered 28,000 casualties, mostly from enemy action, but a large number had died suddenly from non-violent causes and without any detectable symptoms. On account of this phenomenon a pathologist – who an army doctor (Hans Dibold) serving in 6th Army described as a 'distinguished anatomist and a senior physician'[6] – was flown into the Kessel from Berlin to determine, by means of autopsies, how so many soldiers had died a sudden death without any apparent cause. Doctor Dibold relates that:

(After) the pathologist arrived, the corpses were thawed out in an operation bunker – an earth hole lined and faced with boards. The autopsies were made, and the findings were these:

Hardly a scrap of fatty tissue under the skin and around the internal organs, a watery-jellyish content in the intestines, all the organs very pale, the bone marrow not red and yellow but a glassy, quivering jelly, the liver blocked, the heart small and brown, the right ventricle and auricle greatly enlarged. This distension of the right ventricle was deemed to be the immediate cause of death. The basic complaint was hunger, exhaustion, and lack of warmth.

Much later we were again to observe this distension of the right ventricle in both living and dead. And we used to say, not without a touch of bitterness: 'The heart of the Sixth Army!'

Immediately after the pathologist's visit the doctors of the division were called together to discuss the result of the autopsies. I made a report to this conference, and drew a different conclusion: In peacetime we had found that weakness of the right ventricle was a common cause of the sudden death of old people. Here, in Stalingrad, it caused the sudden death of the German soldier's worn-out prematurely senile body.[7]

The average age of these 'prematurely senile' men was twenty-five! Nonetheless, why the 'sudden death' of inadequately clothed men who had lived for over a month in damp, frozen holes in the ground on a bare snow and fog shrouded steppe in the depths of a bitter Russian winter, on a meagre diet of less than 1,000 calories a day, should require a distinguished anatomist to determine beggars comprehension.

The conditions which 6th Army were enduring are described by Colonel H.R. Dingler, the Intelligence Officer of the 3rd Motorized Division, which was 'dug-in' on the south-western corner of the perimeter – the so-called 'Marinovka nose':

The weather conditions were bearable during the first days of December. Later on heavy snowfalls occurred and it turned bitterly cold. Life became a misery. Digging was no longer possible as the ground was frozen hard and if we had to abandon our lines this meant that in the new lines we would have no dug-outs or trenches. The heavy snow diminished our small gasoline supplies still further. The lorries stuck in the snow and the heavy going meant a larger consumption of gasoline. It grew colder and colder. The temperature remained at a steady 20 or 30 degrees below freezing point and it became increasingly difficult for aircraft to fly in.

Night after night we sat in our holes listening to the droning of the aircraft engines and trying to guess how many German machines were coming over and what supplies they would bring us. The supply position was very poor from the beginning, but none of us thought that hunger would become a permanent thing.

We were short of all sorts of supplies. We were short of bread and, worse, of artillery ammunition, and worst of all, of gasoline. Gasoline meant everything to us. As long as we had gasoline we were able to keep warm. As there was no wood to be found anywhere in the steppe, firewood had to be fetched from the city of Stalingrad by lorry. As we had so little gasoline, trips to the city to fetch firewood had to be limited to the bare minimum. For this reason we felt very cold in our holes in the earth.

Until Christmas, 1942, the daily bread ration issued to every man was 100 grammes. After Christmas the ration was reduced to 50 grammes per head. Later on only those in the forward line received 50 grammes per day. No bread was issued to men in regimental headquarters and upwards. The others were given watery soup which we tried to improve by making use of bones obtained from the corpses of horses we dug up. As a Christmas treat the army allowed the slaughtering of four thousand of the available horses. My division, being a motorized formation, had no horses and was therefore particularly hard hit, as the horseflesh we received was strictly rationed. The infantry units were better off as they were able to do some 'illegal' slaughtering.[8]

On Boxing Day Paulus was forced to cut the scale of the already meagre rations being issued to the troops. The starvation diet now consisted of two ounces of bread per day per man – one portion of soup without fat for lunch and one can of tinned meat, when available, for the evening meal or another portion of watery soup in lieu (invariably the latter is what the majority received). Painfully aware that such stringent rations were striking a mortal blow at the stamina and morale of his freezing men, Paulus complained to Manstein that his entire army was on the brink of extinction. This fact, passed over the teleprinter link, was made by Colonel von Kunowski, 6th Army's Chief Quartermaster:

+++Today (26 December), by 1700, we received 38 Ju-52s and 3

He-111 (transports), carrying seventy tons, among them food, mainly bread. We have only enough bread for two days, edible food for one day, fat is gone already. Complete food supplies must be flown in immediately, in balanced proportions, for 250,000 men.... We depend only on what arrives by air.... We are also out of fuel, tomorrow we will give out the last 20 cubic meters.... I beg you by all means to see to it that tomorrow 200 tons be flown in, 150 tons of which is food, and 50 cubic meters in fuel. Otherwise we shall not make it.

+++(answer) We shall do our utmost.

+++(Kunowski's final comment was) No more from here. I have never sat so deep in shit. Kind regards.[9]

This was to be one of the last messages passed over the teleprinter link, for just after Christmas Soviet tanks overran and captured the decimeter relays on the steppe east of Manstein's HQ which had maintained the fragile semi-personal means of contact between Gumrak and Novocherkassk. The rupture of this umbilical cord of effective communication was an ominous augury for Paulus and his staff. Indeed, one of the General's aides, Captain Winrich Behr, began to wonder if Hitler was using 6th Army as a sacrificial pawn in his maniacal game of chess, with the object of tying down as many Russian units as possible to allow Manstein to stabilize the torn and reeling front line.

Behr voiced this nagging possibility in a letter to Major Nikolaus von Below, Hitler's adjutant at the Wolfsschanze:

At the moment we feel somewhat betrayed and sold out. To wait and to persevere is a matter which goes without saying, even if no further orders come through. I just want to tell you quite simply that there is nothing here to eat, with the exception of a few thousand horses, which may last until January, but with which one cannot alone feed an army of 250,000 men. Now there is only enough bread left for tomorrow. With my knowledge of the German soldier we have to foresee that their physical resistance will be lowered to the point that the moment will come when each many will say: 'I don't give a shit about anything,' and will either freeze to death or be captured. The men have the desire to hold fast and it is incomprehensible how they have held out so far. Heating is a very big problem. Everything has to be fetched from Stalingrad, but there is no gasoline available for that. In other words, the cat eats its own tail all around. It may have been decided in view of the situation to give us up, which is not unthinkable — although it is hard to fathom the consequences....

I write this to you so you don't think that we are griping unnecessarily. What I am telling you is based not only on my personal experience, but also on messages and daily conversations with friends at the front (of the Kessel). It is as bad as I say it is. No miracle on the steppe can help us here, only good old Aunt Ju (Ju-52s) and the He-111s (transport planes) if they come – and come often.... Here at the top, especially on days like this one, looking into an empty barrel, the responsibility weighs heavy.[10]

Behr was perceptive, because Hitler now fully intended to sacrifice 6th Army. Faced with the bald fact that it was now impossible 'to re-occupy the positions held prior to the Russian counter-offensive', and stubbornly maintaining that his original decision to hold Stalingrad had been the correct one in the circumstances, he now justified himself by arguing that, by continuing to hold Stalingrad, 6th Army was tying down large Russian forces which were, consequently, prevented from carrying out large-scale operations elsewhere. The whole *raison d'etre* of 6th Army, in Hitler's brutal game of strategic chess, was now to buy time, to allow Manstein to create a new and stable front line. He was, Zeitzler recalls, 'quite unmoved by the mounting tragedy in the Kessel.'

During Christmas week a number of the transport planes delivering supplies into the Kessel had been crammed with nothing other than cumbersome Christmas trees! Festive decorations had been given priority over food, in a situation where men were starving to death! But hunger, gnawing, agonizing hunger, was only one of the nails crucifying 6th Army. Wounds and frostbite were also taking a fearsome toll, as extracts from these letters written by two wretches at Stalingrad portray:

I am in the field hospital in Gumrak, waiting to be transported home by plane. Although I am waiting with great longing, the date is always changed. That I will be coming home is a great joy for me and for you, my dear Elise. But the condition in which I'll get home won't be any joy to you. I am in complete despair when I think of lying before you as a cripple. But you must know sometime that my legs were shot off. I'll be quite honest in writing about it. The right leg is totally shattered and amputated below the knee. The left one is amputated in the thigh. The doctor thinks that with prosthesis I should be able to get around like a healthy man.... Over eighty men are lying in this tent; but outside there are countless others. Through the tent you can hear their screaming and moaning, and no one can help them.... Next to me against the wall of the tent lies a soldier from Breslau who has lost an arm and his nose, and he told me that he wouldn't need any more handkerchiefs. When I asked him what he would do if he had to cry, he answered me, 'No one here, you and me included, will have a chance to cry any more. Soon others will be crying over us.'[11]

It is well that this letter should reach you, and that you know, in case

I should turn up some day, that my hands are ruined and have been since the beginning of December. I lost the little finger on my left hand, but worse still is the loss of the three middle fingers of my right hand through frostbite. I can hold my drinking cup only with my thumb and little finger. I am quite helpless; only when one has lost his fingers does one notice how much they are needed for the simplest tasks. The thing I can still do best with my little finger is shoot. Yes, my hands are wrecked. I can't very well spend the rest of my life shooting, simply because I'm no good for anything else. Perhaps I could make out as a game warden? But this is gallows humour; I only write it to calm myself.[12]

'Every seven seconds a German soldier dies in Russia. Stalingrad — mass grave.' Moscow time was two hours ahead of German clocks, and at precisely 2200, according to German watches, on Thursday 31 December, 1942, the icy darkness was suddenly rent by thousands of brilliant orange and red flashes, followed in a second by an ear-splitting roar of thunder, as the Russian artillery surrounding the Kessel celebrated with a fifteen-minute bombardment to welcome in a New Year that promised glory for the Soviet Union.

An hour and forty-five minutes later — midnight by German time — someone in the 24th Panzer Division, on the north-eastern front of the encirclement, fired a volley of tracer into the night sky. Others spontaneously followed suit, despite the acute shortage of ammunition, and a flickering band of bright yellow tracer was fired skywards by unit after unit, until the whole perimeter of the Kessel became a huge circle of glowing lights climbing lazily towards the heavens. Thus did 6th Army welcome in 1943 — a New Year shorn of hope. Destiny was knocking loudly on the door.

THE ROAD TO PERDITION

On the morning of 1 January, 1943, Hitler sent a New Year greetings message to Paulus:

To you and your brave army I send, also in the name of the German people, my warmest New Year's wishes. I am aware of the difficulty of your responsibility. The heroic attitude of your troops is appreciated. You and your soldiers should begin the New Year with a strong faith that I and the High Command of the Wehrmacht will use all strength to relieve the defenders of Stalingrad and make their long wait the greatest triumph of German military history.[13]

Tagged on was a message which Hitler ordered to be conveyed to every soldier in the Kessel: 'The men of the Sixth Army have my word that everything is being done to extricate them.'[14] This bare-faced lie cut no ice with the majority. Even those of strong Nazi persuasion had lost faith in the

Führer's word, as evinced in a letter a former member of the Hitler Youth wrote to his sister:

Well, now you know that I shall never return. Break it to our parents gently. I am deeply shaken and doubt everything. I used to be strong and full of faith [in Hitler]; now I am small and without faith. I will never know many of the things that happen here; but the little that I have taken part in is already so much that it chokes me. No one can tell me any longer that the men died with the words '*Deutschland*' or '*Heil Hitler*' on their lips. There is plenty of dying, no question of that; but the last word is 'mother' or the name of someone dear, or just a cry for help. I have seen hundreds fall and die already, and many belonged to the Hitler Youth as I did; but all of them, if they still could speak, called for help or shouted a name which could not help them anyway.

The Führer made a firm promise to bail us out of here; they read it to us.... Even now I still believe it, because I have to believe in something. If it is not true, what else could I believe in? I would no longer need spring, summer, or anything that gives pleasure. So leave me my faith [in Hitler], dear Greta; all my life, at least eight years of it, I believed in the Führer and his word. It is terrible how they doubt here, and shameful to listen to what they say without being able to reply, because they have the facts on their side.

If what we were promised is not true, then Germany will be lost, for in that case no more promises can be kept. Oh, these doubts, these terrible doubts, if they could only be cleared up soon![15]

What scant vestige of hope remained amongst the doomed men, now rested entirely on the air-lift. During the ten-day period, 12 to 21 December, while Wintergewitter was under way, the Luftwaffe succeeded in reaching an all-time high in the amount of supplies flown into the Kessel. Yet the tonnage delivered was still woefully inadequate; the total of 1,377 tons (an average of 137.7 tons per day) represented only 27.54 per cent of the minimum requirement necessary to sustain 6th Army. By 21 December, the twenty-seventh day of the air-lift, the cumulative deficit resulting from the failure to deliver the minimum requirement of 500 tons a day amounted to 10,687 tons.

The relative improvement in the rate of deliveries during this ten-day period was aided by a temporary abatement in the fog and blizzards, which made flying hazardous or impossible, and a large number of Soviet aircraft being diverted from the interdiction of the transports to help repulse the relief attack by Armeegruppe Hoth. For example in the four days 18 to 21 December alone, the Russian 8th Air Army flew 758 sorties against German tanks and infantry.

The situation began to deteriorate again on 22 December, when dense freezing fog closed in once more over the airfields and the flight paths to the Kessel. To make matters worse, within a period of nine days the Russians overran the two main bases of the supply operation situated at Tatsinskaya and Morozovskaya.

By 23 December the Soviet 24th Tank Corps (54 tanks strong), of the First Guards Army, had reached a position only eight miles to the north of Tatsinskaya, having advanced 150 miles since the launch of Malyi Saturn eight days earlier. General Fiebig, in command of the air-lift, immediately requested permission for the airfield to be abandoned, but von Richthofen, acting under instructions from Göring that the airfield was to be held until it actually came under direct enemy fire, had no choice but to deny Fiebig's request. At stake was the whole fleet of Ju-52 transports – some 180 aircraft – all grounded at Tatsinskaya on account of dense fog, which, for all their inadequacies, represented the backbone of the supply operation.

At 0520 on Christmas Eve the first Russian shells began falling on the northern perimeter of the airfield. Two Ju-52s were hit and exploded in flames, while the rest began frantically revving up their engines ready for the order to take off. But, unwilling to order the evacuation on his own responsibility, Fiebig wasted valuable time trying desperately to contact von Richthofen over the telephone to obtain the vital order from higher authority, unaware that the telephone exchange in the nearby village had been destroyed by Russian shelling.

At 0525 a Volkswagen command car came racing over the airfield with Fliegerkorps VIII Chief of Staff Colonel Lothar von Heinemann aboard. With Captain Jahne and Lieutenant Drube he had till now been manning Corps HQ in the village. After alerting the air crews, he had ordered those of the ground personnel for whom there was no room in the waiting aircraft to assemble for departure on the airfield's southern perimeter. He himself had reached the airfield just as the first Ju-52s went up in smoke. No one knew, in the shifting fog, where the shells came from, and the sounds of battle were drowned by the howl of aero-engines. Men who till now had been quietly waiting for orders, suddenly started rushing wildly about and crowding the aircraft. Panic had taken over.

Bursting into the shelter, Heinemann reported all this to Fiebig. 'Herr General,' he panted, 'you must take action! You must give permission to take off!' 'For that I need Luftflotte [Richthofen's] authority, cancelling existing orders,' Fiebig countered. 'In any case it's impossible to take off in this fog!' Drawing himself up, Heinemann stated flatly: 'Either you take that risk or every unit on the airfield will be wiped out. All the transport units for Stalingrad, Herr General.

The last hope of the surrounded 6th Army!' Fiebig yielded. 'Right!' he said, turning to the *Gruppen* [squadron] commanders. 'Permission to take off. Try to withdraw in the direction of Novocherkassk.' It was 0530.[16]

With their engines roaring and snow cascading from their wheels in fountains, the Ju-52s began taxiing for take-off in dense fog which reduced visibility to fifty yards. Two, taking off from completely different directions, collided in the middle of the airfield, burning wreckage being hurled in all directions. Others taxied into each other, tangling their wings or smashing their tail units. Heavily laden with vital servicing equipment and boxes of food and ammunition and canisters of fuel destined for Stalingrad, most of the Ju-52s, in hair-raising escapes, managed to lift off the ground just as the Russian tanks, guns firing, began swarming onto the airfield. One Ju-52, on the point of lift-off, collided with a T-34 tank, both disappearing in a blinding sheet of flame and a roaring explosion.

In all 108 Ju-52 transports and 16 Ju-86 medium bombers managed to lift clear of the unholy mess at Tatsinskaya. The madness of Goring's order not to abandon the airfield until enemy fire actually started falling on the base, and the supineness of Richthofen and Fiebig in not ignoring this insanity, cost the transport fleet 72 Ju-52s and nearly all of the servicing equipment and spare parts. The consequences, which were not long in making themselves felt, were borne by the freezing, starving men cut off on the steppe.

Twenty-seven miles to the east of Tatsinskaya the medium-bomber base at Morozovskaya remained in operation for another nine days, until it was eventually overrun by the armoured vanguard of the Third Guards Army on the 2nd January.

As with the previous débâcle, Colonel Ernst Kühl, in command of the base at Morozovskaya, was forbidden to evacuate the airfield until enemy shell fire made it absolutely imperative. This caused the embittered von Richthofen to comment in his diary that the Reichsmarschall should take over the command of Luftflotte IV, 'since he always asserts [to Hitler] that the situation neither here nor in Stalingrad is as strained as is reported. Motto: The optimistic leader at the place over which he is optimistic.'[17]

Immediately after the fall of the two air-bases, the Ju-52s were transferred to an airfield at Salsk, some 150 miles to the south-east of Kotelnikovo, while the He-111 and Ju-86 medium bombers were transferred to Novocherkassk. However, the relentless westward push of the Soviet armies soon caused these bases to be abandoned, causing the medium bombers to move back to bases at Voroshilovgrad, Stalino and Konstantinovka, and the Ju-52s to an improvised landing field at Zverevo. The latter site was a snow-covered cornfield lying along the railway line north of Shakhty, and a take-off and landing strip, approximately 2,000 feet long and 100 feet wide, was created by hard-packing the snow into a flat, fairly solid surface. As there were no heavy rollers available, the native population was rounded up and put to the task. There were no billeting facilities whatsoever in the vicinity for the exhausted air-crews and ground personnel, and they had to live in snow huts in the sub-zero temperatures until a sufficient number of tents could be flown in.

The dislocation caused by the sudden shifting of bases, along with the loss of a large number of aircraft, servicing equipment and spare parts, caused an inevitable decrease in the amount of supplies flown into the encirclement. Moreover, the Ju-52s were now operating at the very limit of their operational range. Zverevo was 187 miles from Pitomnik, and this increased the distance of the round trip by 110 miles (Tatsinskaya was only 132 miles from Pitomnik). The medium bombers were even worse off. Operating from bases 200 to 275 miles from the Kessel (Morozovskaya was only 105 miles from the Kessel), the distance of their round trip was increased by between 120 to 286 miles. These distances were increased further by the aircraft being compelled to make time-consuming detours, to avoid a continuous line of Russian flak emplacements which had been arrayed along the most direct flight paths to Pitomnik. The effects of the longer flights were cumulative. The aircraft had to carry more fuel and this led to a corresponding reduction in available cargo capacity; and the longer the aircraft were in the air the less the number of flights which could be made, and the greater the maintenance and repair time needed to keep them airworthy.

To add to the difficulties heavy snowstorms, which raged during late December and early January, rendered the improvised airfield at Zverevo useless for days on end. Each of the Ju-52s had to be dug out of the deep snow drifts individually after each storm, and the fresh snow on the landing strip had to be hard-pressed before operations could resume.

The effect of all this was that the rate of delivery to the beleaguered 6th Army, dropped from the daily average of 137.7 tons for the period 12 to 21 December, down to an average of only 105.4 tons per day for the twenty-one day period 22 December to 11 January. The total tonnage flown in during the later period amounted to 2,214 tons, which was only 21.10 per cent of the minimum requirement which should have been delivered (10,500 tons). This increased the cumulative deficit to a total of 18,973 tons.

What was delivered was often not what was needed by the starving army. Moist rye bread, which froze solid and had to be thawed out before it could be eaten, was not an ideal ration for men who had very little or no fuel to make fires. It does not seem to have occurred to anyone that concentrated dried foods, which were supplied to U-boat crews, would have been far more space-efficient to transport, and would have been far more nourishing than frozen meat, rye bread and vegetables whose total weight was three parts water. And this was only one aspect of the inefficiency:

On one day five tons of sweets and a dozen cases of contraceptives arrived; on another two planes were loaded up entirely with marjoram and pepper, to a total of four tons. Cumbersome and unusable engineering gear would be flown in; 200,000 leaflets arrived for the Propaganda Department, a ton of cellophane protective covers for hand grenades, labels, dried herbs and much else. The sweets could at a pinch be issued to the troops, but they had no use for the other items though the Supply Branch did suggest that the pepper was perhaps intended for use in hand-to-hand fighting. It was impossible to pin the responsibility for those ridiculous consignments on any one man. Although there was permanent wireless contact with the Army Group's Chief Quartermaster, he naturally could not check every plane before it left.[18]

Such were the errors and inadequacies that paved the 6th Army's road to perdition.

On the morning of 9 January seven of the huge, four-engined FW-200 Condors landed at Pitomnik. 'The crews were fortunate to land on snow; it cooled the tyres, which otherwise would probably have burst from the strain imposed by the overloaded aircraft. For their cargoes were four or five tons in excess of their permissible carrying capacity of nine tons.'[19] The appearance of these giant aircraft stirred new hope. 'If the Luftwaffe could send in giant machines like these, men thought, perhaps the army was not lost after all.'[20]

This hope was short lived, because within days only two of the Condors remained in operation. One was shot down on a return flight from the Kessel with twenty-one wounded on board; another was badly damaged by flak; and three had to be withdrawn from service on account of mechanical failures. At Stalino airfield, where the Condors were based, there were no hangers and the huge aircraft, trouble-prone at the best of times, had to be serviced in the open in temperatures of 20 to 30 degrees below zero. The parkas protecting the engines froze and broke like glass, and the maintenance teams had to work in icy snowstorms without even screens to protect them against the howling, bitter wind. A mobile hot-air blower, designed to warm up the aircraft engines, had to be constantly used to thaw out mechanics who literally became frozen fast to the machines they were trying to service and repair. However, the two Condors which remained in operation went on supplying the doomed army until the bitter end.

Two Ju-290s – 'Great flying furniture vans' – with a cargo capacity of 10 tons and room to fly out 80 wounded each on the return flights, were also conscripted onto the Stalingrad run, with disastrous results. One, flown by Flight-Captain Hanig, crashed while taking off from Pitomnik at 0045 on 13 January. The four-engined Ju-290 was carrying a full load of wounded men, and seconds after becoming airborne it suddenly reared up into an almost vertical position, rolled over and crashed. Only one NCO survived, and he reported that as a result of the rapid acceleration as the aircraft lifted off the ground the wounded slid back to the stern, making the plane so tail-heavy that it became uncontrollable. The second Ju-290 was attacked by Soviet fighters over the Kessel on its very first sortie, and was so badly shot up that it had to be withdrawn from service.

As a last resort to provide more aircraft, an attempt was made to utilize the seven prototypes of the new, as yet untried and fatally flawed, four-engined He-177 long-range bombers. This stratagem also proved disastrous. Apart from being virtually useless in a transport role (they had only a two-ton cargo capacity) design faults caused all seven to crash in flames, without any attributable enemy action, during the one and only mission they flew to Stalingrad!

The brief hope stirred by the appearance of the giant transports lay still-born amongst the wreckage of the Condors, Ju-290s and He-177s. Colonel Dingler recalls that:

> ...the aircraft crews did a job which can only be called superhuman.
> It is certainly not the crews who should be blamed for the inefficient way in which our supply problem was handled.... At about this time we began to discuss what to do if the worst were to happen. We talked about captivity. We talked about the question of committing suicide. We discussed the question of defending what we held to the last bullet but one.[21]

ALL ROADS LEAD TO PITOMNIK

The scant supplies received by 6th Army all flowed through Pitomnik airfield in the centre of the Kessel. For 29,000 wounded men Pitomnik was also the gateway to salvation from the hell that was Stalingrad: this being the total number that were flown out by the transport planes on their return flights. The airfield was also the way out for 7,000 'specialists' of all kinds – wireless operators, veterinary surgeons, blacksmiths, armourers, postal officials, bridge builders, meteorologists, amongst others – whose presence was no longer of any use in the Kessel, but who were urgently needed in other theatres of war.

But for thousands the roads that led to Pitomnik from all the compass points of the Kessel's perimeter were roads of agony and death. The acute shortage of fuel meant that only stretcher cases could be transported to the airfield in lorries and ambulances. The majority of the sick, the wounded and the victims of frostbite had to walk, and although the distance to Pitomnik from all points of the front line varied from between ten to fifteen miles, the exhausting journey on foot proved to be beyond the strength of many of the starving, freezing, bleeding, broken men with their multitude of wounds and illnesses, who took to the snow-covered, icy roads, which were constantly whipped by the biting, howling wind, and swept by Russian artillery and mortar fire, or machine-gunned and bombed by low-flying aircraft. Many of those hobbling along with death at their heels were so weak and ill that they were reduced, after only a few miles, to crawling on their hands and knees, yard by yard, mile after weary mile. Some with leg wounds or frost-bitten feet were supported by comrades, others were dragged along on tarpaulins or in ammunition cases.

Those who collapsed or were too exhausted to struggle on lay on the road sides waving their arms at passing lorries heading for Pitomnik, screaming and shouting for help, but few lorries stopped: they were already crammed to overflowing with wounded. Their appeals were short-lived, for lying immobilized they quickly and mercifully froze to death, the stiff bodies soon being buried from view by fresh snow storms. No man willingly drove over the snow-shrouded corpses, but in the dark or in blizzards the lorries would jolt over things that splintered and snapped beneath their wheels: frozen bones crack like glass. As the days passed the columns of misery grew longer and the number of corpses lining the roads increased.

The dead huddled close together, as though even in death they still sought warmth. And all the while those who were still a little bit alive hurried or walked or crawled past these little groups of corpses on the road to safety. A few thousand managed to make it, but 14,000 fell by the way, on the death roads to Pitomnik, frozen by the icy wind, their life blood congealed upon gangrenous wounds, their bodies crushed beneath the wheels of the endless procession of fleeing vehicles. No man listened to their prayers or heeded their curses.[22]

Those that made it to Pitomnik found cold succour, and few or no drugs to relieve their pain, in the blue hospital tents that lined the airfield. Here they were classified according to the seriousness of their condition, and had tags tied to their chests nicknamed 'reprieve tickets'. Outside the tents countless bodies, stacked up in neat rows, lay unburied: the frozen earth was too hard to dig graves.

From these tents those who could walk or crawl made their own way to the planes. The others were carried on stretchers. They were supposed to take their turn to be flown out according to their number on a roster, but it seldom worked that way. All too often those wounded capable of walking would storm the aircraft in a frantic attempt to get aboard, many being shot out of hand by officers trying to maintain order. Lieutenant Dieter recalls one harrowing incident:

> There were about thirty of us on the plane, mostly wounded, with stretcher cases piled on top of each other all over the floor. There were also some people, couriers and the like, who were quite unharmed — the sort of people who always, it seems, get themselves out of the tightest scrape by the use of their wits. We started trundling across the ground at an ever increasing speed, with clouds of snow blowing back from the propellers; at intervals one wheel would drop in a crater with a terrible crash. Then to our horror the engines cut and we could feel the brakes coming on. The pilot turned round and started taxiing back.... A lieutenant of the Luftwaffe came through and said that we could not get airborne because of the ground, and that we would have to shed about 2,000 kilos... twenty men would have to get out. At once there was the most terrific din, everybody shouting at once, one claimed that he was travelling by order of the Army Staff, another from the SS that he had important Party documents, many others who cried about their families, that their children had been injured in air raids, and so on. Only the men on the stretchers kept silent, but their terror showed in their faces.[23]

There were cases when desperate soldiers were taken aloft hanging on to the undercarriage or tail wheels of aircraft; they all fell to their deaths.

Pitomnik was the heart-beat of 6th Army, the only airfield in the Kessel capable of receiving the supplies flown in, and the only hope of salvation for the sick and wounded. The beating of this heart, weak yet imperative, was about to cease, violently and abruptly.

THE BEGINNING OF THE END

When the Soviet pincers closed on 6th Army on 23 November, Stalin immediately ordered that the encircled German forces should be destroyed off the march by the seven Soviet armies forming the ring around the Kessel. When a week of bitter fighting failed to crack the perimeter defence, and it became clear that more than three times the numbers of Germans had been trapped than first estimates indicated, Stalin postponed the operation until 18 December, by which time the investing armies would be reinforced by the Second Guards Army. However, when Second Guards had to be diverted to the Mishkova River to block Armeegruppe Hoth's attempt to relieve 6th Army, Stalin was forced to postpone Koltso yet again.

On 19 December Stalin ordered General Voronov, the Stavka 'co-ordinator' of the South-western and Voronezh Fronts, which were exploiting the success of Malyi Saturn, to wind up his work and prepare a new operational plan for the liquidation of 6th Army, which was to be accomplished in the space of five to six days. Voronov was to present the plan no later than 21 December.

Voronov's first act was to unify all seven armies on the perimeter into one force. To this end the three armies of the Stalingrad Front investing the Kessel (Fifty-seventh, Sixty-fourth and Sixty-second Armies) were subordinated to Rokossovsky's Don Front.

Voronov spent some time inspecting the German defence positions and the Soviet forces at his disposal, finding that most of the Russian divisions were down to half their normal strength. The conclusion he reached was that the five to six days stipulated in which to wipe out 6th Army was totally unreasonable, and that in view of the necessity of reinforcing the investing armies the operation could not start until 6 January. The plan he submitted, which envisaged three armies launching an attack from the western flank and advancing on an easterly axis towards Stalingrad with the object of splitting the Kessel in two, came in for some rough handling by the Stavka. In a signal sent to Voronov on 28 December, the Stavka complained that:

> The main shortcoming of the plan you presented for Koltso lies in the fact that the main and the supporting attacks diverge from each other and this factor might prejudice the success of the operation.

> In the Stavka's view, your main task in the initial stage must be the splitting up and annihilation of the western grouping of the encircled enemy forces in the Kravtsov − Baburkin − Marinovka − Karpovka area with the object of turning the axis of the main attack [launched from the west] south from the Dimitrevka − Baburkin area into the Karpovka railway station district, and to direct a supporting attack by the Fifty-seventh Army from the Kravtsov − Skliarov area [on the southern front of the Kessel] to link up with the main attack, so that both join at the Karpovkaya railway station [to put it succinctly the intention was to encircle the German forces in the Marinovka 'nose' on the south-western corner of the Kessel].

> Simultaneously, a secondary attack mounted by the Sixty-sixth Army [on the north-eastern corner of the Kessel] advancing through Orlovka towards the Krasny Oktyaber factory [in northern Stalingrad] must be organized to link up with an attack mounted by Sixty-second Army [holding the slender bridgeheads in the city] with the object of cutting off the factory district from the main enemy forces.

> The Stavka instructs you to revise your plan on the basis of these foregoing suggestions. The Stavka confirms the date for opening operations (6 January, 1943) as presented by you in your plan. The first phase of the operation will terminate 5 − 6 days after its

commencement. The plan for the second stage of operations will be presented through the General Staff on 9 January, utilizing the results of the first stage.[24]

Although he had to redraft his original plan, Voronov had not only succeeded in obtaining a more realistic timetable, he also obtained substantial artillery reinforcements and 20,000 infantry from Stavka reserve with which to strengthen his depleted divisions. However, by the morning of 3 January Voronov found himself faced with a dilemma. It had become apparent that the reinforcements in men and artillery, and the huge ammunition stocks required for the pre-attack barrage, would not be assembled in time, leaving Voronov with the unenviable choice of risking attacking on time without his forces being fully concentrated, or running foul of Stalin by asking for a four-day postponement. He opted for the latter which incurred a stinging rebuke from Stalin over the V Ch line: 'You will sit it out so long down there that the Germans will take you and Rokossovsky prisoner. You don't think about what can be done, only about what can't be done. We need to be finished as quickly as possible there and you deliberately hold things up.'[25] Nonetheless Voronov was grudgingly granted his four days and Koltso was re-scheduled to open on 10 January, 1943.

In the meantime Voronov, in an attempt to expedite matters, conceived the idea of sending an ultimatum to 6th Army either to surrender or be wiped out. Stavka approved the text submitted by Voronov, and on 7 January radio contact was established with 6th Army HQ to arrange the passage of emissaries. Consequently, at 1000 on the morning of 8 January two Soviet officers, Major Smyslov and Captain Dyatlenko, under a white flag approached a sector of the front manned by the 2nd Battalion of the 64th Panzer Grenadier Regiment (3rd Motorized Division). Blindfolded with bandages they carried already prepared in their pockets, the two officers were taken to the 2nd Battalion's command post, where they presented the ultimatum to Major Willig, the battalion commander. Willig thanked them, and after allowing the Soviet officers to return to their own lines, he despatched the ultimatum to 6th Army HQ at Gumrak by courier. The offer, typed on Stavka notepaper, was a mixture of 20th century psychological warfare and 18th century military punctilio:

To the Commander-in-Chief of the German 6th Army, Colonel-General Paulus, or his representative, and to all the officers and men of the German units now besieged in Stalingrad.

The Sixth German Army, formations of the Fourth Panzer Army, and those units sent to reinforce them have been completely encircled since the 23rd of November, 1942.

The soldiers of the Red Army have sealed this German Army Group within an unbreakable ring. All hopes of the rescue of your troops by a German offensive from the south or south-east have proved vain. The German units hastening to your assistance were defeated by the Red Army, and the remnants of that force are now withdrawing to Rostov.

The German air transport fleet, which brought you a starvation ration of food, munitions and fuel, has been compelled by the Red Army's successful and rapid advance repeatedly to withdraw to airfields more distant from the encircled troops. It should be added that the German air transport fleet is suffering enormous losses in machines and crews at the hands of the Russian Air Force. The help they can bring to the besieged forces is rapidly becoming illusory.

The situation of your troops is desperate. They are suffering from hunger, sickness and cold. The cruel Russian winter has scarcely yet begun. Hard frosts, cold winds and blizzards still lie ahead. Your soldiers are unprovided with winter clothing and are living in appalling sanitary conditions.

You, as Commander-in-Chief, and all the officers of the encircled forces know well that there is for you no real possibility of breaking out. Your situation is hopeless, and any further resistance senseless.

In view of the desperate situation in which you are placed, and in order to save unnecessary bloodshed, we propose that you accept the following terms of surrender:

1. All the encircled German troops, headed by yourself and your staff, shall cease to resist.

2. You will hand over to such persons as shall be authorized by us all members of your armed forces, all war materials and all army equipment in an undamaged condition.

3. We guarantee the safety of all officers and men who cease to resist, and their return at the end of the war to Germany or to any other country to which these prisoners of war may wish to go.

4. All personnel of units which surrender may retain their military uniforms, badges of rank, decorations, personal belongings and valuables and, in the case of high-ranking officers, their swords.

5. All officers, non-commissioned officers and men who surrender will immediately receive normal rations.

6. All those who are wounded, sick or frost-bitten will be given medical treatment.

Your reply is to be given in writing by ten o'clock, Moscow time, the 9th January, 1943. It must be delivered by your personal representative, who is to travel in a car bearing a white flag along the road that leads to the Konny railway siding at Kotluban station. Your representative will be met by fully authorized Russian officers in

District B, 500 metres south-east of siding 564 at 1000 on the 9th January, 1943.

Should you refuse our offer that you lay down your arms, we hereby give you notice that the forces of the Red Army and the Red Air Force will be compelled to proceed with the destruction of the encircled German troops. The responsibility for this will lie with you.

The document was signed by Voronov on behalf of the Stavka, and by Rokossovsky as C-in-C Don Front. It was remarkably free of all communist rhetoric, and contained considerable psychological persuasiveness with its references to the horrors of the winter still to come and the promise of food and medical treatment. No less persuasive was the old-fashioned touch echoing the wars of the 18th century with the appeal to the military courtesy of senior officers being allowed to keep their swords.

Paulus immediately had the complete text of the ultimatum transmitted to the Wolfsschanze, requesting freedom of action to accept or reject the Russian offer as he saw fit. Hitler refused point-blank, replying to Paulus that 'every day the Army holds out helps the entire Eastern Front since Russian divisions are being kept away from it.'

Paulus therefore wasted no time in informing the Russians over the radio that he rejected the ultimatum. He also issued an order to all the Corps HQs to the effect that: 'All units are to be instructed that in future all enemy emissaries will be fired on.'

In his memoir on the battle, written after the war, Paulus gave his reasons for not accepting the Russian terms and sparing his troops further afflictions:

The realization of the inconceivable torments which my officers and men were suffering weighed heavily on me when it came to making decisions. In the struggle between obedience to orders which emphasized in the most compelling terms that every added hour of resistance was of vital importance, on the one hand, and the promptings of common humanity, on the other, I felt at the time that obedience had to take precedence. The responsibility placed upon the 6th Army and the contribution it was being called upon to make towards the creation of a new front in the southern sector imposed on us the obligation not voluntarily to give up the struggle in Stalingrad and thus add to the sacrifices on the part of those who were striving to restore the situation.[26].... I believed that by prolonging to its utmost our resistance in Stalingrad I was serving the best interests of the German people, for, if the eastern theatre of war collapsed, I saw no possible prospect of a peace by political negotiation.[27]

In purely military terms Paulus's appreciation was the correct one. If the seven Soviet armies investing the Kessel had been free to add their weight to the westward push against Heeresgruppe Don, then Manstein's front would have collapsed, Heeresgruppe A would have been cut off in the Caucasus, and the whole of the German southern wing in Russia would have been crushed. Paulus had doomed 6th Army by his refusal to break out during the first week of the encirclement. All he could do now was buy time with the lives of his men.

On the same day that the Russian ultimatum was delivered to Paulus, Soviet aircraft dropped thousands of leaflets over the German positions containing the full text of the offer of capitulation. To counter the effect on morale, Paulus appealed for the troops to stand together as comrades in arms and not desert, warning against the uncertainties of captivity, which held the promise of nothing but death from starvation or cold, or life as a prisoner under deplorable, brutal and degrading conditions.

The promise of food and medical treatment caused a few to desert, but the majority determined to sell their lives as dearly as possible in preference to the prospect of a living hell in a Siberian prison camp. Others, in the pit of despair, decided on suicide. In his last letter home one soldier, an actor by profession before being conscripted into the Army, wrote:

You are my witness that I never wanted to go along with it, because I was afraid of the Eastern Front, in fact of war in general. I have never been a soldier, only a man in uniform. What do I get out of it? What do the others get out of it, those who went along and were not afraid? Yes, what are we getting out of it? We, who are playing the walk-on parts in this madness incarnate? What good does a hero's death do us? I have played death on the stage dozens of times, but I was only playing, and you sat out front in plush seats and thought my acting authentic and true. It is terrible to realize how little the acting had to do with real death.

You were supposed to die heroically, inspiringly, movingly, from inner conviction and for a great cause. But here what is death in reality? Here they croak, starve to death, freeze to death — it's nothing but a biological fact like eating and drinking. They drop like flies; nobody cares and nobody buries them. Without arms or legs and without eyes, with bellies torn open, they lie around everywhere. One should make a film of it; it would make 'the most beautiful death in the world' impossible once and for all. It is a death fit for beasts; later they will ennoble it on granite friezes showing 'dying warriors' with their heads or arms in bandages.

Poems, novels and hymns will be written and sung. And in the churches they will say masses. I'll have no part of it, because I have no desire to rot in a mass grave... I have decided to take my fate into my own hands.[28]

Others sought to cheat death and avoid captivity be resorting to desperate expedients, as Corporal Täsch relates:

I had taken out a case of medical supplies to the advanced dressing station at Dimitrevka. It was in a warehouse with the roof open to the sky in places from shell fire. It was absolutely crammed with wounded and most of them were in a bad state, dead and dying together, crying and praying aloud... an orderly told me that they were going to be flown out... just then a Katyusha salvo fell in the street and calls from some more wounded took the orderly and the doctor outside. I went over to a part of the building where the men were quiet. They were so badly injured they were unconscious and some of them had already died. I turned one of them off his stretcher... I fired three shots through my left foot and lay down... it was dark and the pain was frightful... there were no lights in the warehouse... I kept telling myself, 'It will be an hour, a few hours, and then the flight.' Two days passed and the blood round my foot froze solid, but I dared not call for attention... two of the men near me died. Then − Morning of Joy! They started to move us.[29]

But Täsch's elation was short-lived. When he arrived at the casualty clearing station at Pitomnik for examination and a 'reprieve ticket', the doctor noticed powder burns on the skin of his foot indicating that the wounds were self-inflicted. Täsch lost his chance to be flown out, and he was captured two weeks later suffering the agonies of frost gangrene. The Russians saved his life by amputating his left leg at the hip.

In the Kessel the cold, the storms and the ice varied in intensity from day to day, but the wind never ceased to whistle and howl across the steppe. The only sound to dominate it was the steady roar of Russian artillery and mortar fire, which never ceased by day or night. But on the morning of Saturday 9 January, 1943, the Russian guns suddenly fell silent and remained so for twenty-four hours. For the bedraggled German troops huddled in their foxholes and trenches, shivering and nursing their infinity of agonies − lice, dysentery, frost-bite, hunger, and the raging fever of the first typhus cases − the eerie silence of the Russian guns sounded the tocsin of the storm of fire and steel they knew must shortly break upon them.

On the eve of Koltso the strength of Rokossovsky's Don Front amounted to 281,000 men, 257 tanks, 3,770 artillery pieces, some 300 Katyusha rocket launchers, 6,300 mortars, 7,300 machine guns, 30,000 sub-machine guns, 164,000 rifles and 9,400 assorted motor vehicles, which were disposed in seven armies. Each army had an average strength of some 40,200 men, the equivalent of a German army corps. On 9 January, 1943, these seven armies had the following effectives:

Units in Formation	65th	21st	ARMIES 24th	66th	62nd	64th	57th
Rifle divisions	8	7	4	6	6	5	3
Rifle Brigades	-	-	-	2	1	7	-
Tank Brigades	1	-	-	-	-	1	2
Independent Tank Regiments	6	1	1	1	-	2	2
Artillery Reinforcements:							
(a) Artillery regiments of the Stavka reserves	27	2	1	2	4	10	9
(b) Artillery mortar regiments	-	3	-	2	2	-	1
(c) Anti-aircraft artillery regiments	5	4	1	-	1	1	1
Katyusha brigades	4	-	-	-	-	1	-
Katyusha Regiments	9	1	1	2	2	1	1
Fortified Regions	-	-	-	-	-	2	-
Independent machine gun/artillery battalions	-	-	5	5	4	-	5

In addition the 16th Air Army was to throw its entire weight of 400 operational aircraft (including 150 fighters) into the attack (between 10 and 31 January, 16th Air Army flew 4,427 sorties against enemy troops).

By this time the German 6th Army had been reduced to 191,000 men, with 6,200 artillery pieces, 1,500 mortars and 60 tanks. In addition there were an unspecified number of immobilized and badly damaged tanks 'dug in' to provide fire points. On 23 November, 1942, the German and Rumanian forces trapped in the encirclement numbered some 267,000 men. Of this number 29,000 wounded and 7,000 'specialists' had been flown out of the Kessel, while 40,000 had lost their lives during the forty-eight days of the encirclement (up to 9 January) from enemy action, disease, starvation, hypothermia and sheer exhaustion. Included in the total of fatal casualties are 364 soldiers who were shot by firing squads for committing court-martial offences such as cowardice, attempting to desert or the theft of provisions.

The 191,000 men remaining on the steppe were so ravaged by the harsh winter conditions, lack of food and dysentery (which had been rampant in 6th Army since the summer months and was the most common of the myriad diseases) that they were too weak to put up a sustained resistance. Heinz Schröter begs us to pause and consider what these men were suffering:

> Can you imagine what it is like not to have washed for weeks, to have eaten nothing save scraps of stale bread, raw roots, to have drunk only melted snow, to have lived under a constant hail of fire with the thermometer at 35 degrees below zero, and with no hope of ever coming out alive?[30]

In comparison the Red Army troops were warmly clad, adequately fed, and had abundant stocks of ammunition. Although the Russian manpower superiority was only 91,000 men, or a ratio of 1.5:1, the relative physical condition of the opposing forces is better compared to that of a heavyweight boxer, packing a mighty punch, going into the ring against a sick and starving man, only capable of throwing weak and rapidly failing punches.

Just after dawn on the morning of Sunday, 10 January, Rokossovsky and Voronov took up position in the command post of General Batov's Sixty-fifth Army, on the western flank of the Kessel, to watch the spectacle of the heaviest Soviet artillery barrage fired in the war up to that time.

Weather conditions were appalling. The temperature was 35 degrees below zero (centigrade) and visibility was reduced to a few hundred yards by a thick, swirling fog and a driving blizzard which was sweeping across the steppe.

At 0850 Moscow time (0650 German time) signal rockets flickered along the entire perimeter of the Kessel, followed seconds later by a mighty flash and roar as 7,000 Russian guns and mortars opened fire simultaneously. Soviet artillery spotters, correcting the fire through the fog and driving snow, watched the curtain of flame and smoke creep forward over the German positions and then back again, ploughing up the frozen, snow-covered ground into a moonscape of craters. To add to the terrifying maelstrom of thousands and thousands of shells, 400 bombers, ground-attack planes and fighters of the 16th Air Army bombed and strafed the German lines on the perimeter, along with positions in the depth of the Kessel, including Pitomnik airfield which suffered fearful punishment.

After enduring fifty-five minutes of this terrific battering, the dazed and terrified German survivors observed another salvo of signal rockets, which heralded the appearance of tanks and a tidal wave of Russian infantry swarming forward through the driving snow and swirling fog towards the bludgeoned ruins of the German lines – a bloody mishmash of bodies, smashed guns and ploughed up gun-pits, foxholes and dug-outs.

The main attack was made by three armies on the western side of the Kessel. The northern most of these, Galanin's Twenty-fourth Army, flung its weight against the 113th and the 76th Infantry Divisions which were holding the north-western corner of the perimeter. In the centre Batov's

Sixty-fifth Army, advancing on a south-easterly axis towards Karpovka, fell upon the 384th, 44th and 376th Infantry Divisions. In the south Chistyakov's Twenty-first Army advancing due east, and the left flank forces of Tolbukhin's Fifty-seventh Army, advancing north-westwards, cut into the Marinovka 'nose' in the south-western corner of the pocket, which was being held by the 3rd and 29th Motorized Divisions.

In the north the 113th Division, and in the south the 297th Division, were able to fold back their westernmost flanks and pull back eastwards clear of the main Soviet thrusts, but the 76th, 384th, 44th, 376th Infantry Divisions and the 3rd and 29th Motorized Divisions were torn asunder, and almost vanished completely in the maelstrom unleashed against them. The survivors of the bombardment in these six divisions fought with demonic savagery until their last ounce of strength was exhausted. When their ammunition ran out they used their rifle-butts and trenching-tools as clubs in hand-to-hand combat, each man determined to sell his life as dearly as possible.

Within two days the Marinovka 'nose' had been completely overrun, and the western flank of the Kessel had been pushed back to the Rossoshka River. This achievement cost the Don Front 26,000 casualties and the loss of 135 tanks (by the evening of 12 January, only 122 of the original tank force remained in action). These losses bear testimony to the savage resistance put up by the starving ghosts of the six German divisions that had held the western flank. But the losses suffered by these divisions amounted to more than double those incurred by the Russians. All six divisions were smashed into fragments, being reduced from some 10,000 men each to the size of battalions – a mere 600 men.

The pitiful remnants of these divisions fled eastwards towards Stalingrad as best they could, some struggling to drag anti-tank guns and the few precious cases of shells through the deep snow. Detachments paused in their flight in a desperate attempt to hold back the Russian juggernaut pursuing them, fighting to the last shell and bullet before being crushed under tank tracks or overwhelmed by Russian infantry. During the disorderly retreat the troops could not be supplied with their meagre rations, but some were lucky:

> A starving horse, shivering with cold, was standing beneath the straw eaves of a cottage. It had eaten the straw as far as it could reach. Six soldiers appeared from the steppe, leaderless and in flight.... One of the soldiers fired a bullet between the horse's eyes. Six knives and bayonets were drawn, and they wasted no time in hacking meat from the bleeding, quivering carcass, which was divided, packed and bundled under their arms. The whole incident hardly took ten minutes, and the soldiers moved on, rather faster than before.[31]

On 15 January Pitomnik airfield came under heavy Russian artillery fire.

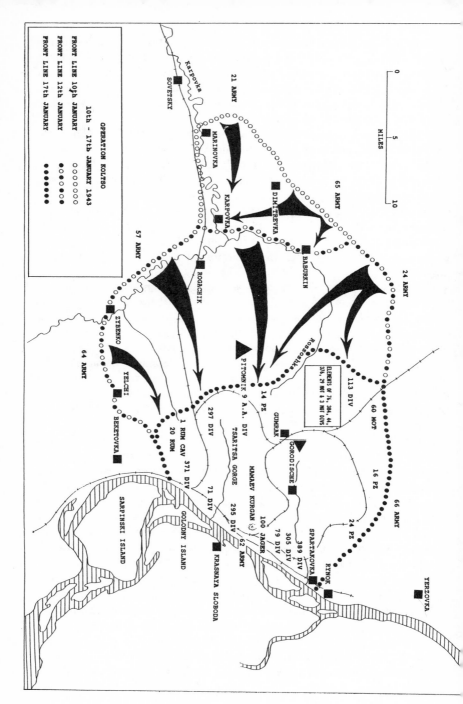

OPERATION KOLTSO
10th - 17th JANUARY 1943

FRONT LINE 10th JANUARY   ○○○○○○○○
FRONT LINE 12th JANUARY   ○○○○●○○○
FRONT LINE 17th JANUARY   ●●●●●●●●

MILES
0
5
10

21 ARMY
65 ARMY
24 ARMY
57 ARMY
64 ARMY
60 MOT
66 ARMY
62 ARMY

Karpovka
SOVETSKY
MARINOVKA
KARPOVKA
DIMITREVKA
BABURKIN
ROGACHIK
ZYBENKO
YELCHI
BEKETOVKA

PITOMNIK 9 A.A. DIV
14 PZ
113 DIV
16 PZ
24 PZ
GUMRAK
GORODISCHE
MAMAEV KURGAN
SPARTAKOVKA
RYNOK
YERZOVKA

ELEMENTS OF 76, 384, 44,
376, 29 MOT & 3 MOT DIVS

1 RUM CAV
20 RUM
371 DIV
297 DIV
71 DIV
TSARITSA GORGE
295 DIV
100 JAGER
79 DIV
305 DIV
389 DIV

SARPINSKI ISLAND
GOLODNY ISLAND
KRASNAYA SLOBODA

Rossoshka

200

That night the ground staff began evacuating the airfield, along with the staff of the field-hospital adjacent to the runway who were forced to abandon hundreds of sick and wounded men to the mercy of the advancing Russians. That same night four transport planes landed; two were immediately hit by shells and exploded in sheets of flame. They formed a funeral pyre of all remaining hope, for on the following day Pitomnik fell to the Russians, and the heart of Festung Stalingrad stopped beating.

On 17 January the Russians paused to regroup and replenish with ammunition in preparation for phase two of Koltso — the complete destruction of 6th Army. By this time they had reduced the Kessel to a third of its original size. The western flank had been pushed back to within five miles of Paulus's HQ at Gumrak, and Stalingrad was only twelve miles distant.

This pause in the eastward Russian drive allowed 6th Army a breathing space in which to throw together a hastily formed defence line on the open steppe. To defend the western approaches to Stalingrad the 113th and 297th Infantry, 14th Panzer and the 9th Anti-aircraft Divisions, along with the exhausted remnants of the six divisions which had been smashed asunder on 10 January, formed a thin but continuous line stretching for twenty miles from north to south. For five days, burrowed into shallow holes scooped in the snow, they shivered and died on the exposed steppe, too weak to dig foxholes and dug-outs in the frozen ground, waiting for the 'God of War', as Stalin called the artillery, to beat another merciless tattoo upon them. The despair and horror of it all is expressed in a letter written by one of their number:

On Tuesday I knocked out two T-34s with my mobile anti-tank gun. Curiosity had lured them behind our lines. It was grand and impressive. Afterwards I drove past the smoking remains. From a hatch there hung a body, head down, his feet caught, and his legs burning up to his knees. The body was alive, the mouth moaning. He must have suffered terrible pain. And there was no possibility of freeing him. Even if there had been, he would have died after a few hours of torture. I shot him, and as I did it, the tears ran down my cheeks. Now I have been crying for three nights about a dead Russian tank driver, whose murderer I am. The crosses of Gumrak shake me and so do many other things which my comrades close their eyes to and set their jaws against. I am afraid I'll never be able to sleep quietly, assuming that I shall ever come back to you, dear ones. My life is a terrible contradiction, a psychological monstrosity.

I have now taken over a heavy anti-tank gun and organized eight men.... The nine of us drag the cannon from one place to another. Every time we change position, a burning tank remains on the field.

The number has grown to eight already, and we intend to make it a dozen. However, I have only three rounds left, and shooting tanks is not like playing billiards. But during the night I cry without control, like a child. What will all this lead to?[32]

Three days after the opening of Koltso, yet another Soviet offensive, launched by Golikov's Voronezh Front against the northern flank of Heeresgruppe B, swept away the 2nd Hungarian Army and the remnants of the 8th Italian Army. Axis casualties totalled 151,000 (including 89,000 taken prisoner) and a 120-mile breach was punched out of the German front line. The situation in the Caucasus had also became untenable, and the 1st Panzer and the 17th Armies (forming Heeresgruppe A) began retreating towards the Crimea under intense Soviet pressure.

Hitler was wrestling with these problems when he received the following message from Paulus, once again appealing for freedom of action:

The combat capability of the troops is sinking fast as a result of the catastrophic situation with regard to food, fuel and ammunition. At present there are 16,000 wounded who are receiving no care whatsoever. With the exception of those on the Volga [in Stalingrad], the troops have no suitable positions, billets or firewood. There are signs that morale is sinking. Once again I request freedom of action in order to continue to resist as long as possible or cease military activity if it cannot be continued.[33]

Hitler's reply was short, unequivocal and brutal:

Capitulation is out of the question. Sixth Army is fulfilling its historic obligation by its staunch resistance, to facilitate the creation of a new front at Rostov and the withdrawal of the Caucasian Army Group.[34]

The situation on the southern wing of the Eastern Front was now so catastrophic that it had become doubly imperative that 6th Army continue to pin down the seven Soviet armies investing what remained of the Kessel for as long as possible. However, in Zeitzler's opinion, Hitler was also 'a prisoner of his stubborn conviction that where the German soldier once sets his foot, there he remains.'[35]

On this double count the troops on the steppe were given no choice but to fight on, with each day bringing a renewed dose of hunger, privation, bitter cold, loneliness of soul, hopelessness, fear of freezing or starving to death, and the fear of suffering wounds which could not be tended. But the end of the nightmare was in sight, for the life of 6th Army was rapidly ebbing away. The frozen bodies of the dead and dying soldiers were simply not enough to build a dyke to hold back the relentless flood tide of the inevitable.

9

EXTREME UNCTION

'He who leads into captivity shall go into captivity; he who kills
with the sword must be killed with the sword.'

(Revelation 13:10).

MILCH'S IMPOSSIBLE MISSION

The length of time that 6th Army could continue to resist was directly
equatable with the amount of supplies it received from the Luftwaffe. To
this end Hitler, on 14 January, instructed Field-Marshal Erhard Milch, the
Secretary of State for Air and Inspector-General of the Luftwaffe, to take
over the command of the air-lift, endowing him with special powers to issue
orders to every military command. Hitler stressed the strategic importance
of the mission to Milch; he was to do everything possible to raise the delivery
of supplies to a minimum of 300 tons a day, which, Hitler believed, would
sustain 6th Army sufficiently to fight on for another six to eight weeks.

After a five-hour flight from Berlin, the aircraft carrying Milch touched
down at Taganrog airfield on the evening of 16 January, in a heavy snow
storm and an icy gale: it was a fitting introduction to the problematic mission
with which he had been entrusted. When he boarded Richthofen's warm,
well-equipped command train, which served as the HQ of Luftflotte IV,
Milch immediately summoned the Luftflotte staff to make a full report on
the situation.

When he learned that Milch had been given command of the supply
operation, Richthofen noted in his diary that: 'Nothing would delight me
more than that Milch should chance upon the Philosopher's Stone which our
supreme authorities evidently believe is lying round here somewhere.
Certainly we have not found it.'[1]

During the conference Milch learned that Pitomnik airfield had fallen to
the Russians earlier in the day, and he was mortified to find that far fewer
transport aircraft were serviceable than was assumed at Hitler's
headquarters. On 16 January only 15 of the 140 remaining Ju-52s, and only
41 of the 140 of the medium-bombers and two FW-200 Condors were
operational: a total of 58 aircraft (20.56 per cent of those available) in flying
condition.

Milch also learned that on account of the weather on that particular day only seven of the Ju-52s and eleven of the He-111s had actually made the flight to the Kessel, and being unable to land at Pitomnik had been forced to drop their supplies from the air. Richthofen advised Milch that he had warned all along that the air-lift was impossible, and now that Pitomnik, the lynchpin of the operation, had been overrun it was madness to continue. Although the situation seemed hopeless, Milch determined to do all he could to improve the rate of deliveries, refusing to act as though Stalingrad was already lost.

With the fall of Pitomnik everything now depended on the primitive airstrip at Gumrak; but throughout the duration of the encirclement 6th Army had made no attempt to ready it to receive transport planes. In fact the army staff had positively discouraged any attempt to improve the airstrip, on the grounds that it would attract Russian bombing raids and thus endanger 6th Army HQ which was situated close by.

By the time Pitomnik fell, the Gumrak airstrip was buried under deep snow, and the troops were so weakened by hunger and privation as to be physically incapable of packing it down firmly enough to support the impact of repeated landings by the heavily laden transport planes. The deplorable condition of the airstrip is evinced by the fact that when six Me-109 fighters evacuated Pitomnik to escape the Russian advance, five of them crashed while attempting to land at Gumrak on account of shell and bomb craters and the deep snowdrifts. The sixth fighter veered off and escaped to the west.

Nonetheless a few transports braved the landing and survived, including one FW-200 Condor which successfully put down in a snowstorm which had reduced visibility to 50 yards. This remarkable feat was accomplished by Lieutenant Hans Gilbert, and although the Condor's tail-skid was smashed during the landing, the intrepid pilot managed to fly out again carrying General Hube, the one-armed commander of the 14th Panzer Corps, who was evacuated on Hitler's instructions to act as an adviser on Milch's staff.

To add to Milch's problems, a heavy Russian air-raid on Zverevo on 17 January resulted in ten Ju-52s being completely destroyed, with a further twenty being too badly damaged to take any further part in the supply operation. During the raid the Rumanians who were manning the anti-aircraft batteries around the airfield abandoned their weapons and sought cover in slit-trenches, leaving a single German-manned battery, equipped with 20mm guns, to protect the airfield: they bagged a single Soviet fighter.

On this same day Milch decided to fly into the Kessel to investigate complaints made by the crews of the few planes which had risked a landing at Gumrak, who reported that they had found no ground organization to unload their cargoes, and that they had handed over the foodstuffs and ammunition they were carrying to troops who happened to be passing by.

While driving to Taganrog airport through a fierce blizzard, Milch's staff car became jammed on a railway crossing and it was struck by a train travelling at 40 Mph. The car was hurled across an embankment and Milch was lucky to escape with his life. But within three hours, despite suffering from concussion, loss of blood from a deep gash in his head and several broken ribs, he was back in the command train propped up at his desk with his head swathed in a bandage and his chest and back encased in plaster.

Major Thiel, the commander of one of the He-111 squadrons, was chosen to undertake Milch's mission to the Kessel with orders to report back on the conditions prevailing at Gumrak. Thiel's subsequent report made grim reading:

The air-strip is easy to pin-point from 4,500 − 5,000 feet owing to its rolled runway, its wreckage and the numerous bomb craters and shell holes. The landing cross was covered with snow. Directly my machine came to a standstill the airfield was shot up by ten enemy fighters − which, however, did not come lower than 2,500-3,000 feet owing to the light flak that opened up on them. Simultaneously it was under artillery zone fire. I had just switched off the engines [of a He-111 medium bomber] when my aircraft became an object for target practice. The whole airfield was commanded by both heavy and medium guns situated − so far as one could judge from the open firing positions − mainly to the south-west.

Technically speaking, the airfield can be used for daylight landings, but at night only by thoroughly experienced air-crews. Altogether thirteen aircraft wrecks litter the field, in consequence of which the effective width of the landing area is reduced to eighty yards. Especially dangerous for night landings of heavily laden aircraft is the presence of the wreck of an Me-109 [fighter] at the end of it. Immediate clearance of these obstacles has been promised. The field is also strewn with numerous bomb-canisters of provisions [ejected by transports which did not risk a landing], none of them saved, and some already half covered with snow.

When I returned to my aircraft [after reporting to General Paulus] I found that it had been severely damaged by artillery fire, and my flight mechanic had been killed. A second aircraft of my section stood off the runway in like condition. Though I had landed at 1100, by 2000 no unloading team had appeared and my aircraft had neither been unloaded nor de-fuelled despite the crying need for fuel by the Stalingrad garrison. The excuse given was the artillery fire. At 1500 Russian nuisance planes [U-2 light reconnaissance aircraft] began to keep watch on the airfield in sections of three or four. From the outset I made it my business to look into the air control system and established that before 2200 it was quite impossible to land a single plane. If one approached, the seven lamps of the flare path would be switched on, offering a target visible for miles, whereat it would be bombed by the nuisance raiders above. The only possible measure was a short flash to enable the aircraft to position its bomb-canisters of provisions to be ejected from the air.[2]

During Thiel's conference with Paulus, in which he endeavoured to explain to the General the manifold and insuperable difficulties which were besetting the supply operation, he was met with bitterness and despair. 'If your aircraft cannot land,' Paulus pointed out, 'then my army is doomed. Every machine that does so can save the lives of 1,000 men. An air drop is no use at all. Many of the canisters are never found because the men are too weak from hunger and exhaustion to look for them, and we have no fuel to send out transport to collect them. I cannot even withdraw my line a few miles because the men would fall out from exhaustion. It is four days since they have had anything to eat. Heavy weapons cannot be withdrawn for lack of petrol, and are therefore lost to us. The last horses have been eaten up. Can you imagine what it is like to see soldiers fall on an old horse carcass, beat open the head and swallow the brains raw? What should I, as commander-in-chief of an army, say when a simple soldier comes up to me and begs: '*Herr Generaloberst*, can you spare me one piece of bread?' Why on earth did the Luftwaffe ever promise to keep us supplied? Who is the man responsible for declaring that it was possible? Had someone told me that it was not possible, I would not hold it against the Luftwaffe. I could have broken out when I was strong enough to do so. Now it is too late.'[3]

Paulus seems to have forgotten that when the 6th Army was threatened with encirclement in mid-November, all of the forward Luftwaffe commanders – von Richthofen, Fiebig and Pickert – had warned him that attempting to supply 250,000 men from the air in the depths of the Russian winter was an impossible undertaking. He also seems to have forgotten that, despite the entreaties of all his corps commanders, he had refused to break out during the first week of the encirclement, refusing to act in defiance of the Führer's will. It was somewhat ironic then that Paulus now thundered at Thiel that: 'The Führer gave me his firm assurance that he and the whole German people felt responsible for my army, and now the annals of German arms are besmirched by this fearful tragedy, just because the Luftwaffe has let us down! We already speak from a different world to yours, for we are dead men. From now on our existence will be in the history books. Let us try to take comfort that our sacrifice may have been of some avail.'[4]

Deeply upset by this confrontation, Thiel flew back to Taganrog, and made a full report to Milch. The Field-Marshal did what he could to alleviate the long-drawn-out death throes of 6th Army, even resorting to the threat that 'any pilot aborting his mission to Stalingrad without good reason will be stood before a court-martial'. But other than instructing the squadron commanders in the correct cold-start procedure for the engines, a simple but effective technicality of which most seemed to be in ignorance, and dispatching a set of flare-path equipment to Gumrak to aid night landings, there was little he could do to meet Hitler's expectation of raising the delivery rate to 300 tons a day.

During the five-day period 12 to 16 January, prior to Milch taking over command of the operation, only 300 tons had been flown into the Kessel (an average of 60 tons a day). For the subsequent seven-day period, 17 to 23 January, starting the day after Milch took command, the daily average flown in rose by a mere 9.28 tons to 69.28 tons a day. The total delivered amounted to 485 tons - a mere 23 per cent of the 300 tons a day demanded by Hitler, and a paltry 13 percent of the 500 tons minimum requirement decided upon at the outset of the air-lift. By 23 January the cumulative deficit of the shortfall on the minimum requirement since the inception of the operation had risen to 24,188 tons. Typically, Hitler's expectation that 6th Army could hold out for a further six to eight weeks had nothing to do with the reality of the situation.

ON THE EDGE OF THE PRECIPICE

At dawn on Friday, 22 January the Russian artillery unleashed another fearsome bombardment on the German positions. On the western flank alone 4,100 guns and mortars rained down a hurricane of steel and high explosive, heralding the final onslaught against the human wreckage manning the twenty-miles of the Kessel's western front.

The German batteries and battalions fought to the last round, but the slender dyke of starving men and the clumps of dead frozen to brittle stiffness were simply swept away by the five Soviet armies which crashed into them. Russian tanks churned over unit after unit, wiping out weapon-pits and grinding the defenders under their tracks, squashing them in their shallow holes in the snow. An impression of the ferocity of the Russian onslaught can be gauged from the amount of ammunition expended by the Don Front during Koltso (10 January to 2 February): 911,000 artillery rounds; 990,000 mortar shells and 24,000,000 machine-gun and rifle rounds.[5]

That night Paulus, in the pit of despair, radioed to Hitler that:

Rations exhausted... What orders should I give to troops who have no more ammunition and are subjected to mass attacks supported by heavy artillery fire? The quickest decision is necessary since disintegration is already starting in some places.[6]

Humanitarian considerations now dictated that 6th Army should surrender. By 22 January continued resistance had become senseless, because 6th Army was no longer performing any useful strategic purpose. Manstein had managed to halt the Soviet offensive on the Donets, and it was already clear that Heeresgruppe A was going to make its escape from the Caucasus through Rostov and the Crimea. But Hitler having boasted that 'where the German soldier sets foot, there he remains,' and that 'nobody will ever drive us away from Stalingrad,' was more concerned with his personal prestige and his obsession with the ideological titular deeds inherent in the name of Stalingrad than with humanitarian considerations.

To these ends he replied to Paulus that:

> Surrender is out of the question. The troops will defend themselves to the last. If possible, the size of the fortress is to be reduced so that it can be held by the troops still capable of fighting. The courage and endurance of the fortress have made it possible to establish a new front and begin preparing a counter-operation. Thereby, Sixth Army has made an historic contribution to Germany's greatest struggle.[7]

Throughout the night of the 22nd/23rd flotsam from the shattered German line began to struggle eastwards in desperate flight towards the smoking ruins of Stalingrad. Gumrak airfield, which had rendered only minute aid to the dying army, fell on the 23rd. Paulus and his staff hurriedly evacuated the HQ at Gumrak and retreated into Stalingrad to set up a new command post in the cellars of the wrecked Univermag department store in the administrative centre of the fire-blackened city, situated between Red Square and the western bank of the Volga.

One of the last Ju-52s to fly out of Gumrak before it was overrun carried seven mailbags containing the last letters written by the doomed men of 6th Army. They were written on the backs of maps, on the dotted lines of wireless and teleprinter pads, on wrapping paper and the insides of envelopes, anything that came to hand. But none of the letters, the last testaments of the damned, was destined to reach those to whom they were addressed – parents, wives, sweethearts, children, friends. On Hitler's orders they were impounded and used to ascertain the morale of the troops. When the aircraft carrying the mail landed at Novocherkassk, the seven mail bags were seized and opened by the Army Field Censorship Department. The address and the sender's name were removed, and they were classified by content and general tenor into a statistical breakdown of the troops, feelings concerning the way the war was being conducted. The results showed:

(a) In favour		2.1%
(b) Dubious		4.4%
(c) Sceptical, deprecatory		57.1%

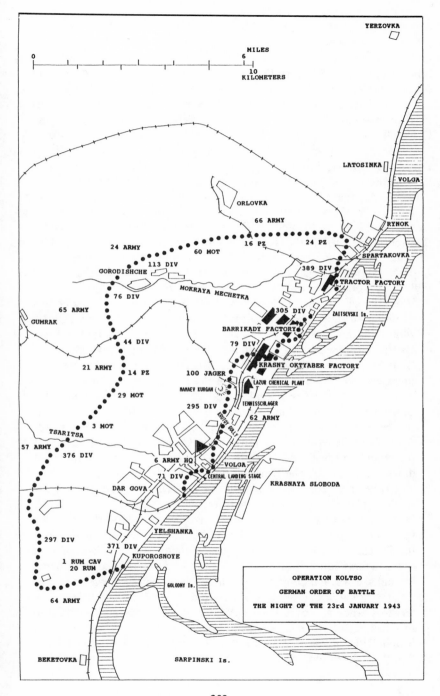

MILES

KILOMETERS

YERZOVKA

LATOSINKA

VOLGA

ORLOVKA

66 ARMY

RYNOK

24 ARMY

60 MOT

16 PZ

24 PZ

SPARTAKOVKA

GORODISHCHE

113 DIV

389 DIV

TRACTOR FACTORY

MOKRAYA MECHETKA

76 DIV

305 DIV

ZAITSEVSKI Is.

65 ARMY

BARRIKADY FACTORY

GUMRAK

44 DIV

79 DIV

21 ARMY

14 PZ

KRASNY OKTYABER FACTORY

100 JAGER

29 MOT

MAMAEV KURGAN

LAZUR CHEMICAL PLANT

TENNISSCHLAGER

295 DIV

62 ARMY

3 MOT

TSARITSA

57 ARMY

376 DIV

6 ARMY HQ

VOLGA

71 DIV

CENTRAL LANDING STAGE

KRASNAYA SLOBODA

DAR GOVA

YELSHANKA

297 DIV

371 DIV

KUPOROSNOYE

1 RUM CAV
20 RUM

GOLODNY Is.

OPERATION KOLTSO

GERMAN ORDER OF BATTLE

THE NIGHT OF THE 23rd JANUARY 1943

64 ARMY

BEKETOVKA

SARPINSKI Is.

209

(d) Actively against   3.4%

(e) No opinion, indifferent   33.0%

Once they had been processed, the bundled letters and the accompanying report were sent to Berlin and placed in the custody of the Army Press Corps for use by Heinz Schröter, who was instructed by Joseph Goebbels to write a documented account of the battle. The Supreme Command hoped to find itself exculpated in this work, but when Schröter's account was read by Goebbels he suppressed it. It was, Goebbels commented, 'Unbearable (*untragbar*) for the German people.' Most of the letters were burned, but a few found their way into the army archives in Potsdam, being removed a few days before Berlin fell to the Russians to be preserved for posterity.

On the day that Gumrak fell, Major Coelestin von Zitzewitz arrived at the Wolfsschanze, having been evacuated by aircraft from the Kessel, on Zeitzler's orders, on 20 January. Zeitzler hoped that a first-hand account of the conditions inside the Kessel might induce Hitler to recant his no surrender order. Zitzewitz's account of the meeting illustrates not only Hitler's callous disregard for the suffering of the troops, but also the nightmare world of unreality in which he was living:

When we arrived at the Führer's Headquarters General Zeitzler was admitted at once, while I was made to wait in the anteroom. A little while later the door was opened, and I was called in. I reported present. Hitler came to meet me and with both his hands gripped my right hand. 'You have come from a deplorable situation,' he said. The spacious room was only dimly lit. In front of the fireplace was a large circular table, with club chairs around it, and on the right stood a long table, lit from above, with a huge situation map of the entire Eastern Front. In the background sat two stenographers taking down every word. Apart from General Zeitzler only General Schmundt and two personal Army and Luftwaffe ADCs were present. Hitler gestured to me to sit down on a stool by the situation map, while he sat down facing me. The other gentlemen sat down in the chairs in the dark part of the room. Only the Army ADC stood on the far side of the map table. Hitler was speaking. Time and time again he pointed to the map. He spoke of a tentative idea of making a battalion of entirely new tanks, the Panther, attack straight through the enemy towards Stalingrad in order to ferry supplies through in this way and to reinforce Sixth Army by tanks. I was flabbergasted. A single Panzer battalion was to launch a successful attack across several hundred miles of strongly held enemy territory when an entire Panzer Army had been unable to accomplish this feat (a reference to Armeegruppe Hoth). I used the first pause which Hitler made in his exposé to describe the hardships of Sixth Army; I quoted examples, I read off figures from a slip of paper I had prepared. I spoke about the hunger, the frost-bite, the inadequate supplies, and the sense of having been written off; I spoke of wounded men and lack of medical supplies. I concluded with the words: 'My Führer, permit me to state that the troops at Stalingrad can no longer be ordered to fight to their last round because they no longer have a last round.' Hitler regarded me in surprise, but I felt that he was looking straight through me. Then he said, 'Man recovers very quickly.' With these words I was dismissed.[8]

Just how the starving, freezing men of 6th Army, whose ammunition was almost entirely spent and who were being pounded to pulp by a numerically superior enemy, were supposed to 'recover very quickly' Hitler failed to explain. No such illusions existed at Stalingrad. 'Sooner or later according to rank and temperament, they realized the senselessness of the orders which they had received from Hitler and the deceitful nature of the promises which he had made to them.'[9]

After the fall of Gumrak the supply situation went from bad to worse. With nowhere to land, the aircraft could only deliver their precious cargoes by air-drop. For the ten-day period 24 January to 2 February, a total of 779 tons of food, ammunition and medical supplies were dropped in bomb-canisters (metal containers shaped like bombs which could be packed with 250 kilograms of supplies). The daily average of 77.9 tons for this the final period represented an increase of 8.62 tons over the amount delivered in the penultimate period. But, it is estimated, only some 50 per cent of the bomb-canisters dropped were actually recovered by the troops on the ground, which reduced the daily average actually received to some 39 tons. The reasons why so many bomb-canisters went unrecovered are as follows:

1) The encircled troops had no means of marking the drop areas properly.

2) The drop areas were often difficult to recognize from the air due to poor visibility. When the cloud ceiling was very low, a frequent occurrence, the canisters had to be dropped blind.

3) The wind frequently blew a number of the canisters off course, and many fell behind Russian lines.

4) The canisters were often so deeply buried in snow or amongst the ruins of the city that the troops could not find them.

5) Because of their weakened condition the troops were unable to collect many of the canisters.

6) Some of the canisters were smashed by the landing impact and the contents were too badly damaged for use.

By 2 February the Luftwaffe had delivered a total of 6,591 tons of supplies: a daily average for the entire 70-day duration of the air-lift of 94.15 tons, which was a mere 18 per cent of the minimum daily requirement. By the time 6th Army had ceased to exist the cumulative deficit of the minimum requirement, which the Luftwaffe had failed to deliver, amounted to 28,409 tons.

This effort by the Luftwaffe, a supreme effort despite its failure, cost the lives of 1,000 air-crew and the loss of 487 aircraft (69 per cent of the total which took part): 266 Ju-52s, 165 He-111s, 42 Ju-86s, 5 FW-200 Condors, 7 He-177s and 2 Ju-290s. Among the pilots lost were some of the Luftwaffe's finest, who had provided the nucleus of the air transport fleet and the cream of the air training schools. It was a blow from which the Luftwaffe never fully recovered. Goering later remarked that: 'There died the core of the German bomber fleet.'

When, on 3 February, Milch and General Hube reported to Hitler in the Wolfsschanze in East Prussia, Hitler suspiciously inquired of Hube whether Milch had done everything possible to improve the delivery rate to 6th Army. Hube replied that if the Führer had sent Milch to Taganrog fourteen days earlier than he did, Stalingrad would not have fallen. 'That,' Hitler regretted, 'is a judgement on me.'[10]

Hube was obviously protecting Milch from Hitler's wrath, for it was pure nonsense to suggest that Milch could have prevented the fall of Stalingrad. Even if he had been appointed to command the air-lift from the very beginning, the most he could have done would have been to marginally improve the delivery rate. The bald fact was that, as the forward Luftwaffe commanders had warned at the very start, it was impossible to supply a quarter of a million men from the air in the depths of a Russian winter.

When Milch reported to Hitler, he made no bones about his view that, had he been in Paulus's shoes, he would have disobeyed orders and broken out of the Kessel during the first week of the encirclement. Hitler retorted that in that case he would have been obliged to lay Milch's head at his feet. 'My Führer,' Milch snapped, 'it would have been worth it! One field-marshal sacrificed to save three hundred thousand men!'[11] And that remark serves as a very apt indictment of Paulus, whose rigid adherence to the 'virtues of obedience, discipline and loyalty, at the expense of initiative and incisiveness, had condemned his army to perdition.

SURRENDER IS FORBIDDEN

By 24 January all of the German forces which had held the western, northern and southern flanks of the Kessel, had been pressed back into the shattered remains of Stalingrad, which, after four months of bombardment and bombing by both sides, had the appearance of a landscape in hell. By this time the size of the Kessel had been reduced from its original 900 square miles to a mere 36 square miles; and although, on 6th Army situation maps, all of the original 22 divisions which had been encircled on 23 November were still shown defending the perimeter defence line, most of them had been slashed to the size of battalions.

At 1645 on the evening of the 24th, 6th Army's chief of operations radioed a message to Manstein which spelled out the horror of the situation:

Attacks in undiminished violence against the entire western front which has been fighting its way back eastward in the Gorodische area since the morning of the 24th in order to form hedgehog in the tractor works. In the southern part of Stalingrad the western front along the city outskirts held on to the western and southern edge of Minina until 1600 hours. Local penetrations in that sector. Volga and north-eastern fronts unchanged. Frightful conditions in the city area proper, where about 20,000 unattended wounded are seeking shelter among the ruins. With them are about the same number of starved and frost-bitten men, and stragglers, mostly without weapons which they lost in the fighting. Heavy artillery pounding the whole city area. Last resistance along the city outskirts in the southern part of Stalingrad will be offered on 25 January under the leadership of energetic generals fighting in the line and of gallant officers around whom a few men still capable of fighting have rallied. Tractor works may possibly hold out a little longer.[12]

When Manstein read the signal, he immediately telephoned Hitler to point out that since 6th Army was no longer able to tie down any appreciable enemy forces, the Führer should grant Paulus freedom of action to surrender. His appeal was in vain, as Zeitzler records: 'Hitler remained adamant. Neither the commander of the Army Group (Manstein) nor I could move him an inch. The unvarnished facts reported by Paulus did not affect him at all. The statistics of dead and wounded, the state of the food and ammunition supplies left him totally unmoved. Even the dramatic descriptions of the hell that was raging in Stalingrad, that was becoming more atrocious every day, left him quite cold. Nothing could convince him or make him change his point of view. He simply repeated that each day's resistance by 6th Army brought great benefits to the rest of the Eastern Front.'[13]

At 1000 on the morning of 25 January three Russian emissaries under a white flag approached outposts held by the remnants of the 297th Infantry Division, which had been forced back on to the southern outskirts of the city. Despite Paulus's order of 9 January that 'all enemy emissaries will be fired on,' the Germans held their fire, but refused to parley with the Russians because they had no officer with them. The Russians duly reappeared at midday led by a major of a guards division. In an attempt to end the slaughter they handed in a further ultimatum:

Further resistance is useless. On 26 January we shall make a heavy attack on the German positions in the south. You can work out for

yourselves how many of you are likely to survive. The Red Army offers
you the chance of making an honourable surrender. All officers may
retain their side-arms, ample supplies of food will be given you and the
wounded will be cared for and fed.[14]

By stressing that they intended to make a heavy attack on the German
positions in the south of the city, the Russians obviously hoped that, even
if Paulus rejected the ultimatum, the commanders of the divisions upon
which the attack was to fall might surrender their forces on their own
volition.

Predictably, when Paulus received the ultimatum, instead of grasping the
nettle and acting unilaterally to bring an end to the agony of his troops, he
merely radioed the text of the ultimatum to Hitler, asking him to authorize
an immediate capitulation so that at least the remaining lives might be saved.
Equally, depressingly, predictable was the Führer's reply:

Surrender is forbidden. Sixth Army will hold their positions to the last
man and the last round and by their heroic endurance will make an
unforgettable contribution towards the establishment of a defensive
front and the salvation of the Western World.[15]

However, the Russians had been perceptive in stressing the threat to the
divisions holding the southern sector of the German line. On the evening of
the 25th, General Hartmann (commanding the 71st Division), General
Stempel (commanding the 371st Division) and General Drebber
(commanding 297th Division), held a council of war in Drebber's
headquarters. Shivering from the intense cold in the candle-lit bunker, a
hole in the ground which was sparsely furnished with make-shift beds, a
table made from planks and packing cases, and ammunition boxes serving
as seats, the three generals considered their response to the Russian
ultimatum. They were constantly showered with earth as the ground above
them heaved and shook under the concussion of exploding shells and bombs.
The decisions they made were acted out on the following morning. General
Stempel blew his brains out with his revolver. General Hartmann, intent on
dying with honour, climbed up onto an exposed position on a railway
embankment and standing upright fired at a group of advancing Russians
with a rifle until he was cut down by a burst of sub-machine-gun fire. Only
General Drebber opted to surrender. At dawn he led the 1,800 survivors of
the 297th Division, with blankets and rags draped over their heads and
shoulders, towards the Russian lines where they were taken prisoner by the
38th Guards Division. Two months earlier Drebber's division had numbered
some 10,000 men.

THE ABYSS
The attacks launched by the Don Front on the morning of Tuesday the

26th were of particular ferocity. A storm of artillery and mortar fire from all flanks, including the batteries ensconced on the far bank of the Volga and on the mid-river islands, shrieked down upon the 25 miles of devastation that was Stalingrad. To add to the carnage, Soviet aircraft dropped hundreds of tons of bombs on to the German positions. Over 400 tons of bombs were dropped on the ruins on the Dzerhezinsky Tractor Factory alone.

Advancing from the west, the leading tanks and infantry of Batov's Sixty-fifth Army smashed through the flimsy German defences between the commanding height of Mamaev Kurgan and the gutted remains of the Krasny Oktyaber small arms factory, and linked up with General Rodmitsev's 13th Guards Rifle Division. The latter was a part of Chuikov's legendary Sixty-second Army, which for a total of 136 days had held the battered bridgeheads on the western bank of the Volga. Chuikov describes the momentous moment:

At dawn it was reported from an observation point that the Germans were rushing about in panic, the roar of engines could be heard, men in Red Army uniforms appeared... Heavy tanks could be seen coming down a hillside. On the tanks were inscriptions: Chelyabinsk Collective Farmer, Urals Metal-Worker...

Guardsmen of Rodmitsev's division ran forward to greet them with a red flag. This joyous, moving encounter took place at 0920, near the Krasny Oktyaber settlement. Captain A. F. Gushchin of the 13th Guards Division handed representatives of the units of Batov's Sixty-fifth Army the flag, on the red cloth of which was written: 'A token of our meeting on 26.1.1943.' The eyes of the hardened soldiers who met were filled with tears of joy. Guards Captain Usenko told General Rodimtsev, who had now arrived on the scene, that he had accepted the flag from his renowned guardsmen. 'Tell your commander (Batov),' said Rodimtsev, 'that this is a happy day for us; after five months of heavy and stubborn fighting we have finally met!' Heavy tanks came up, and the crews, leaning out of the turrets, waved their hands in greeting. Then the powerful machines rolled on, guns firing, towards the factories.[16]

Later that same morning forward elements of Chistyakov's Twenty-first Army and Shumilov's Sixty-fourth Army also linked up with units of Sixty-second Army. The German forces had been firmly split into two separate pockets. In the centre of the city, grouped around Paulus's command post in the Univermag cellars, were what remained of the 4th, 8th, 51st Corps and 14th Panzer Corps, while ten miles to the north the mangled 11th Corps clung grimly to a small area around the shattered wreck of the Tractor Factory. With the 6th Army *in extremis* the Stavka began withdrawing whole divisions from the Don Front, sending them westwards to reinforce other Fronts.

Conditions in the two German pockets were appalling. Those too weak, sick, or wounded to go on fighting sought shelter in the cellars and basements of the ruined buildings, where the tons of rubble overhead provided protection from the constant rain of artillery shells and bombs. There, in the darkness and icy cold, the sick, the mad, the dead and the dying lay crowded together. Above them, on the tallest of the ruins, fluttered the Reich's red, white and black swastika battle flag, symbolizing both defiance and the cause of 6th Army's agony.

During the last days of the struggle the cellars of the ruined buildings in the two pockets became scenes of unimaginable horror and torment: each one was a miniature hell in which men died *en masse*.

A description of the conditions in the cellars buried under the rubble of what had been Simonovitch's warehouse serves as an example of the hundreds of anonymous cellars that became charnel houses during 6th Army's agonizing death throes. 'Eight hundred men lay pressed against the walls and all over the damp and dirty floor. Their bodies littered the stairs and blocked the passages. All men were equal here: rank and class had been shed as the dead leaves fall from the November trees. In the Simonovitch cellars they had reached the end of life's weary journey, and if there were any distinctions to be drawn between them it was only in the severity of their wounds or in the number of the days that they still had to live.'[17] Frost-bitten feet turned gangrenous and the putrid smelling, rotting flesh spread rapidly up the legs of those so inflicted. Dysentery, typhus, tetanus, spotted fever, pneumonia, gangrene and the extremes of dehydration and starvation all took their fearsome toll.

Simonovitch's cellars 'stank of fetid blood and gangrenous flesh and suppurating pus, and over all was the sickly smell of decaying bodies and iodine and sweat and excrement and filth. The air was well-nigh unbreathable, lungs and throats were parched, and eyes streamed tears.'[18] Men shook with fever or shivered from the merciless cold, fear and icy despair. They moaned and screamed until death, their only friend, stilled their torment.

'The lice were the worst, they bit through the men's skin, crawled into open wounds, and prevented the sleep so desperately needed. In their thousands they swarmed over the men's bodies and filthy, tattered underwear; only when death came, or high fever, did they depart, like rats leaving a sinking ship. A disgusting grey, swarming crowd would then move across to the next man and settle on him.'[19]

Amongst the screaming and moaning, the cellars echoed with calls for water and food; they called for a priest, a doctor, an orderly, for morphia, bandages, for their mother, wife or children, and some asked for a revolver. For the lucky ones sometimes a revolver was available, the only request that could be granted, and they were able to put an end to their misery with a bullet through the brain. It is estimated that about a quarter of the total number of men trapped in the two pockets lay in the fetid cellars of Stalingrad. A death sentence was passed on all of them on 28 January, for reasons given in a chilling signal sent to Heeresgruppe Don by 6th Army's Chief of Operations: 'Food situation compels suspension of issue of rations to wounded and sick, in order to keep alive fighting personnel.' This situation had come about because the majority of the heavy bomb-canisters dropped by the Luftwaffe were falling wide of the two pockets, or falling into the tall shells of ruined buildings where the physically exhausted troops could not retrieve them.

Six days earlier, on 21 January, Zeitzler and the senior officers of the Operations Department had voluntarily put themselves on the same scale of starvation rations as the troops in Stalingrad as a gesture of solidarity. But on the 28th they had to abandon this gesture, finding that they could not function properly. The troops in Stalingrad had lived on that scale for over three months!

During the course of Thursday the 28th, the Russians split the southern pocket in two. On Paulus's situation maps the following dispositions were now recorded:

Northern Pocket: 11th Army Corps, consisting of the 60th Motorized, 16th and 24th Panzer, 389th Infantry, and the 100th Jäger Divisions.

Central Pocket: 8th and 51st Corps, consisting of the 113th, 76th, 79th, 295th, 305th and 384th Infantry and the 29th and 3rd Motorized Divisions.

Southern Pocket: 4th Corps and 14th Panzer Corps, consisting of the 71st and 371st Infantry Divisions, which were grouped around Paulus's command post in the Univermag cellars.

Only fifteen of the twenty-two original divisions which had been encircled were now listed, although, in reality, they existed in name only. The other seven divisions had either surrendered or been completely consumed in the inferno that was incinerating 6th Army.

Above Paulus's command post in the cellars of the wholly gutted Univermag, the remains of a staircase, which had once led to the now nonexistent upper floors, trembled nakedly in the icy north-easterly wind. The fragments of the outer walls that still stood were cracked and in imminent danger of collapsing every time a shell or mortar exploded among the ruins of the once huge department store. Below this pile of fire-raked devastation Paulus lay on his camp-bed prostrate with dysentery and nervous collapse. It was General Arthur Schmidt, the die-hard Nazi, who now held the reins of the pathetic wreck of the once huge army which had numbered 330,000 men the previous summer. What the living skeletons of this once proud army thought of a radio message sent by Goering on the evening of the 28th, whose vain boast that he could supply them from the air was partly responsible for their desperate situation, is unrecorded but can easily be imagined:

> The fight put up by the 6th Army will go down in history, and future generations will speak proudly of a Langemarck of dare-devilry, an Alcazar of tenacity, a Narvik of courage, and a Stalingrad of self-sacrifice.[20]

Throughout the 29th the three pockets were constantly pounded by thousands of shells, mortars and bombs. These already devastated areas of the city were churned up in a massive upheaval of explosions, raging fires and vast palls of smoke which hung over each pocket like black funeral shrouds. Thousands died in the conflagration and 'he who fell, fell and the stars will not reveal his name nor the place of his death. The numbers of those who died, a thousand more or a thousand less, do not matter.'[21]

At noon on Saturday 30 January, 6th Army was treated to another sickening piece of bombast from Goering, when he made a speech, broadcast over German radio, celebrating the tenth anniversary of the Nazi seizure of power:

> There came the day when for the first time Panzer Grenadiers forced their way into the Stalingrad stronghold and gained a foothold along the Volga. This will go down in history as our greatest and most heroic battle. What our grenadiers, engineers, artillery-men, anti-aircraft gunners and others in that city, from the generals on down, have achieved is without precedent. Although most of them were racked with weariness and exhaustion, they continued to fight with undiminished courage against overwhelmingly superior forces. A thousand years hence Germans will speak of this battle with reverence and awe, and will remember that in spite of everything Germany's ultimate victory was decided there.... In years to come it will be said of the heroic battle on the Volga: when you come to Germany, say that you have see us lying at Stalingrad, as our honour and our leaders ordained that we should, for the greater glory of Germany. It may sound harsh to say that it was necessary that soldiers must die at Stalingrad, in the African desert or in the icy wastes of the north; if we soldiers are not prepared to risk our lives, then we would have done better to enter a monastery.... A soldier who goes into battle must know that he will probably not return. If he does come back, he should be thankful for his good fortune.[22]

While this, their funeral oration, was being broadcast, the men at Stalingrad were filled with disgust to hear that their appalling end was being disguised from the German public under hypocritical phrases concerning necessity and honour. On his own initiative a radio operator in the northern pocket gave vent to his feelings by sending the following message over the air-waves: 'Premature funeral orations are not appreciated here.'

THE END IN THE CENTRAL POCKET

While Goering was making his speech the Russians set about destroying the central pocket, launching heavy attacks simultaneously from the north and west. By nightfall on 30 January, the few survivors in this pocket who not been blown to pieces by artillery firing over open sights at point blank range, threw away their weapons and surrendered. Amongst those taken prisoner was General von Seydlitz-Kurzbach who had done everything possible to persuade Paulus to break out during the first few weeks of the encirclement, He entered captivity cursing the Nazis and Hitler's insanity. Three corps, 8th, 51st and 14th Panzer, had ceased to exist.

Two hours before the forces in the central pocket surrendered, General Schmidt, having only a vague idea of what was going on, radioed to Manstein from 6th Army's command post that:

> The remains of the Sixth Army closely confined in the three fortresses still hold some built-up areas west of the railway station and south of the water-works. 4th Army Corps (southern pocket) no longer exists. 14th Panzer Corps has surrendered. No information concerning 8th and 51st Corps. Final collapse cannot be delayed for more than twenty-four hours.[23]

When Hitler was made aware that Schmidt considered final collapse imminent, he immediately showered promotions on 6th Army's senior officers. The promotion of 117 officers up to and including the rank of Major-General was radioed to 6th Army HQ, while Paulus was given the supreme honour of being elevated to the rank of Field-Marshal. But Hitler had an ulterior motive. On the previous evening he had remarked to Field-Marshal Keitel that: 'There is no record in military history of a German Field-Marshal being taken prisoner.' He was obviously hoping that Paulus would take the hint and either die fighting or take his own life rather than surrender to the Russians. Unaware of Hitler's motive Paulus replied:

> To the Führer!
> On the anniversary of your accession to power, the Sixth Army sends greetings to its Führer. The swastika flag still flutters over Stalingrad. Should our struggle be an example to present and future generations never to surrender, even when all hope is gone, then Germany will be victorious. *Heil, mein Führer!*[24]

THE END IN THE SOUTHERN POCKET

During the night of 30/31 January, Russian assault troops infiltrated into Red Square, a literal stone's throw away from Paulus' subterranean command post under the Univermag, which was being defended by the survivors of the 194th Infantry Regiment of the 71st Division. At 0130 that night Hitler instructed Zeitzler to send the following message: 'The Führer asks me to point out that each day that Festung Stalingrad holds out is of importance.'[25] Important that is to Hitler's prestige, for no other reason now existed. In response Schmidt radioed:

In the basement ruins of Red Square, Stalingrad, surrounded by the thunder of enemy gunfire, we have read our Führer's proclamations. It has given us courage and resolution for these last hours of the battle for the ruins of the Red Citadel on the Volga. Above us flies the swastika banner. The orders of our Supreme Command are being obeyed to the end. We turn our thoughts loyally to the Fatherland. Long live the Führer!'[26]

When Schmidt sent this message the defence perimeter around the Univermag had been reduced in circumference to a three-hundred yard 'hedgehog,' which was surrounded by the tanks and infantry of the Soviet 38th Motorized Brigade of General Shumilov's Sixty-fourth Army.

At 0615 on the morning of the 31st the radio operator in Paulus's command post sent the following message: 'Russians are at the door. We are preparing to destroy the radio equipment.' An hour later the last transmission was made from the command post: 'We are destroying the equipment.' This message signalled the end of the southern pocket and the capture of Paulus and his staff.

The man who 'captured' Paulus was twenty-one-year-old Lieutenant Fedor Ilchenko. At 0715 a Russian-speaking German officer climbed out of the Univermag cellars and waved a white flag. He shouted to Ilchenko: 'My big chief wants to talk to your big chief.' Ilchenko replied: 'I am the big chief here. Take me to your man.' As Ilchenko, accompanied by fifteen Russian soldiers, started to walk towards the Univermag some Germans yelled out that the entrance was mined. They led the Russian party to a side entrance to the cellars, which were packed with German soldiers who had sought shelter from the artillery and mortar fire. After pushing his way through the throng Ilchenko finally came face to face with General Arthur Schmidt, and negotiations began.

Three Soviet witnesses recount the details of what subsequently transpired. Lieutenant-General Laskin, the Chief of Staff of Sixty-fourth Army, records that:

On the morning of Sunday 31 January, 1943, General Shumilov received a report from Colonel Burmakov, commander of the 38th

Motorized Brigade, that the building of a department store, where the headquarters of the German 6th Army was housed, had been encircled and that Lieutenant Ilchenko was negotiating with a representative of Paulus who had left the store carrying a white flag.

At about 0840 Colonel Burmakov and I arrived at the forward edge of the Brigade. Coming up to the department store, we descended to an unilluminated basement and then entered a large cellar. A German general standing at the table reported that he was Lieutenant-General Schmidt, Chief of Staff of the 6th Army. I stated that I was a responsible representative of General Rokossovsky (Commanding the Don Front) and was authorized to conduct negotiations on surrender.

We presented a demand that an order should be given immediately to the troops to cease fire, then we asked about the whereabouts of Colonel-General Paulus. Schmidt replied that Paulus had been promoted to the rank of Field-Marshal and at the time was in another room in the same basement. We suggested that Schmidt call Paulus to our room.

Having presented our ultimatum to Paulus, I requested that he should immediately order the German troops in the northern pocket to cease fire, and also that he should tell us about the latest instructions issued by Hitler to the 6th Army. Paulus said that his army had been cut into two isolated groups and the army's headquarters had no contact with the northern pocket. In view of this, the question of each group's surrender, he held, had to be decided by the group commanders. As to Hitler's latest instructions, Paulus replied: 'The demand was repeated that we carry on resistance in the hope that the Manstein grouping would battle its way to Stalingrad.'[27]

From the Univermag Paulus and his staff were driven to General Shumilov's headquarters at Beketovka on the southern outskirts of the ruined city. Shumilov records that:

At about noon on 31 January, Paulus, Schmidt and Adam (Paulus's adjutant) were escorted into my room. Before me was the first German Field-Marshal taken prisoner by the Red Army. All of a sudden the three of them shot up their right arms, saying 'Heil Hitler!' I snapped back: 'There's no Hitler here. Before you is the commander of the Sixty-fourth Army whose troops have taken you prisoner, so please salute in a manner befitting the situation.' The three men complied. I invited them to take seats.

In reply to my request: 'Present your documents,' Paulus gave me a soldier's service book and it had no meaning for me at all. Paulus said that he was a soldier of the German Army. To this I objected that I was a soldier of the Red Army but held a definite post in its ranks.

After this he showed me his identity card of Commander of the 6th Army. I said that we had learnt about him having been promoted to the rank of Field-Marshal, and asked whether this was true. Lieutenant-General Schmidt jumped to his feet and said: 'We have received Hitler's order by radio saying that Paulus has been awarded the rank of Field-Marshal.' I asked: 'May I report this to my Supreme Command?' Both men answered in the affirmative.

Several more questions were asked after which we went to the canteen. On our way Paulus asked me: 'Tell me, General, what is the explanation of the fact that your soldiers attack day and night and lay in the snow when the frost reaches minus 35-40 degrees below zero?' A soldier was standing nearby. I called him up and said to Paulus: 'Just look at the way our soldiers are dressed.' The man wore felt boots, quilted trousers, warm underclothes, a sheepskin coat, a fur-cap with ear-flaps and warm mittens. The Field-Marshal's face became distorted: he evidently recalled the picture he had seen when he was being driven to my headquarters. On his way he passed a mass of German POWs who plodded along, stooping, with heads covered with whatever they could lay their hands on: old rags, sacks or pieces of felt. On their feet they had worn-out boots tied round with straw to prevent them from falling apart.[28]

After dining in the canteen, Paulus and his staff were sent to the Don Front headquarters at Ivanovka fifteen miles to the south of Stalingrad. General Voronov, Stavka's representative at Rokossovsky's HQ, recalls that:

On the evening of 31 January the captive Field-Marshal Paulus was summoned for an interrogation. The door to the big room where Rokossovsky and I were waiting opened. Paulus walked in, stopped and saluted. 'Take a seat here at the table,' I told him. An interpreter translated my words. Paulus walked in and sat in the chair. Before us was a tall, elderly man with a thin pale face and tired eyes. He seemed somewhat confused and at a loss. The left side of his face twitched and his hands trembled. He did not know what to do with them. I offered him a cigarette. He nodded his gratitude but did not take it. Then I said: 'We suggest that you order the grouping still fighting (the northern pocket) to cease fire in order to avoid unnecessary bloodshed.' Paulus listened attentively to the interpreter, sighed heavily and then spoke unhurriedly in German. He said that he regretted he could not accept our suggestion because he was now a prisoner of war and his orders would not be valid. I was forced to warn Paulus that by refusing to order the surrender of the surrounded German group he would be held responsible to history and the German people for the senseless death of his subordinates who were in a hopeless position.

After this I asked him what diet he needed to sustain his health. A look of surprise came into his face. Slowly choosing his words he replied that personally he needed nothing special. His only request was that our command should not maltreat wounded and sick German officers and men. I told him the Soviet Army was always humane towards prisoners, particularly to the wounded and sick, but stressed that our medical service was encountering difficulties because the German medical personnel had abandoned hospitals filled with wounded. 'The Field-Marshal must understand,' I added, 'how hard it is to organize quickly the normal medical treatment of wounded German officers and men under such conditions.' This statement strongly impressed Paulus. He was silent for a long time and then said with an effort: 'In war one sometimes finds a situation in which orders are not carried out.' I replied: 'I want the Field-Marshal to know that through his fault many German officers and men [in the northern pocket] will be killed tomorrow.' The conversation ended there. Paulus silently got up, straightened his shoulders, turned and slowly walked out of the room.[29]

During the night of 31 January the Russians published a special communique, announcing the surrender and giving the names of all the senior officers who had been captured. Hitler was furious when he learned that Paulus had not put a pistol to his head as he expected him to do, commenting that he had done an about-face on the threshold of history. He simply could not understand how Paulus could have chosen the Tartarus of Soviet captivity rather than accept the Valhalla he, Hitler, had opened unto him.

At the midday situation conference held in the Wolfsschanze on 1 February, Hitler voiced his fears of what would follow along with his contempt for Paulus:

They have surrendered there formally and absolutely. Otherwise they would have closed ranks, formed a hedgehog, and shot themselves with their last bullets. ...The man [Paulus] should have shot himself just as the old commanders who threw themselves on their swords when they saw that the cause was lost... Even Varus gave his slave the order: 'Now kill me!'

His venom toward Paulus for deciding to live became more poisonous as he ranted on:

You have to imagine: they'll be brought to Moscow — and imagine that rat-trap there. There they will sign anything, and they'll blurt out orders for the northern pocket to surrender too. They'll make confessions, make proclamations — you'll see. They will now walk down the slope of spiritual bankruptcy to its lowest depths... You'll see — it won't be a week before Seydlitz and Schmidt and even Paulus are talking over the radio... They are going to be put into the Lubianka (prison), and there the rats will eat them. How can one be so cowardly? I don't understand it...

What is life? Life is the Nation. The individual must die anyway. Beyond the life of the individual is the Nation. But how can anyone be afraid of this moment of death, with which he can free himself from this misery, if his duty doesn't chain him to this Vale of Tears....

So many people have to die, and then a man like that besmirches the heroism of so many others at the last minute. He could have freed himself from all sorrow and ascended into eternity and national immortality, but he prefers to go to Moscow!...

What hurts me most, personally, is that I promoted him to field-marshal. I wanted to give him this final satisfaction. That's the last field-marshal I shall appoint in this war. You must not count your chickens before they're hatched.[30]

The underlying reason for Hitler's outrage was the fear that Paulus, Schmidt and Seydlitz would slander him and his regime in radio broadcasts from Moscow. This fear was only partly realized. General Arthur Schmidt remained loyal throughout the twelve years eight months of his captivity (he was released in October, 1955). Despite being kept in solitary confinement for long periods and suffering physical abuse, he doggedly refused to co-operate with the Soviet authorities and denounce Hitler.

Initially Paulus also refused to co-operate with his captors, who wanted him to make anti-Nazi radio broadcasts. It was only at the end of July, 1944, when he heard the news of the abortive 'bomb-plot' to assassinate Hitler, and that old and trusted friends like Field-Marshal von Witzleben, Generals Höpner and Fellgiebel and Major von Stauffenberg had been arrested by the Gestapo, that he was finally persuaded to make broadcasts over the radio urging the German troops on the Eastern Front to desert or disobey Hitler's 'murderous orders'. His first broadcast was made on 8 August, 1944, the day on which von Witzleben and Höpner were tried by the Peoples' Court in Berlin, convicted and hanged.

General von Seydlitz-Kurzbach, the most enlightened of the three, was the first to denounce Hitler over Moscow radio. He made his first broadcast during the summer of 1943. He was also the prime mover in the creation of the *Bund Deutsche Offiziere* (The Federation of German Officers), a part of the communist-inspired *Nationalkomitee Freies Deutschland* (National Committee of Free Germany), an anti-Fascist group of Germans in Russian captivity dedicated to the overthrow of the Third Reich.

The indecent haste with which Hitler reviled and maligned Paulus and the others — men who had obeyed his insane, murderous orders to the bitter end — heralded 'the beginning of the debasement of the concept of soldierly devotion to duty, to the extent that the *espirt de corps* of the German Officer Corps was shattered. It was the most baleful heritage resulting from the Stalingrad catastrophe. Not only did the superstitious and incomprehensible belief in the exceptional abilities of Hitler, the amateur who had usurped full control of the Armed Forces, melt away, but mutual distrust began to spread among the senior ranks of the German officers. It was from this point that a common front began to form among some of the younger officers of the General Staff against Hitler's senseless methods of waging war. And this is the most significantly fateful feature which the battle contributed to the history of the German Army in the Second World War.'[31]

FINALE IN THE NORTHERN POCKET

The agony being endured by the remnants of General Karl Strecker's 11th Corps in the northern pocket dragged on for two days after the fall of the southern pocket. During the course of Monday, 1 February, Russian aircraft showered leaflets over the pocket showing photographs of Paulus as a prisoner. It was to no avail. Despite the fact that the bitter fighting around the ruins of the Dzerhezinsky Tractor Factory no longer had any significance whatsoever, Hitler insisted on its continuation in a signal sent to Strecker during the night of 31 January, which was complete with a pathetic attempt at justification: 'The German people expect you to do your duty exactly as did the troops holding the Southern Fortress. Every day, every hour that is won benefits the rest of the front decisively.'[32] As a result the slaughter went on, and a further 4,000 German soldiers died. Units were blown sky-high, or buried beneath the ruins as shells, mortars and bombs shrieked down in a terrifying torrent on the Tractor Factory and its immediate surrounds throughout the day and night of 1 February.

At 0500 the following morning the surviving senior officers of the five shattered divisions still holding out were called to a council of war in the headquarters of the 16th Panzer Division. This had been set up in a cellar of a small factory a thousand yards to the south-west of the Tractor Factory. Twenty officers, unshaven, some with dirty blood-stained bandages covering a variety of wounds, wearing tattered camouflage capes, leather coats or wind-jackets, crowded into the candle-lit cellar where they were addressed by General Strecker: 'Gentleman, the battle is almost over. The Sixth Army no longer exists. We have done our duty to the end. I thank you. My last task is to release you from all of your duties. Each man must now decide for himself what he will do. If any of you should succeed in making your way through to our own lines, give my greetings to Germany.'[33] In effect, Strecker, realizing that further bloodshed was

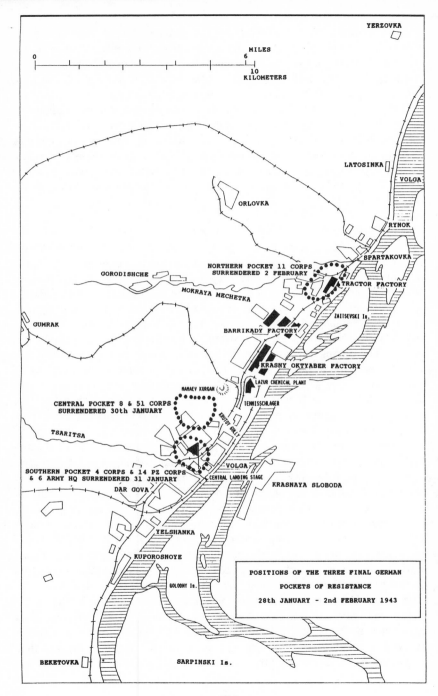

22. General Konstantin Rokossovsky. He commanded the seven Soviet armies on the Don Front, which launched the final offensive to destroy the 6th Army on 10 January, 1943

23. On 26 January, 1943, units of the Soviet 65th Army linked up with 62nd Army. The latter had held the vital bridgeheads in Stalingrad for 136 blood-soaked days. Russian soldiers are shown placing the Red Flag over a recaptured building in the centre of the ruined city

24. After surrendering to the Russians on the morning of 31 January,
1943, Field-Marshal Paulus, Colonel Adam and General Schmidt were
driven to General Shumilov's H.Q. at Beketovka.

25. Dirty and exhausted, Paulus enters the Don Front H.Q. at Ivanovka, 15 miles to the south of Stalingrad, to be interrogated by Generals Voronov and Rokossovsky.

26. Freezing German prisoners shuffling into captivity through the streets of Stalingrad, after the surrender of the central pocket.

27. The survivors of the northern pocket being herded into captivity through the ruined city. All were emaciated and their clothes were infested with vermin. Some were barefoot and the temperature was 30 degrees below freezing.

28. The face of defeat. Of the 91,000 German and Rumanian troops taken prisoner, only 5,000 survived the long, arduous years of captivity in Russian camps. Two thousand of these were not repatriated until 1955, twelve years after the battle.

senseless, had given each officer freedom of action to surrender with their units or attempt to escape to the west.

At 0840, Heeresgruppe Don received the following message: 'Eleventh Corps, with its divisions have fought to the last man against vastly superior forces. Long live the Führer! Long live Germany!'[34] Strecker had called it a day.

Consequently, when at noon on 2 February, whole Soviet divisions from Chuikov's Sixty-second, Zhadov's Sixty-sixth and Galanin's Twenty-fourth Armies attacked the pocket simultaneously from the west, north-west and east respectively, they met with very little resistance. The majority of the German troops waved scraps of white rag and clambered out of the ruins with their hands above their heads. Only a few diehards fought on and they paid with their lives. Chuikov recalls that:

We watched hundreds of prisoners go by... All the privates and non-commissioned officers were emaciated, and their clothes were infected with vermin. Most wretched of all were the Rumanian soldiers; they were dressed so badly it was terrible to look at them. Although the temperature was thirty degrees below zero some of them were barefoot. The German officers, on the other hand, were well-fed and had pockets stuffed with cold sausage and other food, obviously left over after the meagre rations had been issued.

At the Sixty-second Army's last observation post, in the shattered offices of the Krasny Oktyaber factory, the Military Council, divisional and some regimental commanders met. We joyfully congratulated one another on the victory, and remembered those who had not lived to see it.[35]

At 1235 Heeresgruppe Don picked up what proved to be the last wireless message sent by 6th Army. It was sent by a meteorological unit in the northern pocket: 'Cloud base 15,000 feet, visibility seven miles, clear sky, occasional scattered nimbus clouds, temperature minus 31 degrees centigrade. Over Stalingrad fog and red haze. Meteorological station now closing down. Greetings to the homeland.' [36] After that there was silence.

At 1500 that afternoon Milch received a signal from Luftflotte IV: 'No sign of any fighting at Stalingrad.'[37] Milch, nonetheless, ordered a further ten supply planes to fly to Stalingrad to ascertain if any German troops were still holding out. At 1830, when eight of the ten planes returned from their mission the squadron leader reported that: 'Four planes observed no activity of any kind where the German front was assumed to be. Two planes were not able to report with any degree of certainty. The other two jettisoned their loads because they thought they had seen movement.'[38] To make absolutely sure that the end had indeed come, Milch ordered yet another six transports to make the flight. The results were reported at 2200:

'Anti-aircraft defences are very strong. It is no longer possible to identify any sort of a German-held pocket, nor is there any sign of artillery fire. Horse-drawn and motorized enemy columns are moving through the town in every direction and star shells of all colours are being fired without any apparent meaning or purpose.'[39]

When Milch passed on this report to Hitler, the small blue circle round the Tractor Factory in Stalingrad on 'Map 4 East' was struck through in red. The life of 6th Army had run its course.

On the evening of 2 February, Rokossovsky sent the following dispatch to Stalin:

Carrying out your orders, the troops of the Don Front at 1600 on February 2nd, 1943, completed the rout and destruction of the encircled group of enemy forces at Stalingrad. Twenty-two divisions have been destroyed or taken prisoner... The prisoners number 91,000, including 2,500 officers and 24 generals, among them 1 field-marshal, 2 colonel-generals, the rest lieutenant-generals and major-generals... As a result of this final liquidation of the enemy forces, the military operations in the city and the area of Stalingrad have ceased.[40]

After 164 days of carnage the guns finally fell silent and peace returned to the fire-blackened shell that in August, 1942, had been the home of 600,000 souls. During the five months of fighting that began on 23 August, 1942 and ended on 2 February, 1943, ninety-nine percent of Stalingrad had been reduced to rubble: 41,000 homes, 300 factories, and 113 hospitals and schools had been completely destroyed. The severity of the street fighting is attested to by the fact that from amongst the ruins of the city the Russians removed the corpses of 147,200 Germans and 46,700 Russian troops and civilians.

On 3 February the text of a special Oberkommando der Wehrmacht communique was read out over the German radio. It was preceded by muffled roll on the drums and followed by the playing of the funeral march from the second movement of Beethoven's Third Symphony:

The battle of Stalingrad has ended. True to their oath .to fight to the last breath, the Sixth army under the exemplary leadership of Field-Marshal Paulus has been overcome by the superiority of the enemy and by the unfavourable circumstances confronting our forces. The enemy's two demands for capitulation were proudly rejected. The last battle was fought under a swastika flag flying from the highest ruin in Stalingrad. Generals, officers, non-commissioned officers and men fought shoulder to shoulder to the last bullet. They died that Germany might live.[41]

Hitler proclaimed three days of national mourning. All of the theatres, restaurants, cinemas and places of entertainment throughout the Reich were closed. The normal radio broadcasts were suspended and replaced by three days of droning funeral music. The German population and armed forces alike were profoundly shocked by the disaster at Stalingrad. Never before in Germany's history had so large a body of troops come to so dreadful an end. But Hitler, the architect of the disaster seemed, according to Zeitzler, 'to be utterly unaffected by the bloody tragedy of Stalingrad, by the cruel sufferings of hundreds of thousands of his soldiers or by the misery inflicted upon their families. He seemed to shake it all from him, and was soon planning enthusiastically for the future. "We shall create the Sixth Army anew," he said. This was his solution.'[42]

ELEGY

On the day the German population learned of the defeat at Stalingrad, Russian newspapers published photographs of long grey columns of German prisoners, shuffling through the snow towards temporary POW camps that had been constructed near Beketovka on the southern outskirts of the wholly ruined city. Amongst the 91,000 prisoners were a lot who had already contacted typhus, and when they were herded together in the make-shift camps an epidemic quickly spread through their ranks. Enfeebled by cold and hunger thirty-four thousand succumbed to the disease. They were buried in mass graves. Those who survived had to endure a hundred-mile march to Saratov, where they were herded on to trains destined for twenty separate prison camps, which were scattered throughout the Soviet Union from the Arctic circle to the southern deserts near the border with Afghanistan.

Many died during the long march over the frozen steppes. Time and again the columns of misery were raided for personal belongings, sometimes by Red Army troops but more often by civilians. The prisoners were only lightly guarded and those who dropped out through sickness or exhaustion were left to the mercy of the marauding bands of armed civilians who followed the columns. None of those who dropped out were ever seen again. Thousands more died during the long train journeys across Siberia. At each stop the dead were unloaded from the cattle trucks and only fifty per cent of those who had entrained arrived at their destinations. It is estimated that by May, 1943, only 15,000 of the 91,000 taken prisoner on 2 February remained alive. Of these only 5,000 survived the long, bitter, arduous years of captivity to see Germany again, 2,000 of these not being repatriated until 1955, twelve years after the battle.

Except for a brief visit to Nuremburg, where he appeared as a Soviet prosecution witness against the senior commanders of the German Armed Forces during the War Trials held in 1946, Paulus was held captive for ten years by the Russians, albeit in quite comfortable conditions on the outskirts of Moscow. When he was finally released in November, 1953, he chose to live in Dresden, East Germany. For a short while he served as an inspector in the 'People's Police'. But only two years after his release he contracted 'amyelstrophic lateral sclerosis' (motor neurone disease) and he died in a Dresden clinic on 1 February, 1957, at the age of sixty-two. He was destined never to be reunited with his wife, Elena Constance Paulus. She was imprisoned by the Gestapo when Paulus began his anti-Fascist broadcasts from Moscow in August, 1944, on Hitler's personal orders under the terms of *Sippenhaft*, the Nazi law of collective family responsibility of anyone who opposed the regime. Liberated from an Alpine detention centre by American soldiers at the end of the war, Elena died of natural causes at Baden-Baden in 1949. Paulus had two sons: Alexander, who was killed at Anzio in 1944, and Ernst, who committed suicide in 1970 at the age of fifty-two (his father's age when he surrendered at Stalingrad).

Of the 267,000 German and Rumanian troops surrounded in the Stalingrad Kessel on 23 November, 1942, 29,000 wounded and 7,000 'specialists' were evacuated by air and 140,000 were killed by enemy action, disease, starvation and exposure. Of the 91,000 taken prisoner only 5,000 survived, which brought the eventual death toll to 226,000. In addition some 15,000 troops of 6th Army were killed during the Russian Kontrudar between 19 and 23 November, bringing the total 6th Army death toll to 241,000. But this was only a part of the cost of Hitler's obsession with Stalingrad. Outside the Kessel, but as a direct result of the dispositions on the Stalingrad axis, the 4th Panzer Army, the 3rd and 4th Rumanian Armies, and the 8th Italian and 2nd Hungarian Armies, had been destroyed, wiping a further 300,000 men from the Axis order of battle, for a grand death total of 541,000 men. Soviet casualty figures have never been made known, but at a conservative estimate they must, due to the ferocity of the fighting, have at least equalled the Axis total. Stalingrad had cost well over a million lives.

It was a blow from which the Wehrmacht never recovered, for although Stalingrad cost the Soviet Union as much in spilled blood and military hardware, Stalin was able to cover the cost on account of the huge well of reserves and resources at his disposal. In comparison Hitler's assets were tottering into bankruptcy.

Coupled with El Alamein and the Anglo-American landings in North Africa, Stalingrad marked one of the great turning points of the Second World War. The high tide of German conquest which had rolled over most of Europe to the frontier of Asia on the Volga and in Africa almost to the Nile, had began to ebb and would never flow back again. Although the German Army would launch desperate counter-offensives at Kursk in the spring of 1943 and in the Ardennes in December, 1944, they formed part of a defensive strategy bolstered by an unrealistic hope of regaining the initiative. At Stalingrad the initiative passed out of Hitler's hands for ever, and his dream of Lebensraum — the very *raison d'etre* of the war — lay buried so deep under the rubble of the fire-blackened, blood-soaked city sprawled along twenty-five miles of the Volga that it could never be resurrected.

The consequences of the Stalingrad disaster on Hitler's allies was equally profound. The governments of Rumania and Hungary, whose countries lay athwart the Soviet road to the west, began looking to their own salvation. During the spring of 1943 they began casting about for contacts and understandings with the Western Allies who, they hoped, might shelter them from the full consequences of a Soviet victory.

After the war Stalingrad was completely rebuilt according to plans drawn up in 1945, which eliminated many of the old city's shortcomings. The riverside was freed of industrial structures, storehouses and the like which had cut off the residential regions from the river. The centre of the modern city, which was renamed Volgograd in 1961, is formed by a system of squares and boulevards dispersed along one axis parallel to the Volga. Volgograd is now the home of 1,000,000 people and its new apartment buildings and factories extend for more than 40 miles along the western bank of the Volga. To honour the Russian dead of the great battle, a huge 200-feet-high female statue, cast in a classical style, holding a sword aloft — 'Motherland Calls' — was erected on the top of Mamaev Kurgan (the Tartar burial mound) during the years 1963-67. Apart from a museum filled with artifacts of the battle, the only other reminder of the momentous event is a marble slab affixed to the wall of the new Univermag department store, which carries the inscription: 'In this building, on the 31st of January, 1943, the commanders of the fascist invaders surrendered to the heroes of the Red Army.'

Unlike other theatres of war, there are no German war cemeteries in or near Volgograd, or anywhere else in the Soviet Union for that matter. All of the 147,200 German dead removed from the rubble of Stalingrad were burned and their ashes thrown into the Volga. The same fate was awarded to the thousands of unburied frozen German corpses which littered the steppe to the west of the city within the area of the Kessel. The German cemeteries which did exist on the Don — Volga isthmus (the resting places of those killed in the early months of the battle) were disinterred, and the corpses cast into mass graves with nothing to mark the spot. At the end of October, 1942, Hitler had boasted that 'where the German soldier sets foot, there he remains... You may rest assured that nobody will ever drive us away from Stalingrad.' This boast was vindicated, but with the proviso that those who remain do so in hundreds of unmarked graves.

The few fortunate German survivors of the battle and the subsequent captivity were haunted by the spectre of Stalingrad for the rest of their lives. In their dreams and memories they heard again the harsh clangour of war, and the howling wind sweeping across the steppe; they saw again the hellish pyrotechnics of war that by night, those 'howling, bleeding, screeching nights,' illuminated the vast ruin of the city in the garish glow of flares, tracer, explosions and the giant fires which swept the streets; they also saw the ghostly, hollow-eyed faces of their dead comrades mutilated by starvation, disease, bullets, shells, grenades and bombs. And whenever their dreams and memories transported them back to those terrible days an intense cold gripped their hearts — a deeper chill than they ever experienced during the agony of Stalingrad.

APPENDIX I

SOVIET ORDER OF BATTLE INVOLVED IN THE KONTRUDAR (Counter-Blow) 19 – 20 NOVEMBER, 1942. SOUTH WESTERN FRONT

First Guards Army:
  1st, 153rd, 197th, and 203rd, 266th & 278th Rifle Divisions. 1st Guards Mechanized Corps (composed of the 1st, 2nd, & 3rd Guards Mechanized Brigades and the 16th & 17th Guards Tank Regiments)*. 22nd Motorized Rifle Brigade.
(*The 1st Guards Mechanized Corps was not fully concentrated on 19 November).

******

Fifth Tank Army:
  14th, 47th & 50th Guards Rifle Divisions. 119th, 159th & 346th Rifle Divisions. 8th Cavalry Corps (composed of the 21st, 55th & 112th Cavalry Divisions). 1st Tank Corps (composed of the 89th, 117th, & 159th Tank Brigades and the 44th Motorized Rifle Brigade). 26th Tank Corps (composed of the 19th, 157th & 216th Tank Brigades and the 14th Motorized Rifle Brigade). 8th Guards Tank Brigade. 8th Motorcycle Regiment. 510th & 511th Independent Tank Battalions.

******

Twenty-first Army:
  63rd, 76th, 96th, 277th, 293rd & 333rd Rifle Divisions. 3rd Guards Cavalry Corps (composed of 5th & 6th Guards Cavalry & 32nd Cavalry Divisions). 5th Independent Engineer Brigade. 1st, 21st, 60th & 99th Independent Anti-tank Battalions. 4th Tank Corps (composed of 45th, 69th & 122nd Tank Brigades and 4th Motorized Rifle Brigade). 1st, 2nd & 4th Guards Independent Tank Regiments.

******

17th Air Army: 388 aircraft.
2nd Air Army: 144 aircraft.
Totals of Formations in South-western Front:
Rifle Divisions 18
Tank Corps 3

DON FRONT

Twenty-fourth Army:
    49th, 84th, 120th, 173rd, 214th, 233rd, 260th, 273rd, & 298th Rifle Divisions. 54th Fortified Region (UR). 58th & 61st Guards Independent Anti-tank Battalions. 16th Tank Corps (composed of 107th, 109th & 164th Tank Brigades and 15th Motorized Rifle Brigade). 10th Tank Brigade. 134th, 224th & 229th Independent Heavy Tank Battalions.

★★★★★★

Sixty-fifth Army:
    4th, 27th, & 40th Guard Rifle Divisions. 23rd, 24th 252nd, 258th, 304th & 321st Rifle Divisions. 54th & 64th Independent Anti-tank Battalions. 59th & 121st Tank Brigades. 59th Independent Heavy Tank Regiment.

★★★★★★

Sixty-sixth Army:
    64th, 99th, 116th, 226th, 299th & 343rd Rifle Divisions. 63rd Independent Anti-tank Battalion. 58th Tank Brigade.

★★★★★★

16th Air Army: 260 aircraft.
Formations Attached to
The Don Front:
    159th Fortified Region (UR). 65th, 66th, 97th, 98th, 99th, 100th, 101st & 102nd Independent Anti-tank Battalions. 64th & 148th Tank Brigades. 39th, 40th & 377th Independent Anti-aircraft Armoured Regiments.

★★★★★★

Totals of Formations in Don Front.
Rifle Divisions..24
Fortified Regions (UR)...2
Tank Corps 1
Independent Tank Brigades...6

234

STALINGRAD FRONT

Twenty-eighth Army:
 34th Guards Rifle Division. 248th Rifle Division. 52nd, 152nd & 159th Rifle Brigades. 78th & 116th Fortified Regions (UR). Independent Cavalry Regiment (without number). 6th Guards Tank Brigade. 565th Independent Tank Battalion. 35th Independent Heavy Tank Battalion. 30th, 33rd & 46th Independent Heavy Tank Regiment.
******

Fifty-first Army:
 15th Guards Rifle Division. 91st, 126th & 302nd Rifle Divisions. 76th Fortified Region (UR). 4th Cavalry Corps (composed of 61st & 81st Cavalry Divisions). 4th Mechanized Corps (composed of 36th, 59th and 60th Mechanized Brigades and the 55th & 158th Tank Regiments). 38th Motorized Rifle Brigade. 254th Tank Brigade.
******

Fifty-seventh Army:
 169th & 422nd Rifle Divisions. 143rd Rifle Brigade. 45th, 172nd & 177th Independent Machine-gun/Artillery Battalions (URs). 13th Mechanized Corps (composed of the 17th, 61st & 62nd Mechanized Brigades). 90th & 235th Tank Brigades. 156th Independent Naval Infantry Battalion.
******

Sixty-second Army:
 13th, 37th & 39th Guards Rifle Divisions. 45th, 95th, 112th, 131st, 138th, 193rd, 284th & 308th Rifle Divisions. 42nd, 92nd, 115th, 124th, 149th, & 160th Rifle Brigades. 84th Tank Brigade. 506th Independent Tank Battalion.
******

Sixty-fourth Army:
 7th Rifle Corps (composed of 93rd, 96th & 97th Rifle Brigades). 36th Guards Rifle Division. 29th, 38th, 157th & 204th Rifle Divisions. 66th & 154th Naval Infantry Brigades. 20th Independent Engineer Brigade. Composite Cadet Regiment. 118th Fortified Region (UR). 13th & 56th Tank Brigades.
******

8th Air Army: 535 aircraft.
Formations attached to
The Stalingrad Front:
 300th Rifle Division. 77th, 115th & 156th Fortified Region (UR). 85th Tank Brigade. 166th Independent Tank Regiment.

235

Totals of Formations on Stalingrad Front:
Rifle Corps..1
Rifle Divisions...24
Rifle Brigades...15
Motorized Rifle Brigade..1
Independent Engineer Brigade 1
Fortified Regions (UR)...7
Independent Rifle/Cavalry Regiments..2
Cavalry Corps 1
Cavalry Divisions...2
Tank Corps 1
Mechanized Corps..1
Independent Tank Brigades...8
Independent Tank Regiments 2
Independent Tank Battalion 1
Independent Heavy Tank Regiments..4
(Source: A. Samsonov, Stalingradskaia bitva).

APPENDIX II

DENSITY OF THE ATTACK AND BREAK-THROUGH FRONTAGE OF THE SOVIET FORCES INVOLVED IN THE KONTRUDAR 19th-20th NOVEMBER, 1942

		Frontage (miles)	
	Total	Attack Zone	Break-through Sector
South-western Front:			
First Guards Army	109	6	—
Fifth Tank Army	21	16	6
Twenty-first Army	24	11	7
TOTAL	154	33	13
Don Front:			
Sixty-fifth Army	50	10	4
Twenty-fourth Army	24	3	3
Sixty-Sixth Army	19	—	—
TOTAL	93	13	7
Stalingrad Front:			
Sixty-second Army	25	—	—
Sixty-fourth Army	22	8	8
Fifty-seventh Army	22	10	10
Fifty-first Army	81	8	8
Twenty-eighth Army	130	—	—
TOTAL	280	26	26
GRAND TOTAL	527 miles	72 miles	46 miles

(Source: Voenno istorichesky zhurnal, No.3 of 1968, p 72.

APPENDIX III

ORDER OF BATTLE OF GERMAN DIVISIONS TRAPPED IN THE STALINGRAD KESSEL: 23 NOVEMBER, 1942.

44th Infantry Division.
Home Station: Vienna.
Commanding Officer: Lieutenant-General Heinrich Deboi.
Carrying the honorary title 'Reichsgrenadierdivision Hock und Deutschmeister', this was an Austrian division whose troops were drawn from Northern Austria and the southern districts of Czechoslovakia.
Composition: 131st, 132nd and 134th Infantry Regiments; 95th Artillery Regiment; 44th Fusilier Battalion; 46th Anti-tank Battalion; 80th Engineer Battalion; 64th Signal Battalion.

71st Infantry Division.
Home Station: Hildesheim (Hanover).
Commanding Officer: Lieutenant-General Alexander von Hartmann.
Composition: 191st, 194th and 211th Infantry Regiments; 171st Artillery Regiment; 171st Reconnaissance Battalion; 171st Anti-tank Battalion; 171st Engineer Battalion; 171st Signal Battalion.

76th Infantry Division.
Home Station: Berlin.
Commanding Officer: Lieutenant-General Karl Rosenburg.
Composition: 178th, 203rd and 230th Infantry Regiments; 176th Artillery Regiment; 176th Reconnaissance Battalion; 176th Anti-tank Battalion; 176th Engineer Battalion; 176th Signal Battalion.

79th Infantry Division.
Home Station: Koblenz.
Commanding Officer: ?
Composition: 208th, 212th and 226th Infantry Regiments; 179th Artillery Regiment; 179th Reconnaissance Battalion; 179th Anti-tank Battalion; 179th Engineer Battalion; 179th Signal Battalion.

94th Infantry Division.

Home Station: Dresden.
Commanding Officer: Lieutenant-General George Pfeiffer.
Composition: 267th, 274th, and 276th Infantry Regiments; 194th Artillery Regiment; 194th Reconnaissance Battalion; 194th Anti-tank Battalion; 194th Engineer Battalion; 194th Signal Battalion.

100th Jäger Division.
Home Station: Vienna.
Commanding Officer: Lieutenant-General Sann.
The Jäger (light) divisions differed from infantry divisions in that their equipment, particularly in artillery and anti-tank guns, was of a lighter scale and smaller calibre, and they were composed of two instead of three regiments. They were created as pursuit divisions.
Composition: 54th and 227th Jäger Regiments; 83rd Artillery Regiment; 100th Reconnaissance Battalion; 100th Anti-tank Battalion; 100th Engineer Battalion; 100th Signal Battalion. Attached to this division was the 369th Reinforced Croatian Infantry Regiment.

113th Infantry Division.
Home Station: Nuremberg (Bavaria).
Commanding Officer: Lieutenant-General Hans Heinrich Sixt von Armin.
Composition: 260th, 261st and 268th Infantry Regiments; 87th Artillery Regiment; 113th Reconnaissance Battalion; 113th Anti-tank Battalion; 113th Engineer Battalion; 113th Signal Battalion.

295th Infantry Division.
Home Station: Hanover.
Commanding Officer: Major-General Dr. Otto Korfes.
Composition: 516th, 517th and 518th Infantry Regiments; 295th Artillery Regiment; 295th Reconnaissance Battalion; 295th Anti-tank Battalion; 295th Engineer Battalion; 295th Signal Battalion.

297th Infantry Division.
Home Station: Vienna.
Commanding Officer: Major-General Moritz von Drebber.
Composition: 522nd, 523rd and 524th Infantry Regiments; 297th Artillery Regiment; 297th Reconnaissance Battalion; 297th Anti-tank Battalion; 297th Engineer Battalion; 297th Signal Battalion.

305th Infantry Division.
Home Station: Konstanz.
Commanding Officer: Major-General Kurt Oppenlaender.

Composition: 576th, 577th, 578th Infantry Regiments; 305th Artillery Regiment; 305th Reconnaissance Company; 305th Anti-tank Battalion; 305th Engineer Battalion; 305th Signal Company.

371st Infantry Division.
Home Station: Munster.
Commanding Officer: Lieutenant-General Richard Stempel.
Composition: 669th, 670th and 671st Infantry Regiments; 371st Reconnaissance Company; 371st Anti-tank Battalion; 371st Engineer Battalion; 371st Signal Company.

376th Infantry Division.
Home Station: Munich.
Commanding Officer: Lieutenant-General Alexander Edler von Daniels.
Composition: 672nd, 673rd and 766th Infantry Regiment; 376th Artillery Regiment; 376th Reconnaissance Company; 376th Anti-tank Battalion; 376th Engineer Battalion; 376th Signal Company.

384th Infantry Division.
Home Station: Dresden.
Commanding Officer: Lieutenant-General Eccard Freiherr von Gablenz.
General von Gablenz and the headquarters staff of this division escaped encirclement. The three infantry regiments, which were virtually destroyed in the retreat across the Don, were attached to the 44th Infantry Division, while the other units were attached to the 76th Infantry Division.
Composition: 534th, 535th and 536th Infantry Regiment; 384th Artillery Regiment; 384th Reconnaissance Company; 384th Anti-tank Battalion; 384th Engineer Battalion; 384th Signal Company.

389th Infantry Division.
Home Station: Wiesbaden.
Commanding Officer: Major-General Martin Lattman.
Composition: 544th, 545th and 546th Infantry Regiment; 389th Artillery Regiment; 389th Reconnaissance Company; 389th Anti-tank Battalion; 389th Engineer Battalion; 389th Signal Company.

3rd Motorized Infantry Division.
Home Station: Frankfurt-on-the-Oder.
Commanding Officer: Lieutenant-General Helmuth Schlomer.
Composition: 103rd Panzer Battalion; 8th and 29th Motorized Grenadier Regiments; 3rd Motorized Artillery Regiment; 103rd Panzer

Reconnaissance Battalion; 3rd Anti-tank Battalion; 3rd Motorized Engineer Battalion; 3rd Motorized Signal Battalion.

60th Motorized Infantry Division.
Home Station: Danzig.
Commanding Officer: Lieutenant-General Otto Kohlermann.
Composition: 160th Panzer Battalion; 92nd and 120th Motorized Grenadier Regiments; 160th Motorized Artillery Regiment; 160th Panzer Reconnaissance Battalion; 160th Anti-tank Battalion; 160th Motorized Engineer Battalion; 160th Motorized Signal Battalion.

14th Panzer Division.
Home Station: Dresden.
Commanding Officer: ?
Composition: 36th and 108th Panzer Grenadier Regiments; 4th Panzer Artillery Regiment; 64th Motorcycle Battalion; 40th Panzer Reconnaissance Battalion; 4th Anti-tank Battalion; 13th Panzer Engineer Battalion; 13th Panzer Signal Battalion.

16th Panzer Division.
Home Station: Munster.
Commanding Officer: Lieutenant-General von Angern.
Composition: 2nd Panzer Regiment; 64th and 79th Panzer Grenadier Regiments; 16th Panzer Artillery Regiment; 16th Motorcycle Battalion; 16th Panzer Reconnaissance Battalion; 16th Anti-tank Battalion; 16th Panzer Engineer Battalion; 16th Panzer Signal Battalion.

24th Panzer Division.
Home Station: Frankfurt-on-the-Oder.
Commanding Officer: Lieutenant-General Arno von Lenski.
Composition: 24th Panzer Regiment; 21st and 26th Panzer Grenadier Regiments; 89th Panzer Artillery Regiment; 24th Panzer Reconnaissance Battalion; 40th Anti-tank Battalion; 40th Panzer Engineer Battalion; 86th Panzer Signal Battalion.

SOURCE NOTES

Introduction
(pp. 1-8)

1. *Trial of the Major War Criminals before the International Military Tribunal* (hereafter cited as IMT), vol xxvi 789-ps, 329.
2. Domarus, Hitler: *Reden und Proklamationen, 1932-1945*, vol 1, pp 642-3.
3. Rauschning, *Hitler Speaks*, pp 47-8.
4. Leach, *German Strategy Against Russia, 1939-41*, (hereafter cited as Leach), p 227.
5. Halder, *Hitler as Warlord*, p 11.
6. Hubatsch & Schramm, *Die Deutsche Militärische Führung in der Kriegswende*, p 37.
7. *IMT* xxvi 846-ps, 379.
8. Klee, *Das Unternehmen Seelöwe*, p 189.
9. *Documents on German Foreign Policy 1918-1945*, Series D, X-370-74.

Chapter One
(pp. 9-24)

1. *Marcks Plan*, quoted in Leach, pp 250-254.
2. Ibid.
3. Ibid.
4. Görlitz, *Paulus and Stalingrad*, p 116.
5. Ibid, pp 118 & 120.
6. Jacobsen, *Generaloberst Halder: Kriegstagebuch*, vol 2, p 211.
7. Warlimont, *Inside Hitler's Headquarters*, p 138.
8. *OKH Final Deployment Plan*, quoted in Cooper, *The German Army 1933-45*, p 271.
9. Quoted in Liddell Hart, *The Other Side of the Hill*, p 272.
10. Statistics obtained from US Department of the Army, Pamphlet 20-261a, *The German Campaign in Russia — Planning and Operations 1940-42*.
11. Milward, *The Germany Economy at War*, p 6.
12. Gisevius, *Adolf Hitler: Versuch einer Deutung*, p 471.
13. Liddell Hart, *History of the Second World War*, p 170.
14. Hillgruber, *Staatsmänner*, vol 1, p 600.

15. Quoted in Carell, *Hitler's War on Russia*, p 204.
16. Fest, *Hitler*, p 971.

Chapter Two
(pp. 25-47)

1. Quoted in Liddell Hart, *The Other Side of the Hill*, pp 295-6.
2. Quoted in Warlimont, *Inside Hitler's Headquarters*, p 240.
3. Hubatsch, *Hitler's Weisungen Für die Kriegsführung*, Directive (*Weisung*) 45.
4. Ibid.
5. Ibid.
6. Halder, *Kriegstagebuch*, vol 2, p 358.
7. Görlitz, p 156.
8. *Istoriya Vtoroi Mirovoi voyny, 1939-1945*. All statistics regarding Soviet forces are taken from this 12 vol work (hereafter cited as *IVMV*).
9. Quoted in Görlitz, pp 47-48.
10. Quoted in Liddell Hart, *The Other Side of the Hill*, p 306.
11. Hubatsch, *Weisung Nr.45*.
12. Ibid.
13. General Kurt Zeitzler, *Stalingrad*, in *The Fatal Decisions*, p 116.
14. *IVMV*, vol V, pp 166-167.
15. War Diary 6th Army, *AOK 6, Ia Kriegstagebuch, Armeebefehl für den Angriff auf Stalingrad*.
16. War Diary 4th Panzer Army, *AOK 4, Ia Kriegstagebuch, Der Oberbefehlshaber der 4. Panzerarmee, an General Hüsinger, 19.8.42*.

Chapter Three
(pp. 48-71)

1. *AOK 6, Ia Kriegstagebuch*.
2. Vasilevsky, *Delo Vsei Zhizni*, p 236.
3. Samsonov, *Stalingradskaya bitva*, (hereafter cited as Samsonov) p 152.
4. Erickson, *The Road to Stalingrad*, p 506.
5. Quoted in Schröter, Stalingrad, (hereafter cited as Schröter) pp 34-35.
6. *Marshal Zhukov's Greatest Battles* (hereafter cited as Zhukov) pp 132-133.
7. AOK 6, *Ia Kriegstagebuch*.
8. Ibid.
9. Zhukov, p 135.
10. Ibid, p 136.
11. Ibid, p 136.
12. Ibid, p 138-139.
13. Samsonov, pp 160-161.

14. Zhukov, p 140.
15. Görlitz, p 64.

Chapter Four
(pp. 72-101)

1. Doerr, *Der Feldzug Nach Stalingrad*, pp 66-67.
2. Quoted in Mellenthin, *Panzer Battles*, p 164.
3. Rotundo, *The Soviet General Staff Study of the Battle For Stalingrad*, p 62 (hereafter cited as Rotundo).
4. Hoffman diary, quoted in Chuikov, *Nachalo puti*, pp 251-253.
5. Ibid.
6. Quoted in Schröter, p 37.
7. Ibid.
8. Zeitzler, *Stalingrad* (in *The Fatal Decisions*), p 127 (hereafter cited as Zeitzler).
9. Ibid. p 121.
10. Ibid. p 123.
11. Ibid. p 127.
12. *Voenno istoricheskiy zhurnal*, No.3 of 1968, p 69.
13. Ibid. p 67.
14. Quoted in Clark, *Barbarossa*, p 241.
15. Schröter, p 47.
16. Quoted in Clark, *Barbarossa*, p 238.

Chapter Five
(pp. 102-122)

1. Schröter, p 63.
2. Plocher, *The German Air Force Versus Russia*, 1942, p 231.
3. Batov, P.I., *V pokhodakh i boyakh*.
4. Zeitzler, p 129.
5. Ibid. p 129.
6. AOK 6, *Ia Kriegstagebuch*.
7. AOK 4, *Ia Kriegstagebuch*.
8. Schröter, p 78.
9. Carell, *Hitler's War on Russia*, pp 584-585 (hereafter cited as Carell).
10. Ibid. p 585-586.
11. Adams, *Der schwere Entschluss*.
12. Zeitzler, p 130.
13. AOK 6, *Ia Kriegstagebuch*.
14. Fest, *Hitler*, p 987.
15. Ibid.
16. Carell, p 587.

17. AOK 6, *la Kriegstagebuch*.
18. *OKH, GenStd H, Op. Abt. Kriegstagebuch* (General Staff Operations Branch, War Diary).
19. Zeitzler, p 131.
20. Werth, *The Year of Stalingrad*, p 355-356.
21. AOK 6, *la Kriegstagebuch*.

Chapter Six
(pp. 123-144)
1. Rotundo, pp 141-142.
2. Chuikov, *Nachalo puti*, p 232.
3. Werth, p 358.
4. Quoted in Carell, p 599-601.
5. Zeitzler, p 131.
6. Ibid.
7. Ibid. p 131-132.
8. *AOK 6, la Kriegstagebuch*.
9. Zeitzler, p 138.
10. *OKH, GenStd H, Op Abt. Kriegstagebuch*.
11. *AOK 6, la Kriegstagebuch*.
12. Zeitzler, p 141.
13. Ibid, p 142.
14. Ibid.
15. Ibid.
16. Ibid.
17. Quoted in Carell, pp 597-596.
18. Schröter, p 110.

Chapter Seven
(pp. 145-172)
1. Quoted in Bekker, *The Luftwaffe War Diaries*, p 283.
2. Carell, p 606.
3. Manstein, *Lost Victories*, pp 553-554 (hereafter cited as Manstein).
4. Ibid, p 311.
5. Ibid, p 319.
6. *Voenno istoricheskiy zhurnal*, No.1 of 1966, p 19 (hereafter cited as *VIZ*).
7. Quoted in Mellenthin, *Panzer Battles*, p 184.
8. Quoted in Ziemke, *Stalingrad to Berlin*, p 63.
9. *VIZ* (No.3), pp 28-29.
10. *VIZ* (No.3), pp 29-30.
11. Manstein, p 333.
12. Ibid, p 334.

13. Ibid.
14. Manstein, p 335.
15. *Heeresgruppe Don, la Kriegstagebuch* (War Diary Army Group Don).
16. Ibid.
17. Ibid.
18. Ibid.
19. Ibid.
20. Zeitzler, pp 150-151.
21. Kerr, *The Secret of Stalingrad*, p 238.

Chapter Eight
(pp. 173-202)

1. Quoted in Craig, *Enemy At The Gates*, pp 288-289.
2. *Letzte Briefe aus Stalingrad* (hereafter cited as *Letzte Briefe*).
3. Ibid.
4. *Heeresgruppe Don, 1a Kriegstagebuch.*
5. *Letzte Briefe.*
6. Dibold, *Doctor in Stalingrad*, p 27.
7. Ibid, pp 28-29.
8. Quoted in Mellenthin, *Panzer Battles*, pp 188-189.
9. *Heeresgruppe Don, 1a Kriegstagebuch.*
10. Quoted in Craig, *Enemy At The Gates*, p 299-300.
11. *Letzte Briefe.*
12. Ibid.
13. *AOK 6, 1a Kriegstagebuch.*
14. Ibid.
15. *Letzte Briefe.*
16. Bekker, *The Luftwaffe War Diaries*, p 286 (hereafter cited as Bekker).
17. Quoted in Murray, *Luftwaffe: Strategy for Defeat*, p 216.
18. Schröter, p 153.
19. Bekker, p 289.
20. Ibid.
21. Quoted in Mellenthin, *Panzer Battles*, p 199.
22. Schröter, p 185.
23. Quoted in Clark, *Barbarossa*, p 285.
24. *VIZ*, No 5 of 1962.
25. *VIZ*, No 5 of 1962.
26. Quoted in Görlitz, p 272.
27. Ibid, p 285.
28. *Letzte Briefe.*
29. Quoted in Clark, *Barbarossa*, p 286.
30. Schröter, p 200.

31. Ibid, pp 194-195.
32. *Letzte Briefe.*
33. Quoted in *VIZ*, No 2 of 1960.
34. Ibid.
35. Zeitzler, p 157.

Chapter Nine.
(pp.203-232)

1. Quoted in Irving, *The Rise and Fall of the Luftwaffe*, p 185 (hereafter cited as Irving).
2. Bekker, p 292.
3. Ibid, pp 292-293.
4. Ibid.
5. *Istoriya Velikoi Otechestvennoi voiny Sovetskovo Soyuza*, Vol 3, p 62.
6. *OKH, GenStd H, Op Abt. Kriegstagebuch.*
7. Ibid.
8. Quoted in Carell, pp 620-621.
9. Zeitzler, p 160.
10. Irving, p 196.
11. Ibid.
12. *Heeresgruppe Don, 1a Kriegstagebuch.*
13. Zeitzler, p 161.
14. Quoted in Schröter, pp 228-229.
15. Ibid.
16. Chuikov, *Nachalo puti*, pp 258-259.
17. Schröter, p 242.
18. Ibid, p 243.
19. Ibid.
20. Quoted in Schröter, p 249.
21. Ibid, p 252.
22. Ibid, pp 249-250.
23. *Heeresgruppe Don, 1a Kriegstagebuch.*
24. *OKH, GenStd H, Op Abt. Kriegstagebuch.*
25. Ibid.
26. Ibid.
27. Quoted in the *Soviet Military Review*, January, 1973.
28. Ibid.
29. Ibid.
30. Felix Gilbert, *Hitler Directs His War*, pp 17-22.
31. Görlitz, p 84.
32. *OKH, GenStd H, Op Abt. Kriegstagebuch.*

33. Quoted in Schröter, p 258.
34. *Heeresgruppe Don, 1a Kriegstagebuch.*
35. Chuikov, *Nachalo puti*, p 262.
36. *Heeresgruppe Don, 1a Kriegstagebuch.*
37. *OKH, GenStd H, Op Abt. Kriegstagebuch.*
38. Ibid.
39. Ibid.
40. Quoted in Werth, *The Year of Stalingrad*, p 435.
41. Domarus, *Hitler, Reden und Proklamationen*, Vol II, p 1985.
42. Zeitzler, p 165.

BIBLIOGRAPHY

Unpublished Archive Material:
The War Diaries of the German 6th Army (*Armee Oberkommando, 1a Kriegstagebuch* — cited as *AOK 6, 1a Kriegstagebuch*); the War Diaries of Army Group Don HQ (*Oberkommando des Heeresgruppe Don* — cited as *Heeresgruppe Don, 1a Kriegstagebuch*); the War Diaries of the Army General Staff Operations Section (*Oberkommando des Heeres* — cited as *OKH, GenStd H, Op Abt. Kriegstagebuch*); along with the files of the German Eastern Front intelligence gathering section (*Fremde Heere Ost*), are on microfilm in the United States National Archives and Records Administration, Washington, D.C.

United States, Department of the Army, Historical Pamphlets:
20-230.— Russian Combat Methods in W.W.II. (1950).
20-233.— German Defence Tactics Against Russian Break-throughs, (1951).
20-234.— Operations of Encircled Forces: German Experiences in Russia. (1952).
20-261A.— The German Campaign in Russia: Planning and Operations, 1940-1942. (1955).
20-290.— Terrain Factors in the Russian Campaign. (1951).
20-291.— Effects of Climate on Combat in European Russia. (1952).
20-701.— War (Military) Economy of the U.S.S.R. in W.W.II. (1955).

Published Official Works:
Documents on German Foreign Policy, 1918-1945, from the Archives of the German Foreign Ministry; Series D, 13 vols. (Washington, 1949).
Istoriya Vtoroi Mirovoi voyny, 1939-1945, 12 vols. (Moscow, 1973-1982).
Istoriya Velikoi Otechestvennoi voiny Sovetskovo Soyuza, 1941-1945, 6 vols. (Moscow, 1965).
Kriegstagebuch de Oberkommandos der Wehrmacht. Band I, 1940-1941 (Hans-Adolf Jacobsen, ed.); Band II, 1942 (Andreas Hillgruber, ed.). (Frankfurt 1961-1965).
The Great Patriotic War of the Soviet Union, 1941-1945. (Moscow, 1974).
The Soviet Air Force in World War II: The Official History. (London, 1974).
Trial of the Major War Criminals before the International Military Tribunal, 42 vols (Nuremberg, 1947).

General and Semi-Official Works.

Adam, W. *Der schwere Entschluss.* (Berlin, 1965).

Barnett, Correlli (Ed). *Hitler's Generals.* (London, 1989).

Bekker, Cajus, *The Luftwaffe War Diaries.* (London, 1967).

Bialer, S. *Stalin and his Generals: Soviet Military Commanders Memoirs of W.W.II.* (New York, 1969).

Carell, Paul. *Hitler's War on Russia*, 2 Vols (vol 1 as cited, vol 2 Scorched Earth). (London, 1964-70).

Carver, Field-Marshal Lord. *Twentieth Century Warriors: The Development of the Armed Forces of the Major Military Nations in the Twentieth Century.* (London, 1987).

Chuikov, Marshal Vasili Ivanovich. *Nachalo puti* (Moscow, 1959). English translation — *The Beginning of the Road: The Battle for Stalingrad.* (London, 1963).

Clark, Alan. Barbarossa: The Russian-German Conflict 1941-1945. (London, 1965).

Cooper, Matthew. *The German Army 1933-1945: Its Political and Military Failure.* (London, 1981).

Cooper, Matthew. *The German Air Force 1933-1945: An Anatomy of Failure.* (London, 1981).

Craig, William. *Enemy At The Gates: The Battle for Stalingrad.* (New York, 1973).

Dawidowicz, Lucy. *The War Against The Jews 1933-1945.* (London, 1975).

Deutscher, Isaac. *Stalin.* (London, 1972).

Dibold, Hans. *Doctor at Stalingrad. The Passion of a Captivity.* (London, 1958).

Doerr, Hans. *Der Feldzug Nach Stalingrad. Versuch eines Operativen Uberblickes.* (Darmstadt, 1955).

Domarus, Max. *Hitler, Reden und Proklamationen, 1932-1945.* 2 volumes. (Wurzburg, 1962 & 1963).

Einsiedel, Count Heinrich von. *The Shadow of Stalingrad.* (London, 1953).

Ellis, John, *Brute Force: Allied Strategy and Tactics in the Second World War.* (London, 1990).

Erickson, John. *The Road to Stalingrad and The Road to Berlin* (Vols 1 & 2 of *Stalin's War with Germany*). (London, 1975 & 1983).

Fest, Joachim C. *The Face of the Third Reich.* (London, 1970)

Fest, Joachim C. *Hitler.* (London, 1974).

Gisevius, Hans Bernd. *Adolf Hitler: Versuch einer Deutung.* (Munich, 1963).

Görlitz, Walter. *Paulus and Stalingrad.* (London, 1963).

Grove, Eric. *World War II Tanks.* (London, 1976).

Guderian, General Heinz. *Panzer Leader.* (London, 1952).

Higgins, T. *Hitler and Russia: The Third Reich in a Two Front War,*

1937-1943. (New York, 1966).

Hillgruber, Andreas. *Staatsmanner und Diplomaten bei Hitler*. 2 vols. (Frankfurt am Main, 1967-70).

Hubatsch, Walter. *Hitler's Weisungen Für die Kriegsführung, 1939-1945*. (Frankfurt, 1962).

Hubatsch, Walter & Schramm, Percy E. *Die deutsche militärische Führung in der Kriegswende*. (Cologne/Opladen, 1964).

Irving, David. *Hitler's War*. (London, 1977).

Irving, David. *The War Path: Hitler's Germany 1933-39*. (London, 1978).

Jacobsen, Hans-Adolf (Ed.). *Generaloberst Halder: Kriegstagebuch*. 3 vols. (Stuttgart, 1963).

Jacobsen, Hans-Adolf & Rohwer, Jurgen (Eds.). *Decisive Battles of World War II: The German View*. (London, 1965).

Jukes, Geoffrey. *Stalingrad: The Turning Point*. (New York, 1978).

Keegan, John. *The Mask of Command*. (London, 1988).

Kehrig, M. *Stalingrad: Analyse und Dokumentation einer Schlacht*. (Stuttgart, 1974).

Kerr, Walter. *The Secret of Stalingrad*. (London, 1979).

Klee, Karl. *Das Unternehmen 'Seelöwe'. Die geplante deutsche Landung in England, 1940*. (Göttingen, 1958).

Leach, Barry A. *German Strategy Against Russia 1939-1941*. (Oxford 1973).

Liddell Hart, B.H. *The Other Side of the Hill*. (London, 1951)

Liddell Hart, B.H. *Strategy: The Indirect Approach*. (London, 1954).

Liddell Hart, B.H. *History of the Second World War*. (London, 1970).

Madej, W.V. (ed.) *Southeastern Europe Axis Armed Forces Handbook* (Allentown, Pennsylvania, 1982).

Madej, W.V. (ed.) *Red Army Order of Battle: 1941-1943*. (Allentown, 1983).

Madej, W.V. (ed.) *German Army Order of Battle: The Replacement Army, 1939-1945*. (Allentown, 1984).

Madej, W.V. (ed.) *German Order of Battle: Field Army and Officer Corps, 1939-1945*. (Allentown, 1985).

Madej, W.V. *Italian Army Order of Battle, 1940-1944*. (Allentown, 1990).

Manstein, Field-Marshal Erich von. *Lost Victories*. (Elstree, 1987).

Mayer, Arno J. *Why Did The Heavens Not Darken: The Final Solution In History*. (New York, 1990).

Mellenthin, Major General F.W. *Panzer Battles*. (London, 1956).

Milward, Alan S. *The German Economy at War*. (University of London, 1965).

Mitcham Jr., Samuel W. *Hitler's Legions: German Order of Battle in World War II*. (London, 1985).

Mitcham Jr., Samuel W. *Hitler's Field-Marshals and Their Battles*. (London, 1989).

Moll, Otto E. *Die deutschen Generalfeldmarschaelle, 1939-1945*, (Baden, 1961).

Morzik, Generalmajor a. D.F. *German Air Force Airlift Operations*. U.S.A.F. Historical Division, Study 167. (New York, 1961).

Perrett, Bryan. *A History of Blitzkrieg*. (New York, 1983).

Piekalkiewicz, Janusz. *Moscow 1941: The Frozen Offensive*. (London, 1985).

Plocher, Generalleutnant Hermann. *The German Air Force Versus Russia, 1942*. U.S.A.F. Historical Division, Study 154. (New York, 1965).

Rauschning, Hermann. *Hitler Speaks*. London, 1939.

Richardson, W & Freidin, S. (Eds.) *The Fatal Decisions*. (London, 1956).

Rokossovsky, K.K. (ed.). *Velikaya pobeda na volge*. (Moscow, 1965).

Rotundo, Louis (Ed.). *Battle of Stalingrad: The 1943 Soviet General Staff Study*. (London, 1989). Samsonov, Aleksandr M. Stalingradskaya bitva (Moscow, 1968).

Schröter, Heinz. *Stalingrad... biz zur letzten Patrone*. (Lengerich, 1953). English translation, *Stalingrad*. (London, 1958).

Seaton, Albert. *The Russo-German War 1941-1945*. (London, 1971).

Seaton, Albert. *Stalin as Warlord*. (London, 1976).

Seaton, Albert. *The Fall of Fortress Europe 1943-1945*. (London, 1981).

Seaton, Albert. *The German Army 1933-1945*. (London, 1982).

Seth, Ronald. *Stalingrad: Point of Return*. (London, 1959).

Shirer, William L. *The Rise and Fall of the Third Reich*. (London, 1959).

Taylor, A.J.P. *The Origins of the Second World War*. (London, 1961).

Vasilevsky, A.M. *Delo vsei zhizni* (Moscow, 1975).

Vasilevsky, A.M. & Others, *Two Hundred Days of Fire: Accounts by Participants and Witnesses of the Battle of Stalingrad*. (Moscow, 1970).

Warlimont, General Walter. *Inside Hitler's Headquarters*. (London, 1964).

Werth, Alexander. *The Year of Stalingrad: An Historical Record And A Study of Russian Mentality, Methods & Policies*. (London, 1946).

Zhukov, Georgi K. *Marshal Zhukov's Greatest Battles*. (London, 1969).

Ziemke, Earl F. & Bauer Magna E. *Moscow To Stalingrad: Decision In The East*. US Army Historical Series. (New York, 1988).

Ziemke, Earl F. *Stalingrad To Berlin: The German Defeat In The East*. US Army Historical Series. (Washington, 1968).

Anon, *Letzte Briefe aus Stalingrad*. (Guetersloh, 1954).

Periodicals.

Armies and Weapons: B. Hooton, *Stalingrad: Beginning of the End*, in issues No 34 (May, 1977); No 35 (June, 1977); No 36 (July, 1977).

Army Quarterly (April, July, October 1949 issues): Col. H. Selle, *The Tragedy of Stalingrad*.

Australian Army Journal (March, 1970): G.M. Brown, *The Significance of*

Stalingrad in W.W.II.

Military Affairs (April, 1986): A.R. Sunseri, Stalingrad: *An Oral History Interview.*

Pakistan Army Journal (Dec. 1984): Lt.-Col. I.U. Khan, *The Battle of Stalingrad: A Study in the Higher Direction of War.*

Revue Internationale d'Histoire Militaire (No 44, 1979): Col. Y.V. Plotnikov, *Exploit at Stalingrad.*

Soviet Military Review: Marshal A.M. Vasilevsky, *Counter Offensive Against Manstein: Stalingrad 1942* (Jan. 1968 issue) & *Stalingrad: The Great Battle* (Jan. 1973 issue).

Voenno istoricheskiy zhurnal (Military History Journal): articles relating to Stalingrad can be found in issue No 5 of 1962; No 3 of 1963; No 10 of 1965; No 1 & 3 of 1966; No 3 of 1968; No 11 of 1972.

INDEX

Adam, Colonel Wilhelm, 112, 221.
Apell, General Wilhelm von, 106.

Balck, General H., 156-157.
Batov, General P. I., 94, 104, 118, 198, 215.
Behr, Captain Winrich, 180-181.
Below, Major Nikolaus von, 180.
Binder, Karl, 173.
Blitzkrieg, strategic doctrine of, 5-7, 12-14, 31.
Blumentritt, General Gunther von, 14, 27.
Bock, Field-Marshal Fedor von, 30, 35.
Brauchitsch, Field-Marshal Walter von, 7, 25.
Bund Deutsche Offiziere, 224.
Busse, Colonel T., 153.

Chistyakov, General I. M., 94, 198, 215.
Chuikov, General Vassili Ivanovich, 63, 73-101 *passim;* 128-129, 215, 227.
Constantinescu, General C. A., 98.

Dibold, Dr. Hans, 178.
Dieter, Lieutenant, 189.
Dingler, Colonel H. R., 82, 178-179, 188.
Dragalina, General C. A., 44.
Drebber, General, 214.
Doerr, General Hans, 76, 134.
Dumitrescu, General P., 93, 98, 132.
Dyatlenko, Captain, 192.

Einsatzgruppen, 18.
Eismann, Major, 164-166.

Fiebig, General Martin, 114, 142, 145-146, 151, 184-185, 206.
Fillipov, Colonel Grigor, 113-114.
Forster, Colonel, 146.
Fremde Heere Ost,
  estimates of Soviet military strength, 15, 17, 26-27, 32, 70.
Führer Directives:
  No. 21, 16; No. 41, 28; No. 45, 37.

Galinin, General I. V., 94, 105, 198, 227.
Gariboldi, General I., 162.
Germany:
  armaments production, 15-16, 27.
  population statistics, 17.

German Army:
  in Polish campaign, 3-4; invades Denmark & Norway, 4; in French campaign, 45; strategic doctrines of, 4-7; strength on eve of Barbarossa, 14-15; casualties in Russian campaign, 20-21, 26; effects of Russian climate on, 21-22; supply problems, 22, 28, 32, 44, 99; fails to capture Moscow, 23; suffers first major defeat, 23; strength in March, 1942, 26; dispositions in Fall Blau, 30-31; dispositions on Stalingrad axis, 46-47, 72-73; tactics in Stalingrad battle, 76-79.
Field Armies:
  2nd Army, 30-32, 35-37 *passim*, 92.
  6th Army, 30-32; assessment of, 33; in Fall Blau, 35-46 *passim*; in battle for Stalingrad 49-101 *passim*; casualties, 70, 83, 123-124, 177-178, 188, 197, 228-230; strength of, 30-31, 72-74, 123-124, 197; encirclement of 103-122 *passim*; forms circular defence, 123-127; supply difficulties, 150-151, 153, 176-179, 186-187, 217; situation in the Kessel, 173-202 *passim*; ammunition expended, 83; suffering of troops in cellars, 216-217; fate of prisoners from, 227-229.
  11th Army, 71.
  17th Army, 30-32, 35-38 *passim*; 71, 202.
Panzer Armies:
  1st PZ Army, 30-32, 35-39 *passim*; 71, 74, 201-202.
  4th PZ Army, 30-32, 35-45 *passim*; 54-71 *passim*; 72-74, 110-111, 132, 134, 152, 192, 230.
Infantry Corps:
  4th Corps, 44, 54, 62, 84, 110-111, 115, 120, 124, 126, 215, 217, 219.
  8th Corps, 41, 54, 62, 84, 110-111, 115-116, 120, 123-124, 215, 217, 219.
  11th Corps, 39, 43, 73, 84, 95, 98, 104-105, 118, 120, 124, 215, 217, 225.
  51st Corps, 39, 42-43, 59-60, 63, 73, 120, 124, 126, 139, 215, 217, 219.
Panzer Corps:
  14th PZ Corps, 39, 41-44, 49, 54, 56, 60, 62, 66, 70, 73, 80, 84, 107, 120, 123-124, 126, 215, 217, 219.
  24th PZ Corps, 39, 41-44 *passim*.

damage to and rebuilding of, 231; renamed Volgograd, 231.
Stempel, General Richard, 214.
Strecker, General Karl, 120, 143, 225-227.

Tasch, Corporal, 195-196.
Thiel, Major, 205-206.
Tolbukhin, General F. I., 94, 198.
Trufanov, General N. I., 94, 160.

U.S.S.R., communication system, 15; armaments production, 16-17, 21, 27; population statistics, 17; climatic conditions, 21-23, 25; aid received from western allies, 27; oil fields, 30, 71.

Vasilevsky, General A. M., 61, 67-69, 93-94, 131, 156, 159.
Vatutin, General N. F., 94, 159-160.
Vernichtungsgedanke,
strategic doctrine of, 6-7, 12-13, 95.
Voronov, General P. N., 161, 190-193, 198, 222.
Voroshilov, General S. S. K., 28.

Wagner, General Eduard, 7, 39.
Warlimont, General Walter, 13.
Weichs, General Maximilian von, 35, 62, 69-70, 93, 105-106, 111-112, 115-117, 132.
Weiner, Lieutenant, 99.
Wenck, Colonel Walther, 132-134.
Wietersheim, General Gustav von, 56, 60, 70, 84, 120.
Willers, Major, 146.
Willig, Major, 192.

Yeremenko, General A. I., 46, 56-57, 59, 63-65, 94, 107-108, 131, 160.

Zeitzler, General Kurt,
criticizes Hitler's strategy, 38, 87-93, 105-106, 112-113, 157, 181, 229; attempts to counter Russian Kontrudar, 105, 112-113, 117; attempts to persuade Hitler to allow 6th Army to break-out, 134-143 *passim,* 151, 169-170, 210, 213.
Zhadov, General A. S., 94, 227.
Zhukov, General G. K., appointed Deputy Supreme Commander of Red Army, 60-61; in battle for Stalingrad, 61-69 *passim,* 80-81; plans the Kontrudar, 68-69, 93-94.
Zitzewitz, Major Coelestin von, 210-211.